Sex, Power, & the Violent School Girl

Sibylle Artz

Trifolium Books Inc.
Toronto

Canadian Cataloguing in Publication Data
Artz Sibylle, 1949–
    Sex, power, & the violent school girl
Includes bibliographical references and index.
ISBN 1-895579-41-4
1. Delinquent girls. 2. Violence. 3. School violence.
I. Title. II. Title: Sex, power, and the violent school girl.
HV9069.A77 1997   362.74'0835'2   C97-932008-9

Printed and bound in Canada
10 9 8 7 6 5 4 3 2 1

Trifolium Books Inc. acknowledges with gratitude the generous support of the Government of Canada's Publishing Industry Development Program (BPIDP) in the production of this book.

Editing/Design/Desktop publishing: Francine Geraci
Cover photo: First Light

Ordering Information
Orders by bookstores, wholesalers, individuals, organizations, and educational institutions: Please contact General Distribution Services, 34 Lesmill Road, Don Mills, Ontario, Canada M3B 2T6; tel. Ontario and Quebec (800) 387-0141, all other provinces (800) 387-0172; fax (416) 445-5967. In the U.S.A., contact General Distribution Services, 85 River Rock Road, Suite 202, Buffalo, NY 14207; tel. 1-800-805-1083; fax (416) 445-5967.

Trifolium's books may also be purchased in bulk for educational, business, or promotional use. For information please telephone (416) 925-0765 or write: Special Sales, Trifolium Books Inc., 238 Davenport Road, Suite 28, Toronto, Ontario, M5R 1J6

CONTENTS

Dedication

This book is dedicated to my parents, Cornelia and Eric Artz, who showed me that it is possible to do the seemingly impossible and still find time to laugh.

Acknowledgments

This book could not have been written without the participation, expertise and goodwill of key people.

To those who participated in this study, I would like to express my heartfelt thanks. Had you not been as willing as you were to talk openly about your sometimes painful and difficult experiences, all those who read this book, and I, would never have been able to learn from the insights you so freely shared. I believe it takes a special kind of courage to give of oneself in the way that you have. I deeply respect and appreciate what you have done.

Next, I wish to acknowledge and thank my research colleague, Dr. Ted Riecken, for encouraging me to undertake this project and for contributing to it in so many ways through his ongoing work with, and his dedication to, the Youth Violence Project, our collaborative undertaking. Without Dr. Riecken, this book and the project that engendered it would not have been possible.

I wish to thank Francine Geraci, my editor, for her immense contribution to making this book a reality, and I wish to thank Grace Deutsch and Trudy Rising of Trifolium Books for never wavering and for bringing this book to publication.

Lastly, I want to say thank you to my partner, Stan Olsen, for his support and patience, and to Stephanie Olsen for her insightful comments.

Introduction

In recent years, in the Western industrialized world, much attention has been paid to youth violence and with it, the ever-increasing participation of school children in all forms of violence and aggression. To combat this growing problem, research and youth violence prevention programs have begun in Europe (e.g., Olweus, Block, & Radke-Yarrow, 1986; Tutt, 1988, 1991; Klicpera & Klicpera, 1993), Australia (Jenkins, 1994; Rigby, 1996), the United States (e.g., Boothe, Bradley, Flick, Keough, & Kirk, 1993), and Canada (Hamilton, 1993). In North America, youth violence and violence in schools have become the object of intense media attention: The topic has been widely discussed in newspapers, magazines, scholarly journals, and television and radio programs; it has also been the focus of academic and community conferences.

Educators and social scientists appear to agree that youth violence, particularly violence in schools, is on the rise at an unprecedented rate, and that this violence is more intense, vicious, and deadly than ever before. In an article entitled "The Violence at Your Door," which distills the findings of a 1993 U.S. national survey of school executives, Boothe et al. (1993) state that "violence has increased markedly in U.S. public schools in the last five years." In Canada, Hamilton (1993) draws on government- and teacher-compiled data to state categorically that

> few young people today have not experienced some form of violence, either first-hand or involving a friend. Bullying, sexual assault, and violent incidents involving children and teens are happening more and more frequently ... in big cities and small towns, in parks and shopping centers, in private and public schools.

These sources and others (e.g., Bibby & Posterski, 1992; Mathews, 1994; Cameron, deBruijne, Kennedy, & Morin, 1994) specifically mention an increase in *violence among school girls*. For example, Mathews, Ryan, and Banner (1994) found that girls had become more directly involved in assault or the use of weapons, either as individuals or in groups or gangs, with most attacks directed against other individual girls or groups of girls. In one school, female students self-reported that they were as likely as male students to rob another student, and more likely than male students to threaten or hurt someone with a weapon. In another school, older females (grade nine) were more likely than males to be perpetrators of most categories of violent offenses, with the exception of sexual violence. Finally, in Canada, murder charges were recently laid against juveniles — among them two 14-year-old girls who were charged with manslaughter — in connection with the slaying of a motorist who had apparently stopped his car to give them a ride.

The overall reported increase in youth violence has made this a hot topic. The involvement of females has made it even hotter.

Females and violence in schools

Hot topics usually generate much literature. When I undertook a search in this area, therefore, I was surprised to find very little. Much of the literature consisted of articles in academic journals that are not readily accessible to front-line workers, educators, parents, or indeed to the girls themselves. The vast majority of articles on school violence failed to address girls' violence, and the major trend on violence in general offered prescriptions without benefit of research.

Antiviolence programs, no matter how well meaning, stand scant chance of success if they do not apply to the individuals and groups they intend to affect. This is particularly true for girls: Little research has been done with respect to violent females because, for the most part, violence and delinquency are seen to be almost exclusively a male problem. As well, the handful of studies that do exist focus on Afro-American or Hispanic-American girls who are marginalized because of color or ethnicity, live in ghettos, and are either members of known youth gangs or heavily involved with the juvenile justice system.

The violent, non-gang, white girl and the violent white school girl who is not in juvenile detention have been virtually ignored. It is as if such girls do not exist — but in fact they do; and they are very much in the forefront of the rise in violence in schools, both as victims and as perpetrators. Nevertheless, most antiviolence programs ignore gender differences and base their interventions on theories derived from research on boys and men. This means that there is a marked lack of information upon which to base meaningful and effective violence prevention aimed at violent girls.

My involvement in the problem

I initially became interested in the topic of youth violence early in 1993, while working with teachers on the conflicts arising from differences in learning and teaching styles. I was struck by the number of times violence was brought into our discussions: Teachers described gang fighting, drug use, vigilantism, and extortion among students, along with an increase in intimidating behavior towards adults.

My response was to seek out more information on school-based violence. I also contacted my colleague, Dr. Ted Riecken. Together, we set out to research the nature and incidence of such violence in order to provide a realistic and concrete understanding of the extent of the problem. The result of our collaboration was an 11-page self-report questionnaire designed to tap into various aspects of students' experiences, which we administered to over 1,500 students aged 13 to 16, both male and female. The results appear in the *Survey of Student Life* (Artz & Riecken, 1994).

The second step in our inquiry involved my spending many days and weeks, for a period of one year, with six violent school girls, their parents, teachers, and counselors, in order to learn about the girls' lives and about how they make sense of their participation in violence. It is on this study that this book is based.

The third step, in which we are now deeply immersed, is the Youth Violence Project, which involves working at the community-based level with 16 schools on violence prevention from the ground up.

The purpose of this book

This book inquires into the life-worlds and practices of school girls who are involved in violence, but who are not involved with the juvenile justice system, nor are they members of a gang or a visible minority group. The girls chosen for this study range in age from 13 to 16 years, because this population shows the highest participation of girls in school-based violence.

This book has the following objectives:

- To provide a well-researched and well-articulated description of the life-worlds of violent school girls.

- To provide an understanding of where the violent school girl stands in relation to her nonviolent female peers and her violent and nonviolent male peers.

- To provide information that may be applied to the design and implementation of programs and interventions that have the power to reach violent girls and help them to stop participating in violence.

Chapter One presents an overview of past and current theories of crime and delinquency, in order to ground the reader in the ways in which the problem of girls' violence has thus far been understood.

Chapter Two, which draws mostly on the extensive data generated by the *Survey of Student Life* (Artz & Riecken, 1994), presents profiles of the adolescent school girl and her violent female peer and the adolescent school boy and his violent male peer, and discusses gender similarities and differences.

Drawing on case study material, Chapters Three through Eight explore the life-worlds of individual violent school girls. These chapters focus on the girls' descriptions of themselves, their families, their social activities, friends, and friendships; on their school activities and relationships with teachers, administrators, and counselors; and on their moral understanding of their own participation in violence.

Chapter Nine summarizes and analyzes the findings described in the preceding chapters, while Chapter Ten ties these findings to existing approaches to violence prevention, points out the gaps, makes suggestions for change, and outlines possibilities for working effectively with violent school girls.

Sibylle Artz
Associate Professor
School of Child & Youth Care
University of Victoria
Victoria, British Columbia, Canada

CHAPTER ONE

Exploring Theories of Female Crime and Delinquency

> Prior to the 1970s researchers treated females as marginal to the study of juvenile delinquency. Albert Cohen (1955), for example, well known for his study of male delinquent subcultures, paid only token attention to females, proposing that male delinquency was "versatile," while female delinquency was "specialized" and limited to "sexual crimes" (p. 144). He concluded that girls became delinquent because they were preoccupied with establishing sexual relationships with boys. (Berger, 1989, p. 375)

In order to ground the reader in theories of female crime and delinquency, a synopsis follows based on the literature reviews produced by Chesney-Lind and Koroki (1985), Ronald Berger (1989), and Chesney-Lind and Shelden (1992). These scholars have written succinct overviews of some 200 articles, reports, and books produced between 1985 and 1991. In summarizing their findings, I consulted other sources, notably Warren (1981) and Flowers (1990); but for the most part, this synopsis is guided by Chesney-Lind and her associates and by Berger.

Mainstream Theories of Crime and Delinquency

Early theorists in this area included Burgess (1928), who studied ecological patterns of crime and delinquency and the effects of social disorganization and deprivation on crime; Thrasher (1927), who studied juvenile gangs; and Shaw and McKay (1942), whose work further investigated the effects of social factors on crime and delinquency. These theorists demonstrated the powerful effects of social disorganization, class, and the breakdown of social conventions on crime and delinquency. Yet for the most part, they overlooked females and concentrated on the experiences of males.

Focusing on inner-city crime, these researchers showed that communities that are (a) largely populated by transitory, economically underprivileged people coming from similar ethnic backgrounds and (b) characterized by a collective inability to make provisions, solve problems, and maintain social control through the adequate use of

organizations, groups, and individuals, invariably give rise to disproportionately high crime rates. The work of these researchers, who focused
primarily on the socially derived motivational aspects of crime, was
seminal for others, notably those who developed "strain" theories of
delinquency and crime. These theories concentrate on the explanatory
power of frustrated social opportunity and its relationship to crime.

STRAIN THEORIES OF CRIME AND DELINQUENCY

Building on Emile Durkheim's (1933) notion of *anomie*, described in
Webster (1975) as "lawlessness: a state of society in which normative
standards of conduct and belief are weak or lacking" (p. 47), and
described by Chesney-Lind and Shelden (1992) as a "breakdown in
moral ties, rules, customs, laws and the like that occurs in the wake of
rapid social change" (p. 64), strain theorists beginning with Robert
Merton (1938) developed theories that "explain juvenile delinquency
as a response of adolescents to their lack of socially approved opportunities" (Flowers, 1990, p. 127).

Merton, focusing on males, noted that unequal opportunity and
limited access to legitimate means for achieving culturally defined
male success goals created "strain" or pressures that pushed some males
into finding alternative means to achieve these desired ends. Merton
postulated five alternative adaptive responses to anomie and strain:
(a) becoming a *conformist*, which implied unquestioning acceptance of
culturally defined success goals and means, with no guarantee of goal
attainment; (b) becoming an *innovator*, which implied acceptance of
commonly held success goals while replacing socially sanctioned
means with deviant means; (c) becoming a *retreatist*, giving up and
rejecting both goals and means; (d) becoming a *ritualist*, or blindly following the means while rejecting the goals, thus following rules only
for rules' sake without attaining the goal; and (e) becoming a *rebel*,
redefining success goals in one's own terms and inventing one's own
means for attaining them (Chesney-Lind & Shelden, 1992; Flowers,
1990).

Other researchers have noted that the most common adaptive
responses used by delinquents are *innovation*, expressed through illegal
means such as theft, fraud, and robbery to achieve material gain;
retreatism, the flight to drugs and alcohol as a means of escape from
frustration; and *rebellion*, the rejection of conventional authority
through aggressive and hostile behavior (Flowers, 1990).

Although Merton's theories may have had explanatory power for males, they do not hold for females, especially in the late 20th century. Given that many females now have success goals similar to those of men (Adler, 1975; Morris, 1987; Simon, 1975), and given also that women's opportunities are still far more limited than those of men (Faludi, 1991), it might be expected, according to Merton, that women would experience more strain than men, and would therefore commit more crime. Yet, this is clearly not the case: women still engage in crime at far lower levels of incidence than men.

Theories that followed on Merton's continued to explore the links between strain, social class and gender, and crime and delinquency. Among these are Albert Cohen's (1955) theories of delinquent sub-culture, which saw delinquency as a phenomenon brought about by the inability of lower-class[1] males to achieve recognition and success commensurate with the standards set by the dominant middle class.

Central to Cohen's thesis is the notion that problems of adjust-ment are different for males and females because each individual's behavior must first of all be in keeping with his or her identity as male or female. Thus, females must preserve their frail and dependent state in order to affirm themselves as feminine and as such, are not inclined towards crime and delinquency. Males, however, must preserve their independent and dominant state in order to affirm themselves as mas-culine, and thus, when thwarted, are more inclined to delinquency. For Cohen, delinquency is a male solution to a male problem:

> ... Both the respectable middle class pattern [for success, i.e., getting an education and success in the business world] and the delinquent response are characteristically *masculine*. Although they differ dramatically, to be sure, they have something in common. This common element is suggested by the words "achievement," "daring," "active mastery," "pursuit." Every one of these terms has, to be sure, a different twist of emphasis or direction when combined with the different values orientations of the respectable and the delinquent culture. ... In both cultures however, one measures his manhood by comparing his *performance*, whether it be in stealing, fighting, athletic contests, work or intellectual achievement, against those of his own sex. (Cohen, 1955, p. 139)

Cohen suggested that because lower-class males were for the most part blocked from ever achieving success as defined by the middle class, they instead inverted middle-class standards and developed a reactive and rebellious subculture. In redefining the rules for success in a way that made it attainable for them, they established themselves as "rogue males," "untrammeled in their masculinity" and therefore free from the domination of others (p. 140). Cohen described the values and standards of this subculture as "short run hedonism" that is "malicious, negativistic and non-utilitarian." Yet, he concluded: "However it may be condemned by others on moral grounds, [this behavior] has at least one virtue: it incontestably confirms, in the eyes of all concerned, [the rogue male's] essential masculinity" (Cohen, 1955, pp. 139–140).

Cohen's claim that a defense of masculinity is at the bottom of crime and delinquency leaves little room for the formation of an understanding of female crime and delinquency. This gap in applicability does not appear to have deterred others from continuing to build theory based exclusively upon male experience. Miller (1958) further explored conflict in class standards and values and argued, much as Cohen did, that a lower-class male focus on trouble, toughness, smartness, excitement, fate, and autonomy ultimately leads to engagement in delinquency and crime. He further suggested that this is often the outcome of males' tendency to seek the company of other males in street-corner groups, which become gangs. This, Miller argued, was the result of the absence of fathers in lower-class households and the inability of mothers to provide adequate male role models, thus forcing young males to learn male behavior from their peers.

Cloward and Ohlin (1960), also concentrating on males and delinquent gangs, elaborated on Miller's (1958) notions and argued that although lower-class males indeed had far less opportunity to achieve success through legitimate means and therefore experienced intense frustration, they still had ample access to illegitimate means (especially because of their propensity to congregate in gangs), which they frequently exercised. Like Miller, Cloward and Ohlin suggested that the underlying cause for delinquency could be found in the absence of males in the life-world of the lower-class adolescent. Lower-class males,

> engulfed by a feminine world and uncertain of their own identification ... protest against femininity ... in the form of robust aggressive behavior, and even malicious, irresponsible, and destructive acts. Such acts evoke maternal disapproval and thus come to stand for independence and masculinity to rebellious adolescents. (Cloward & Ohlin, 1960, p. 49; quoted in Chesney-Lind & Shelden, 1992, p. 67)

Quite apart from the fact that Miller (1958) and Cloward and Ohlin (1960) offer nothing to females — and in some ways, seem to hold females responsible for male deviance — they also overlook the fact that, despite the disproportionate representation of lower-class (or, more appropriately, working-class males in index crime statistics, the vast majority of working-class males are not before the courts for delinquency and crime. According to Flowers (1990), such theories have also been widely criticized for assuming that lower-class males automatically wish to adopt middle-class norms of material success and educational and occupational achievement, and for overlooking the fact that even those who become gang members for the most part eventually abandon their delinquent lifestyle and lead conventional adult lives.

Differential association theories of crime and delinquency

Noting that delinquents tend to gather in groups and gangs, and also that those who engage in delinquency appear to interact more with others who engage in crime than those who do not, Sutherland (1939) and others (Sutherland & Cressey, 1978) argued that deviant behavior, like other human behavior, is learned. Thus, close association with others who engage in such behavior provides opportunities to learn the techniques, motives, and values that facilitate criminal behavior. According to Flowers (1990), differential association theory suggests that

the probability of delinquent behavior varies directly with the priority, frequency, duration, and intensity of a person's contacts with patterns of delinquent behavior, and inversely with their non deviant contacts. Interaction with anti-social elements tends to take place more often when an individual's perception of their circumstances is supportive to violations of the law. (p. 130)

Flowers expands on this by adding:

… the theory contends that delinquency is a social rather than anti-social behavioral pattern. Thus, if most of a juvenile's interaction is with people who frequently violate the law and who express beliefs that seek to justify their behavior, then the juvenile has a greater chance of becoming delinquent or criminal than one who interacts with persons who do not violate the law or disapprove of such violations. (p. 130)

Sutherland, while not confining himself to a study of the working class in that he included white-collar crime and professional theft in his work, did however focus only on males. Despite this, Sutherland's differential association theories hold some promise with regard to females, given that recent research indicates that females who have frequent contact with deviant females appear to engage in deviant behavior to a greater degree than those who do not (Giordano & Cernkovich, 1979). As pointed out by Giordano, Cernkovich, and Pugh (1986; see also Morash, 1986 and Singer & Levine, 1988), females who become involved in deviance and delinquency still participate at lower rates than males, but nevertheless

> adopt a set of attitudes in which they [see] delinquency as appropriate, possible, or desirable ... and a friendship style in which they ... encourage each other as a group to act on these orientations. (Giordano et al., 1986, p. 1,194; cited in Berger, 1989, p. 389)

Social control theories of crime and delinquency

Also promising — from the point of view of understanding female violence — are social control theories of crime and delinquency, which focus on the capacity of all human beings to engage in deviance and crime (although most researchers who conceptualized these theories still focused on males as research subjects). For social control theorists, crime and delinquency have less to do with motivation to deviate from the norm and more to do with the presence or absence of conditions (internal and external) that are favorable to breaking the law. Social control theorists explored personal control or inner containment of deviant urges grounded in a positive self-concept (Reiss, 1951; Reckless, 1961), effective family and other external social controls of deviance grounded in a positive social structure (Nye, 1958; Toby, 1957), and the absence or presence of a social bond (Hirschi, 1969). Both Chesney-Lind and Shelden (1992) and Flowers (1990) select Hirschi as the most influential of the social control theorists, largely because research has borne out his notion that individuals with strong bonds to social institutions (e.g., family and school) are more likely to have lower rates of crime and delinquency.

Hirschi (1969) suggested that the social bond — that which keeps one's deviance in check — is made up of four components: (a) *attachment*, largely emotional, to family, friends, peers, and institutions such as school; (b) *commitment*, or one's personal stake or investment in conformity based in what one would stand to lose if one did engage in crime and delinquency; (c) *involvement*, or one's participation in legitimately sanctioned activities such as school, work, and non-deviant forms of recreation; and (d) *belief*, or one's acceptance that socially sanctioned moral values provide the correct foundation upon which to build one's own standards. Hirschi (again, working exclusively with boys) found that attachment, commitment, and belief were the best predictors of delinquency or the lack of it, while involvement had a lesser effect (Chesney-Lind & Shelden, 1992).

Hirschi's (1969) notions that social bonds, and the social controls exerted by these bonds, had a direct effect on the level of an individual's participation in delinquency and crime generated much further research, including research on females. Jensen and Eve (1976) and Cernkovich and Giordano (1987) found that attachment to conventional others and a belief in the legitimacy of rules had predictive power for both male and female delinquency. Cernkovich and Giordano also found that lower rates of female delinquency could be partly explained by higher levels of parental supervision and intimate communication between parents and daughters.

Hagan, Simpson, and Gillis (1987) and Hagan (1988, 1990) took up the theory of social control and argued that social control or constraint varies across gender, with females experiencing more control especially in more traditional, patriarchal families. Hagan et al. define the "ideal-type patriarchal family" as including "a husband who is employed in an authority position and a wife who is not employed outside the home" (p. 791). They define the "ideal-type egalitarian family" as including a mother and father who are both employed in authority positions outside the home (p. 792). They also define single-parent households headed by women as "a special kind of egalitarian family" which, like other egalitarian households, experiences "freedom from male domination" (p. 793).

It is the contention of Hagan et al. (1987) that whenever males are dominant, as they most often are in the ideal-type patriarchal household, mothers are charged with the task of child-rearing as a result of a division of labor along gender lines. This leaves fathers in control of production (i.e., participation in the work force) and mothers in control of consumption, domestic labor, and the "day-to-day control of their children, especially their daughters" (p. 792). According to

Hagan et al., such families reproduce the gender divisions they model and enforce and allow much less risk-taking behavior in their daughters. As a result, these families produce lower deviance and delinquency rates for females than for males, while ideal-type egalitarian families (which allow more risk taking in their female members) produce higher delinquency rates for females, rates that tend to close the gender gap. Therefore, according to Hagan et al., the more traditional the family, the lower the female delinquency rate.

The argument of Hagan et al. (1987) rests upon two points: one which suggests that mothers who work outside the home (especially in positions of authority) constitute a move away from patriarchy towards a more egalitarian system, and a second which suggests that such a move towards egalitarianism is linked with higher delinquency rates in girls. Therefore, for Hagan et al., the greater the control of men over women and girls in families, the lower the risk for female adolescent deviance. When this is not the case, and adult women in families take up more equal power with males, or find themselves in the position of being single heads of households, girls in these families become more like boys and as a consequence also take more risks, including deviant risks.

In effect, Hagan et al. (1987) appear to suggest that working mothers contribute to higher delinquency in their daughters. But, as Chesney-Lind and Shelden point out,

> no evidence suggests that as women's labor force participation has increased, girls' delinquency has increased. Indeed, during the past decade [the 1980s], when women's labor force participation and the number of female-headed households soared, aggregate female delinquency measured both by self-report and official statistics either declined or remained stable (Ageton, 1983; Chilton & Datesman, 1987; Federal Bureau of Investigation, 1986). (Chesney-Lind & Shelden, 1992, pp. 96–97)

Thus, even if Hagan and his associates are correct in pointing out that gender and patriarchy are important in shaping both male and female behavior, their assumption that a mother working outside the home increases the risk of female delinquency does not appear to hold. This theory, like others that will be discussed below, is an example of backlash theories which, in effect, recommend that women maintain traditional gender roles because in the end, liberation — seen here as a move towards the masculine — carries too great a price.

LABELING THEORIES

One final mainstream theoretical approach that may shed light on female crime and delinquency is labeling theory. Labeling theory is concerned primarily with the selective social construction of certain behaviors as criminal and delinquent rather than with original causes of behavior. Schur (1972) suggests that

> human behavior is deviant to the extent that it comes to be viewed as involving a personally discreditable departure from a group's normative expectation and it elicits interpersonal and collective reactions that serve to isolate, treat and correct or punish individuals engaged in such behavior. (p. 21)

Thus, deviance becomes the creation of those in society whom Becker (1963) called "moral entrepreneurs," that is, those who designate deviance through the creation of certain rules and standards which, when broken, constitute deviance. Deviance, then, is not characterized by certain behaviors, but is rather the consequence of assigning the label of deviance and its differential application.

This theory helps us to understand the social construction of certain behaviors as deviant for females although they are not designated as such for males. A prime example of this is the propensity of those who work in juvenile justice systems to characterize women and girls as deviant based upon the perception that they are engaged in promiscuous sexual behavior and to incarcerate them for status offenses (e.g., running away) and curfew violations because they are designated as "unmanageable" and "beyond control," a standard that is rarely applied to men and boys (Chesney-Lind & Shelden, 1992). Further, labeling theorists, unlike other mainstream theorists discussed thus far, did in fact include women in their theorizing. Schur (1984) extended his theories to women and argued that "women's powerlessness has resulted in an extensive array of labels being used against them to characterize them as deviant and to devalue and objectify the very condition of womanhood itself" (Chesney-Lind & Shelden, 1992, p. 70).

SUMMARY: MAINSTREAM THEORIES

Few mainstream sociological theories appear to have dealt with female crime and delinquency. Content with the assumption that crime and delinquency were masculine forms of behavior, and bolstered in that assumption by statistical evidence of the overwhelming participation of males in such behavior, the majority of theorists (who were them-selves male) focused on males. Those who did address female partici-pation in crime and delinquency still grounded most of their thinking in male experience.

A Brief History of Theories of Female Crime and Delinquency

As outlined above, most researchers treated females as marginal to the study of crime and delinquency prior to the 1970s. Interest in female crime and delinquency arose, in part at least, as the result of two forces: (a) the involvement of more women in scholarship and (b) the possi-bility that female crime and delinquency may be on the rise.[2] A care-ful reading of work focusing on females reveals that most research on female crime and delinquency has been geared towards answering the question, "Why do so *few* girls and women engage in crime and delin-quency?" rather than, "*Why* do girls and women engage in crime and delinquency?" When females are considered, the focus is generally on the gender gap and the proportionally low participation of females, rather than on the conditions or motivations that move females towards crime and delinquency.

Three categories of theory have emerged from the literature:

- those that explain the gender gap in crime and delinquency as given in the *biological differences* between the sexes and explain female deviance in terms of biologically based sexual problems;

- those that explain the gender gap in crime and delinquency as derived from differences in *gender role socialization* and explain the kinds of deviance females do participate in as based on their gen-der roles; and

- those that accept that female deviance is on the rise relative to male deviance and explain this trend in terms of a "*masculiniza-tion" of women* brought on by women's liberation and the feminist movement.

All three categories explain female crime and delinquency as a move away from the feminine towards the masculine. Only Chesney-Lind and her colleagues (1985, 1992) call for a shift away from theories of delinquency that are uncritically grounded in male behavior. In place of such theories, Chesney-Lind et al. suggest a move towards a broader understanding of the lives of deviant girls and women.

Biologically based theories of female crime and delinquency

Early theories of female crime, like early theories of male crime, were strongly affected by social Darwinism. Biology was destiny, and criminal behavior was seen as the result of problems with evolution. Cesare Lombroso, working in 1895, explained all criminal elements in society as biological *throwbacks* resulting from an arrested evolutionary process. According to Lombroso, females were by their very nature less disposed to crime than males because (a) they had evolved less than males and were therefore naturally more childlike, sedentary, weak and passive, and thus not able to participate in challenging and independent activities like crime; (b) their primary functions were childbearing and caretaking, which made them unsuited to criminal activity; and (c) their underdeveloped intelligence, as well as their maternity, piety, and weakness, tempered their often jealous and vengeful natures and prevented them from behaving like criminals. Thus, Lombroso reasoned that if women did choose to become criminals, it was largely because they did not possess a maternal instinct and were most probably degenerate, unwomanly (read, masculine) throwbacks.

The belief that biology is destiny — along with the notion that men and women had natural roles and true natures — outlived Lombroso, although his work has long been, for the most part, discredited. Otto Pollack, working in the 1950s, and Cowie, Cowie, and Slater, working in the 1960s, wrote extensively about imbalances in women's physiology and sexuality as causes of female crime.

For Pollack (1950), the explanation for the consistently low rates of female crime (relative to male rates) lay in the fact that women were naturally more deceitful and secretive, and could therefore get away with far more than men could. He suggested that this ability to deceive has its origins in women's sexual passivity and their ability to conceal or feign sexual arousal — something that men cannot do. Therefore, women's ability to be deceitful, coupled with the various hormonal imbalances brought about by menstruation, menopause, and pregnancy, predisposed women towards criminality and at the same time provided them with the means to escape detection and responsibility for their actions.

As Chesney-Lind and her colleagues (1985, 1992) point out, the notion that biology is destiny lives on in more recent studies. For example, for Cowie, Cowie, and Slater (1968), differences in male and female delinquency were largely explained by anatomy. According to Cowie et al. (1968), two primary forces were responsible: (a) biological, somatic, and hormonal differences, which derived from chromosomal differences between the two sexes, and (b) the natural timidity and lack of enterprise found in females. If females did get involved in criminal activity, Cowie et al. attributed this to an excess of male chromosomes. Of interest here is the notion that what's good for the gander is not good for the goose.

Criminality in males has thus far been described in positive terms as the outcome of males' more advanced evolvement and greater honesty, coupled with their propensity to become involved in challenging and independent activities. However, when females engage in criminality, the tone becomes more negative. They are variously described as lacking in some capacity, especially so-called feminine capacities, such as the maternal instinct, or natural female passivity (which term is used pejoratively), and they are accused of the ultimate faux pas: an excess of male chromosomes, those very same chromosomes that lend strength of purpose to males.

The notion that biological factors exert a strong influence persists among some criminologists to the present day. Slade (1984) and Binder, Geis, and Bruce (1988) proposed premenstrual syndrome (PMS) as a cause for female criminality, although little evidence was brought to bear in support of this claim, and Wilson and Herrnstein (1985) repeated the argument that biological factors determine levels of aggression as well as differentials in male and female law breaking. Konopka (1966, 1983), who was one of the first researchers actually to study adolescent females in order to understand their life-worlds (and who broke more new ground by emphasizing the effects on female crime and delinquency of the changing cultural position of women and the sexual double standard), nonetheless concluded that girls and women were largely controlled by biology and sexuality. As Chesney-Lind and Shelden (1992) point out, Konopka, in noting that most girls come to the attention of the juvenile justice system because of sex-related behaviors, was convinced that "most female delinquency is either 'sexual' or 'relational' rather than 'criminal' in nature" (p. 61) and therefore requires help with sexual adjustment.

The assumption, made by so many researchers, that delinquency in juvenile females is largely sexual delinquency borne of sexual maladjustment, can be explained by the fact that in the United States, the ratio of arrests for prostitution is 50:1 for girls over boys (Chesney-Lind & Shelden, 1992, p. 8). Noteworthy as this arrest pattern may be, it may in fact reflect not girls' sexual deviance, but the American judicial system's preoccupation with girls' sexuality, a preoccupation that mirrors the preoccupation of the culture at large.

Gender role theories of female crime and delinquency

In contrast to and in protest against biologically based theories of crime, gender role theories of delinquency and crime emerged in the 1950s (Grosser, 1951) and have grown in strength and number to the present day (Balkan & Berger, 1979; Hagan et al., 1985, 1987; Hoffman-Bustamente, 1973; Morris, 1965). Given that males are socialized to be more active, aggressive, and independent and are rewarded for flaunting conventional behavior, while females are socialized to be more passive, caring, and dependent and are rewarded for engaging in conventional behavior (Berger, 1989; Gilligan, 1982; Hoffman-Bustamente, 1973), it is reasoned by gender role theorists that male/female differences in aggression and crime can be accounted for by differences in socialization.

The power of gender role theories lies in the clear differentiation that exists between the kinds of crime committed by men and those that are committed by women. Berger (1989) notes that "male juveniles have been consistently more likely than females to be arrested for every crime category (except running away and prostitution)" (p. 378). Citing Federal Bureau of Investigation data from 1987, he states that

> male juveniles accounted for 89% of all juvenile arrests for "index" violent crimes (i.e., murder, non-negligent manslaughter, forcible rape, robbery, aggravated assault) and 79% of all juvenile arrests for index property crimes (i.e., burglary, larceny-theft, motor vehicle theft, arson) as well as 91% of arrests for vandalism and 81% of arrests for disorderly conduct (FBI, 1988). (Berger, 1989, p. 377)

Chesney-Lind and Shelden tell a similar story using self-report data gathered in the United States by Cernkovich and Giordano (1979):

Boys are more likely to report involvement in gang fighting, carrying a hidden weapon, strong-arming students and others, aggravated assault, hitting students, sexual assault [and sex for money]. Boys are also disproportionately involved in serious property crimes; they are much more likely to report involvement in thefts of more than $50. (Chesney-Lind & Shelden, 1992, pp. 16–17)

Again, males show dominance in all areas including trading sex for money, a delinquent behavior traditionally considered "feminine." Comparable data were reported by Figueria-McDonough, Barton, and Sarri (1981), who found significant gender differences in theft, vandalism, fraud, serious fighting, carrying weapons, and prostitution, with males reporting their involvement at ratios of between 3:1 and 6:1 over females.

With regard to official crime statistics, Hindelang, Hirschi, and Weis (1981) also reported stable, offense-specific, male/female differences in U.S. uniform crime reports from 1960 to 1976, with males showing a distinct dominance in burglary, weapons offenses, assault, robbery, and auto theft. Data on admissions to youth corrections facilities gathered in British Columbia (the Canadian province in which the study described in this book was conducted) between 1986 and 1993 show a similar trend.

Figures on the incidence of admission to custody (1986 to 1993) provided by the British Columbia Ministry of the Attorney General show that where youth in custody are concerned, males account for 94% of breaking and entering convictions, 81% of crimes against persons, 84.5% of property crimes, 76.7% of sex crimes, 68.5% of theft by fraud, 69.8% of theft under $1,000, and 89.6% of violent crime on average, over the seven-year period since the Young Offenders Act became law in Canada. Data provided by the Police Services Division, also of the British Columbia Ministry of the Attorney General, tell very much the same story: From 1986 to 1993, males were charged with 85.7% of murders, 82.6% of attempted murders, 96% of sexual assaults, 75% of all other forms of assault, 87% of robberies involving the use of weapons, 93% of breaking and entering, 91% of thefts of motor vehicles, and 68.5% of other thefts (including shoplifting).

Although the data reported here are by no means exhaustive, whether one turns to official crime reports or to self-report data for serious crimes, males clearly participate in significantly greater numbers than females. What must be noted as well is that while the population of adolescents in British Columbia increased at the rate of 6% during this period (1986 to 1993), the number of male youths charged with assault increased 118%, rising from 672 charges in 1986 to 1,468 charges in 1993, and the number of female youth charged increased by 250%, rising from 178 charges in 1986 to 624 charges in 1993. Thus, male young offenders are still in the forefront where assault is concerned, but female young offender participation rates are increasing more rapidly than those of males. In 1986, females accounted for 26% of all assault charges laid against youths in British Columbia. By 1993, this had risen to 42%. Although the seven-year average for assault by female youth in British Columbia still hovers at 25%, this figure masks what appears to be an alarming rise in the participation of female youth in all forms of assault other than sexual assault.

British Columbia is not the only province to record a rise in crime among young offenders, although as with all crime rates in Canada, it continues to lead the way. Data provided by Statistics Canada (Canadian Crime Statistics, 1995) show a similar trend across the country. From 1986 to 1993, the number of female youths charged with assault increased by 190%, rising from 1,728 charges in 1986 to 5,096 charges in 1993, and the number of male youths charged increased by 117%, rising from 7,547 charges in 1986 to 16,375 charges in 1993.

Reports from the United States also paint a grim picture. According to figures released by the U.S. Department of Justice on November 12, 1995, the number of juveniles arrested for weapons violations has more than doubled between 1985 and 1993. The rise in arrests for weapons offenses among juveniles is three times higher than that for adults for the same period. Newspapers report that in the United States, minors under the age of 18 now account for nearly 25% of arrests for violations of laws controlling deadly weapons ("Juvenile weapons arrests double," *Globe & Mail*, November 13, 1995).

Tom Gabor, a criminologist at the University of Ottawa, Ontario, who completed a national survey of school violence for the Solicitor General of Canada in 1994, concluded that school violence and armed students are on the increase and that females are now more often involved in violence than in the past ("Tremendous increase in violence among girls," *Victoria Times Colonist*, October 15, 1993). In view of such reports, it is not surprising that the media, school officials, and ordinary citizens are reporting an escalation in youth violence, particularly for female adolescents.

When theorists attempt to explain the gender gap in youth crime statistics, those who favor gender role theories often explain differences in male/female participation as an outcome of imposing higher moral expectations and greater social controls on girls and women. As Berger (1989) points out,

> family arrangements have kept females, in comparison to males, more cloistered, and females have been expected to provide support and nurturance to others. In the occupational world, these traditions have been reflected in and reinforced by "gender appropriate" occupations such as secretaries, waitresses, teachers, and social workers. As a result, girls have been more closely supervised by their parents than boys and have had less opportunity than boys have had to commit delinquent acts. They have been more likely to accept general moral standards, blame themselves for their problems, feel shame for their misconduct, be taught to avoid risks, fear social disapproval and be deterred by legal sanctions. (p. 377) (See also: Balkan & Berger, 1979; Giallombardo, 1980; Hagan, Gillis, & Simpson, 1985; Mawby, 1980; Morash, 1983; Morris, 1965; Richard & Tittle, 1981.)

Given the consistency of the gender gap in both official crime rates and self-report data, especially for more serious crimes, an understanding of socialization patterns and gender expectations may indeed contribute to an understanding of male/female differences in participation. However, it does not explain either the motivations for females to take up crime and delinquency, nor the engagement of females in so-called male crimes and delinquencies. Therefore, a reliance on socialization patterns and gender expectations "fails to explore motivation and intent as an integral part of female crime. ... While significant in its contribution ... role theory still provides only a limited perspective on female crime and behavior" (Chesney-Lind & Koroki, 1985, p. 7). Further, in bringing into focus the need to understand the differences in social experiences and their effect on behavior for males and females, gender role theories also provide a basis for the feminist backlash notion that a change in women's roles and the emancipation of women will ultimately lead to a greater participation of women in criminal activity.

"Masculinization" theories of female crime and delinquency

Freda Adler (1975) is generally credited with promoting the belief that a convergence of gender role expectations brought about by feminism and the women's movement in the late 1960s and 1970s has contributed significantly to a rise in female crime. Adler claimed that "the phenomenon of female criminality is but one wave in ... [the] rising tide of female assertiveness — a wave which has not yet crested and may even be seeking its level uncomfortably close to the high-water mark set by male violence" (quoted in Berger, 1989, p. 379). Basing her claims on largely unfounded notions that traditional attitudes towards women were rapidly changing and that women were indeed making substantial gains in all areas of the corporate world (Anderson, 1991; Faludi, 1991), Adler contended that

> in the same way that women are demanding equal opportunity in the fields of legitimate endeavor, a similar number of determined women are forcing their way into the world of major crimes ... as the position of women approximates the position of men, so does the frequency and type of their criminal activity. (Quoted in Chesney-Lind & Koroki, 1985, p. 9)

Adler's claims supported those of Simon (1975), who noted a rise in women's arrest rates for white-collar crimes (e.g., embezzlement and fraud) and attributed this to women's greater participation in the workforce.

Adler's (1975) claims created a continuing debate because they appeared to be supported by official arrest statistics for the period between 1960 and 1975, which showed dramatic increases in female crime, especially in non-traditional offenses for females. The primary objection to her thesis came from scholars who disputed her analysis of official crime statistics. Specifically, they argued that although percentage increases in non-traditional crimes for females (murder, aggravated assault, robbery) showed dramatic leaps, these increases were based on very small absolute numbers where even a small change in number could create a large change in percentage (Chesney-Lind, 1992; Miller, 1986).

As well, most increases in female crime were found in non-violent offenses. Simon (1975) found the greatest increases in such offenses as larceny, fraud, and check forgery; he argued that this was the direct result of the feminization of poverty brought on by the rise in single-family households headed by females. This was confirmed by Steffensmeir (1978) and Steffensmeir and Cobb (1981), who found major increases in female crime largely in shoplifting and check forgery, crimes that are consistent with traditional female roles.

Although they and others concurred that female violence for adults and juveniles had risen between 1960 and 1977, Steffensmeir and his associates found that male violence had also increased at an equal rate, thus preserving the gender gap. Steffensmeir's work itself sparked a further debate centering around interpretation of data and methods for calculating comparative changes in crime participation rates (see Berger, 1989).

This debate continues and is reflected in the current alarm about greater participation of females in violence in schools. At the present time, it does appear that both males and females are participating more in all forms of crime and delinquency, and that sex differences are narrowing somewhat, at least with regard to assault (Summary Statistics, British Columbia, 1994).

Although Adler (1975), Simon (1975), and others hold the emancipation of women responsible for an apparent narrowing of the gender gap in crime rates, a number of researchers have found evidence to the contrary. For example, James and Thornton (1980) found that attitudes towards feminism had little to do with the extent and kind of female participation in delinquent behavior. Cernkovich and Giordano (1979) found that positive attitudes towards feminism were not related to participation in delinquency. Rather, they found that feminist attitudes may *inhibit* delinquent behavior, and that more traditional attitudes towards the role of women were associated with increased delinquency. As Chesney-Lind and Shelden (1992) point out,

> serious research efforts to locate the dark side of the women's movement have almost without exception been unsuccessful. Careful analyses of existing data fail to support the notion that girls have been committing nontraditional (i.e., "masculine") crimes. It seems peculiar ... that so many academics would be willing to consider a hypothesis that assumed improving girls' and women's economic conditions would lead to an increase in female crime when almost all the existing criminological literature stresses the role played by discrimination and poverty (and unemployment and underemployment) in the creation of crime. Because rectification of these social injustices has been put forward as a major solution to crime, it is more than curious that in the case of women's crime, the reverse was argued with such ease and received such wide public acceptance. (pp. 77–78)

Despite this, the notion that feminism is responsible for a rise in female delinquency and crime persists, especially in the popular press. Claims such as those made by McGovern (1995) that "prodded by feminism, today's teenage girls embrace antisocial behavior" underline the popular notion that somehow feminism is contributing to a decline in social values (p. 28). As McGovern sees it, "the rate of cultural degeneration seems to be accelerating" because of "new masculinized attitudes [that] permeate girls' attitudes" (p. 29).

Despite the fact that "masculinization" theories of female crime and delinquency have been shown to be inadequate, the "persistent theme ... that masculinity, of one sort or another, is at the core of [female] delinquency" (Chesney-Lind & Shelden, 1992) nevertheless appears to be central to all sociological theories of crime. In every case, female experience is measured against that of males, and theories about female delinquency are constructed out of already existing theories premised upon male experience.

The Implications

If "all theories of delinquency are built around the lives and experiences of males, whose development, behavior, and options are radically different from those of females" (Chesney-Lind & Shelden, 1992, p. 80), how then are we to understand the deviant girl, particularly the violent girl, in her own right?

Chesney-Lind and Shelden suggest turning to the girls themselves and beginning the search for an understanding of female deviance with their personal accounts. They call for a qualitative exploration of the lives of deviant girls by pointing out that much insight into male delinquency grew from the willingness of male researchers to spend large amounts of time interacting with delinquent boys. They note that researchers such as Frederick Thrasher (1927) and Clifford Shaw (1930, 1938) generated volumes of information on the lives of the boys they studied, sometimes devoting an entire book either to one boy or to a small group of boys. Chesney-Lind and Shelden point out that other researchers relied heavily on the work of Thrasher and Shaw, and lament the fact that much of delinquency research on girls, including their own, has taken a quantified view — one that seeks to understand delinquency in terms of sociological and psychological variables and factors, rather than in terms of the essential features of delinquent action as a lived experience. Such a view does not provide the same qualitative basis for understanding that has been granted to theorists of male delinquency.

It appears, therefore, that if we are to understand delinquent girls, we must first of all understand the circumstances of their lives. Few such studies exist. Chesney-Lind and Koroki (1985) interviewed female delinquents in custody in Hawaii. Chesney-Lind and Shelden (1992) mention three others: Bottcher (1986), who interviewed girls in California training schools; Arnold (1990), who conducted a retrospective study of black women's reflections upon turning to criminal behavior in New York; and Gilfu (1988), who studied adult female offenders in Massachusetts. Two of these studies involved talking to women about what it had been like to be deviant girls; they did not involve adolescent females. Locating research that focuses on the life-worlds of delinquent girls, especially those not yet involved with the justice system, proved to be difficult. Where violent school girls were concerned, no such study could be found.

Four independent researchers were located who had produced a total of eight studies, each of which explored the lives of girls who were gang members (Brown 1977; Campbell, 1984, 1986, 1987; Horowitz, 1983, 1986, 1987; Klein, 1971). These studies do not focus directly on girls' violence, but do deal with girls' accounts of their own experience. As such, they contribute to the qualitative basis for the kind of understanding that Chesney-Lind and Shelden call for. However, all these researchers confine themselves to the lived experiences of girls who are struggling at the sociocultural and socioeconomic margins and who are American, mostly black or Hispanic, or — in the case of Chesney-Lind and Koroki's (1985) study — members of a racially mixed Hawaiian group. White school girls have so far not been included, thus leaving the mistaken impression that they have little involvement with violence.

The girls in Chesney-Lind and Koroki's (1985) study were interviewed about a number of dimensions of their lives. They reported coming from extremely troubled homes, in which they experienced divorce, abandonment, death of a parent, problems with stepparents, alcoholism, and frequent moves. They reported feeling lonely and isolated both from peers and family; they also reported feeling suicidal and in some cases, made suicide attempts. All had experienced violence and physical abuse, and six of the ten had experienced sexual abuse. School life was problematic, although only two actually reported not liking school. Despite their school difficulties, they all expected to graduate from high school, and six of the ten wanted to go to college. Their notions of gender were for the most part stereotypical, and their gender role expectations for the future were traditional. Most of the girls were experienced users of drugs and alcohol, and most had been involved in deviant behavior for some time before they were arrested and put into detention. Typically, they reported deliberately adopting a "bad girl" image because this afforded them status, excitement, and a sense of pride. Finding themselves unable to make it in the role of "good" girl, they found a new lease on life in the role of "bad" girl. Here, at least, was a release from boredom — even a chance to shine.

Chesney-Lind and Koroki (1985) point to poverty, severe family problems, and physical and sexual abuse as factors that thrust the girls in their study into difficulties in school and into behavioral patterns that eventually brought them into the juvenile justice system. They also highlight the girls' traditional notions of sex and gender as a contributing factor, in that their participants

> typically hope to escape from their present situation by marriage to men who, like their fathers, stepfathers, and brothers abuse them. Wedded to traditional and rigid sex roles, these girls see no other way out, and their fantasies, while enabling them to deal with the loneliness of the present, guarantee nothing but another generation of "bad" girls in the future. (p. iv)

Chesney-Lind and Shelden (1992), reflecting further upon the Hawaiian study, suggest that for these girls, delinquency was an adaptive move, a way of coping with otherwise dismal life-worlds. When all that one can expect at home is abuse, then running away, truancy, and even trading sex for money, food, or shelter become survival strategies. Chesney-Lind and Shelden (1992) point out that girls, particularly working-class (and especially poor) girls from dysfunctional families[3] (i.e., families characterized by marital discord, violence, and the abuse and neglect of children), are disadvantaged early in life by entrenched stereotypical notions of gender, limited educational prospects, the constraints of the sexual double standard, and by the emotional and psychological impact of physical and sexual abuse.

Campbell (1984, 1991), who studied black and Hispanic girls in New York City, found that her subjects participated in gangs primarily because they were attempting to escape violent and dysfunctional families and the resulting emotional isolation. Typically, they had experienced severe parental alcohol and drug misuse, family disintegration through marital discord or the alcohol- or drug-related death of a parent, and extreme poverty. Added to these factors were the ever-present difficulties they experienced as young women of color. When they joined gangs, they wanted somewhere to belong: a community that would afford them safety, continuity, loyalty, and unconditional acceptance. As well, the support of a gang held out the promise (if not the reality) of improved financial status, albeit through illegal means.

As gang members, these girls engaged in violence as a means of survival and as a way of proving their worth to other members. They participated also because violence was accepted and expected. Typically, they fought for one of two reasons: (a) to settle disputes over boys and (b) to enhance their reputations as "tough girls." Being known as "tough" meant that other girls (and also some boys) would fear them and show them respect. This gave them a sense of worth and power. As one girl in Campbell's (1991) study put it:

> It's true — you feel proud when you see a girl that you fucked up. Her face is all scratched or she got a black eye, you say, "Damn, I beat the shit out of that girl you know." And it makes you feel stronger, then you want to fight more and more … .(p. 263)

All the studies suggest that the subjects' marginality facilitates their participation in a delinquent and/or gang life — and the violence that accompanies it. Missing in the literature are studies that seek to understand the life-worlds and practices of non-marginalized, violent, working-class and middle-class girls — girls who are not found in youth custody and who are not part of an identifiable gang.

Bridging the Gap

The fact that the literature does not as yet address the participation of non-marginalized girls in violent and aggressive behavior helped my colleagues and me to choose the focus of our work. Together we undertook to follow the three-pronged approach outlined in the introduction to this book: We began our study by taking a statistical baseline of students' perceptions of and experiences with violence, and we quite deliberately included questions on a range of their life factors in order to allow us to interpret our findings more fully with respect to violence.

Following this, I undertook a qualitative study that inquired into the life-worlds and practices of school girls who were involved in violence, but who were neither involved with the juvenile justice system nor members of a gang. I sought to answer a number of questions:

- Who are the young women who engage in violence? Where do they come from, and how do they find one another?

- How do they arrange their activities, make decisions, carry out their acts of aggression?

- How do they explain their actions to themselves, to one another, and to others who might oppose them?

- What kinds of home lives do these girls have? What are their families, parents, siblings, grandparents like?

- What stories might the girls tell me? What stories might their parents tell me?

- Who interacts with the girls at school? Whom do they know, and who knows them?

- What forces are at work at home, at school, and in the community that serve to suggest to these young women that aggression and violence are a legitimate means to an end?

- How do these girls make sense of their participation in violence? How do they perceive violence in others and in general?

My main purpose in pursuing these questions was to formulate an understanding of the girls' participation in violence. It is my belief that we do the things we do because we have made sense of ourselves and the world along particular lines and are therefore impelled to act in certain ways. I view action in Michael Novak's (1978) terms, that is, as "a declaration of faith: one cannot act without implicitly imagining the shape of the world, the significance of one's own role, the place at which the struggle is effectively joined" (p. 45). Thus, I concluded that if I wanted to understand violence among teenage school girls, I needed to approach them in ways that would allow me to discover all I could about their "declarations of faith." I needed to learn how they lived their lives and how they made sense of their actions.

Upon completing the analysis of our baseline data and the qualitative study of the *Life Worlds and Practices of Violent School Girls* (Artz, 1995), we became involved in the current phase of the Youth Violence Project: A Community-Based Violence Prevention Project. This phase is a collaborative, community-based initiative designed to address the problem of youth violence in a Vancouver Island school district. It involves teachers, counselors, parents, and students, as well as representatives from health care and social service agencies. It consists of 13 individual antiviolence initiatives that have been developed by school-based health teams located in each of the local school communities for whom these initiatives are intended. Although there are 13 initiatives, these in some cases extend to more than one school; thus, they involve a total of 16 school communities. The school-based health teams include the participation of over 60 parents, 118 students, 60 educators, and 20 local agency workers (some of whom participate on more than one health team). The overall project serves over 5,400 students, their families, educators, and community members. It is intended to educate and train students and community members in a preventative approach to violence that includes helping individuals change their behavior and acquire and master skills that will enable them to act differently in circumstances that previously would have called forth violent responses.

This project will provide us with much needed information about violence prevention. The research dimensions of the project focus on the evaluation of the effectiveness of the various initiatives, using a model of participant-based program evaluation. Because the writing of this book and the implementation and evaluation of the prevention initiatives are concurrent, it is possible to report here only preliminary findings. Nevertheless, much has already been learned about programs and interventions that speak to violent girls.

NOTES

1. "Lower class" refers to a socioeconomic status (SES) category where "lower" means "lower income and status." "Working class" generally refers to the connection between social class and work — in this case, blue-collar work. The distinction between the two terms comes down

to money. "Lower class" always means "having lower socioeconomic levels of income," whereas "working class" refers to the kind of work an individual does regardless of income, as physical or skilled labor is often highly paid.

2. This possibility solidified into a reality in the 1990s, as the statistics presented on pages 13–15 show.

3. Although most of the literature surveyed here focuses on a sociological understanding of female crime and delinquency, it is clear from the material provided by Chesney-Lind and her associates (1985, 1994) and by Campbell (1991) that dysfunctional families are strongly implicated in the deviance and delinquency of their daughters.

Flowers (1990, pp. 133–139), in his overview of the literature on juvenile offenders, states that "many experts believe that it is the interactants of family life that is the greatest predictor of adolescent delinquency" (p. 133). In examining the familial correlates of delinquent behavior, Flowers (1990) cites over 40 studies and notes that child abuse (especially sexual abuse) and physical violence are strongly associated with deviance and delinquency for both males and females. According to Flowers, numerous studies have shown that sexual abuse is strongly linked with prostitution and sex crimes. He also notes that many studies have shown that violent adolescents have often witnessed brutality in their families and experienced it at the hands of their parents or other family members. Such abuse is not only strongly linked to extra-familial violence; it is also linked to intra-familial violence, in that children who have been physically and sexually abused also tend to abuse their parents more than children who have not been abused.

Other familial correlates of delinquent behavior also listed by Flowers are: lax or inconsistent discipline and harsh discipline; lack of parental affection; absence of the kind of parenting that promotes constructive interpersonal communication and encourages the development of normative values and prosocial behavior and of academic and professional skills; the "broken home factor," in which one or both parents are absent through death, desertion, separation, or divorce; and family dissension, where families have remained intact but are characterized by a climate of conflict and discord. With regard to this last correlate, Flowers suggests that "there is indication that intact families beset by conflict and turmoil are more significant in delinquency formation than broken home families" (p. 139). Finally, Flowers includes intergenerational cycles of violence and abuse grounded in "a lifestyle of neglect that comes from sharing and passing on of family misfortunes" as the context in which the familial correlates he itemizes have their anchor (p. 135).

CHAPTER TWO

Profiles of the Protagonists

> More kids from middle to upper middle income backgrounds are committing violent assaults on their own peer group or on the adult group or the teaching staff than they used to. (Auty, Dempsey, Duggan, Lowery, West, & Wiseman, 1993, p. 5)

> Violence: a use of physical force so as to damage or injure ... an abusive use of force ... . (*The New Lexicon Webster's Encyclopedic Dictionary of the English Language*, 1988, p. 1,099)

> Assault: a vigorous armed attack ... a violent critical attack ... an unlawful threat to use force against another person (*The New Lexicon Webster's Encyclopedic Dictionary of the English Language*, 1988, p. 56).

This chapter draws on the findings of the *Survey of Student Life* (Artz & Riecken, 1994) in order to provide profiles of students who report that they engage in violence in schools. In creating these profiles we, like all other researchers, were faced with the task of defining our terms. We had to ask ourselves the following questions:

- What did we mean when we described someone as violent?
- How would we delineate between violent and non-violent youth?
- Given that our study had a broader basis than violence alone, what else did we want to investigate in relation to violence?

How we answered these questions is explained in the section that follows.

Defining Violence and Creating Comparison Groups

Embedded within the *Survey of Student Life* (Artz & Riecken, 1994) was a question consisting of 13 variables that tapped into rule-breaking and deviant or violent behavior. This question has previously been used by Gordon Barnes (1991), a noted Canadian researcher in the fields of family violence, addictions, and substance abuse, in his *Northern Family Life Survey*. Barnes adapted his questionnaire from an earlier one developed by American researcher Richard Jessor (1977), director of the Institute of Behavioral Science and director of the MacArthur Foundation Research Program on Youth at Risk.

Using Barnes's question meant we did not have to re-invent the wheel; it also meant that we were working with a measure that had been previously tested and that lent credibility to our findings. This question investigated such behaviors as smoking without parents' permission, lying about one's whereabouts, various degrees of skipping classes or school, and various levels of stealing, damaging property, violence, and carrying weapons.

Of the 13 variables investigated, the one that spoke most directly to violence reads, "During the past year, how often have you beaten up another kid?," thus defining violence ("beating up another kid"). Students responded by circling the number corresponding to one of four choices: (1) "Never," (2) "Once or twice," (3) "Several times," or (4) "Very often." For purposes of analysis, students' answers were dichotomized into "Never" and "Once or More." These groups were termed "nonhitters" and "hitters," respectively. This dichotomy was deemed to represent the clearest and most natural distinction between the two groups, and was used for both males and females in the creation of the profiles of the protagonists.

Of the 1,466 students who provided an answer to the variable that separated hitters from nonhitters, *51.9% of the males* (i.e., 396 of 763) *and 20.9% of the females* (i.e., 147 of 703) *answered that in the past year, they had beaten up another kid once or twice.* This means that 37% of our sample identified their involvement in physical violence in the past year. Further, the male:female ratios for self-reported participation in violence found in previous research (Hindelang, Hirschi, & Weis, 1981; Berger, 1989) have typically been on the order of 3:1 to 4:1, whereas we are reporting a male:female ratio of slightly under 2.5:1. Given the magnitude of the response rates, the seriousness of violence in schools is not to be underestimated, nor is the participation of girls.

The Overall Picture: Gender-Based Comparisons of Nonhitting and Hitting Students

In order to discover how those who reported beating up another student differed from those who reported that they had not done this, we created four groups: nonhitting females, nonhitting males, hitting females, and hitting males. We tabulated their answers to all other questions in the *Survey of Student Life,* and then compared outcomes for all the groups we created. A chi-square analysis of our data showed that: (a) there were *more differences* between males and females who *had not beaten* up another student in the past year (56/168) than there were between males and females who had beaten up another student in the past year (31/168); and (b) there were *more differences between males* who had and had not beaten up another student (52/168) than there were between females who had and had not beaten up another student in the past year (30/168).

Thus, males and females who do not engage in violence appear to be more distinguishable along gender lines than males and females who engage in violence; males who engage in violence are more readily distinguishable from males who do not; and females who engage in violence, despite showing some similarities with their male counterparts, are still more like girls who don't engage in violence than they are like boys.

To facilitate an overview of the comparisons generated by our database, we have presented our findings using the following categories:

- Relationships and Social Attitudes.
- Personal and Social Concerns.
- Support Systems.
- Sources of Enjoyment and Sources of Concern.[1]
- Experience of Abuse and Victimization (Physical and Sexual).
- Participation in Deviant Behavior.

Relationships and Social Attitudes

In this category, participants were asked to provide information about their perspectives on and experiences with family, peer groups, schools and teachers, interpersonal values, moral judgments, and self-concept.

Family
Eighty-four point four percent of students surveyed were living in two-parent households. The overall breakdown of living arrangements was: 64.5% were living with both biological parents, 11.9% were living with mother and stepfather, 3.8% were living with mother and a common-law partner, 2.8% were living with father and stepmother, 1.4%

were living with father and a common-law partner, 13% were living with mother only, and 2.6% were living with father only.

Most participants' parents were employed, and few were experiencing the deprivation of poverty. As well, the majority of parents were educated at the high school graduation level or better. (See Tables A-1 and A-2 in Appendix I for a breakdown of parental occupation/education for the sample as a whole.)

Neither males nor females who hit reported any significant differences in family configuration, living arrangements, parental employment, or parental education from those reported by males and females overall. Familial differences were, however, found in family dynamics. (See Tables A-3a and A-3b in Appendix I.)

Hitting females and hitting males reported placing significantly less importance upon family life than either nonhitting females or nonhitting males. Hitting females also reported that enjoyment of their mothers was less applicable to them than all other groups, and that they feared being physically abused at home, and were physically abused at home, at significantly greater rates than those reported by all other groups. As well, hitting females smoked without their parents' permission more than all other groups. However, nonhitting females also smoked more often without parental permission than nonhitting males, and at the same rates reported by hitting males.

A similar pattern emerged with regard to lying about one's whereabouts. Hitting females lied more often than nonhitting females and nonhitting males, while nonhitting females lied more often than nonhitting males. Hitting females and hitting males reported lying at about the same rates (i.e., their rates, while numerically different, were not statistically different). Thus, on average, females reported smoking more and lying more than males. Finally, hitting females and hitting males reported the same rates for staying out all night without parents' permission and for deliberately ruining an item of parents' property after an argument, rates that were significantly higher than those reported by nonhitting females and nonhitting males, who reported the same significantly lower rates.

Peer Groups

In the survey, students were asked if they were members of a number of groups including school clubs, youth clubs, sports teams, religious organizations, and specific street groups ("Bangers," "Rappers," or

"Skates"). The only significant differences that emerged with regard to group affiliation and participation centered around self-reported group membership and the differential importance participants placed upon their involvement in dating, party-going, and negative experiences with sex. We found that both hitting males and hitting females reported being members of either the Bangers or Rappers at far higher rates than nonhitting males and nonhitting females. When Skates were also considered, we found that 68.8% of hitting females' and 53.5% of hitting males' group membership could be accounted for. (See Table A-4 in Appendix I.)

The following brief descriptions will help the reader understand those street groups in which hitting participants claimed membership.

Rappers. Rappers are people who listen to rap music, which has its origins in reggae and American inner-city, black-ghetto street music. Rap involves rhyming and dancing; its main appeal is its tribal rhythms. Rap is "cool" in the style of black America; rap is also angry. Rap endorses gangs, crime, machismo, and misogyny, as well as freedom from white dominant-group oppression. Being a Rapper means acquiring an instant style: baggy clothes, designer sneakers, and brandname (and sports-team affiliated) jackets, shirts, and pants. For most adolescents, being a Rapper has more to do with fashion and style than it does with espousing the sentiments expressed in the lyrics of rap music.

Though the main draw with rap is beat and image, Rappers do take a position with regard to violence. Mostly, their message is, "I'm tougher than you." This holds true for both males and females. In the final analysis, a Rapper is loath to back down and must guard his or her reputation for toughness by exhibiting a willingness to fight, especially if "dissed"; that is, if one perceives that he or she is being treated with disrespect.

Bangers. Bangers are people who particularly like heavy metal music. Their favorite bands include Guns 'N Roses, Alice In Chains, and Metallica. Heavy metal music is largely blue-collar and antiestablishment in its origins. Often the music expresses angst, anger, and rage, and sometimes the focus is on a self-absorbed examination of substance abuse. Bangers' values are expressed in their music, and their heroes are heavy metal musicians.

Both male and female Bangers wear T-shirts and tight jeans emblazoned with the names of their favorite music groups. Banger males usually grow their hair long, and females may dye their hair blond. Females often carry large purses or bags in order to carry alcohol and drugs for boys. Bangers believe in male dominance; females "look after" (read, serve and look up to) males. Banger girls, like Rapper girls, are tough, particularly when it comes to beating off competition from other girls vis-à-vis their boyfriends.

SKATES. Skates, or Skaters, are people whose focus is predominantly on the activity of skateboarding and somewhat less on style and music, although they also have a clothing style and music preferences. Skates enjoy thrash, punk, and hip-hop music, and tend to dress in anything they can find, although their preference in sneakers and skateboarding equipment is expensive and brand-name driven. The look they try to achieve is unmistakable: oversize T-shirts, shorts, and pants; long underwear worn under shorts; toques and sometimes baseball hats worn backwards; strategic holes, tears, and cut-off cuffs, sleeves, and pant legs.

Skates are less concerned with toughness and anger than Rappers. In an altercation, they usually take the defensive. They see themselves as outcasts, often in conflict with authority because their skateboarding is rarely welcome. There are many fewer Skater girls than boys, largely because skateboarding appeals more to boys, but also because most adult involvement with the sport is commercially driven and encourages competition and product endorsement aimed very specifically at males. Occasionally, a girl does join a group of Skaters, and in one or two larger urban centers, it's possible to find groups of female Skates. These girls sometimes call themselves "Betties" and congregate in all-female groups. More often, if a girl is a Skate, she became one through her connection with a Skater boy.

Finally, in connection with their self-reported high level of group affiliation, both hitting males and hitting females placed significantly greater importance on belonging to a group or gang, and having the right clothes to fit their group or gang, than did nonhitting males and nonhitting females. (See Table A-5 in Appendix I.)

One final difference reported by those who had beaten up another kid and those who had not was the enjoyment they received from parties: 50.1% of male hitters reported receiving "a great deal of enjoyment" vs. 34.1% for male nonhitters, while 60.0% of female hitters reported receiving "a great deal of enjoyment" from parties, vs. 41.7% for female nonhitters.

School and teachers

Respondents to the *Survey of Student Life* (Artz & Riecken, 1994) were asked how much enjoyment they received from school; whether they agreed that, overall, their teachers were genuinely interested in them; whether they were afraid they would be attacked at school; whether they had ever stayed away from school because they were afraid; if they had ever been attacked on their way to or from school; how often they had damaged school property in the past year; and whether, compared with elementary school, life was safer, less safe, or about the same.

Females hitters and nonhitters and male nonhitters reported the same level of enjoyment from school (75.6% reported receiving at least some enjoyment from school, although all agreed that out of 23 possible items, school ranked lowest as a source of enjoyment). Male hitters also ranked school lowest as a source of enjoyment, and did so at a level (57.8%) that was significantly lower than either nonhitting males or hitting and nonhitting females.

Neither female nor male hitters reported significant differences with regard to any of the following:

- being afraid to go to school because they might be physically attacked (19.6% of all students said they were afraid).
- staying away from school because they were afraid (7.6% of all students said they had stayed away).
- finding life at junior high school safer, less safe, or about the same as life in elementary school (48.9% of all students said it was less safe, while 38.4% said it was about the same).
- agreeing that their teachers were genuinely interested in them (57.6% of all students did not agree).

However, both female and male hitters reported significantly higher levels of damaging school property than their nonhitting peers. They also reported acting up in school if they didn't like their teachers to a significantly greater degree than their nonhitting counterparts. (See Table A-6 in Appendix I.)

Interpersonal social values

A gender-based comparison of the endorsement of selected interpersonal dynamics and social values (friendship, being loved, concern for others, respect for others, forgiveness, honesty, politeness, generosity, and being respected) revealed that where these dynamics and values are concerned, the between-group differences (females to males) are more striking than the within-group differences (males to males and females to females). (See Tables A-7, A-8, and A-9 in Appendix I.)

Nonhitting females endorsed all the relational dynamics and social values listed at significantly higher levels than nonhitting males. However, when nonhitting females were compared with hitting females, the only value that was differentially endorsed by hitting females was honesty. This finding must be interpreted with caution, however, because the difference only approaches significance; that is, given that the level required to claim statistical significance ($p <$ .0001) is almost achieved, we may only speculate that this difference can be attributed to something other than chance.

In contrast to the findings that emerged with regard to females, a comparison of nonhitting and hitting males did yield some differences with regard to self-reported endorsement of interpersonal social values. According to the data provided, respect for others, forgiveness, honesty, politeness, and generosity are *less important* to hitting males than they are to nonhitting males.

An overview of the self-report data provided by the survey respondents showed that females, whether they are nonhitting or hitting, place more importance on all the interpersonal social values explored, but they (like the males) *place more importance on how they themselves are treated than on how they treat others* (e.g., friendship, being loved, and being respected). For females, the only significant difference that distinguishes one group from another in this sample is the differential value placed on honesty when nonhitting and hitting girls are compared.

For males, some interpersonal values do seem to help in distinguishing males who hit from those who do not. It appears that among males, the endorsement of respect for others, forgiveness, honesty, politeness, and generosity seems to contribute to an inhibition against beating up other kids.

The male/female differences in interpersonal social values reported here are similar to those reported by Bibby and Posterski (1992), who tapped into some of these same values and also found that females had a greater commitment to interpersonal values than males did. In view of this, Bibby and Posterski (1992) sounded a warning note: They suggested that "a major trend characterizing life for young people today is the devaluing of personal ideals" (p. 141). The data provided by the participants in this study suggest exactly what Bibby and Posterski (1992) predicted when they wrote:

> Young women in the 90s are … far more likely than males to place a very high value on interpersonal traits, including … honesty, concern for others … politeness and generosity… . The current low proportion, less than one in two, of young males who highly value such interpersonal traits is enough to make one wonder about the confidence people can have in their dealings with these emerging young men. When honesty is downplayed, along with concern and courtesy, the implications for social life are a bit scary. (p. 142)

This statement has implications that cannot be ignored. Social scientists must develop a different understanding of females with regard to the impact of subscribing to interpersonal values, especially because the girls in our study reported participating in violence despite endorsing interpersonal values. For my colleague and me, these findings raised the question: If, for girls, hitting is largely unconnected to differences in interpersonal social values, what, then, helps us to distinguish female hitters from female nonhitters? The answer became clear when we examined survey participants' moral judgments.

Moral judgments

Participants were presented with the following statements in order to gauge their endorsement of the problematic behaviors described:

- If someone has something you really want, it's OK to make them give it to you.
- It's OK to punch or hit someone when you're having an argument.
- Fighting is a good way to defend your friends.
- It's OK to use threats to get what you want.
- If I don't like my teacher, it's OK to act up in school.
- It's OK to damage buildings and property as a way of getting even.
- Right or wrong is a matter of personal opinion.
- The use of marijuana should be legalized.

Responses to these statements provided us with insight into participants' moral judgments with regard to aggressive and violent behaviors and produced significant gender differences, as well as significant differences between nonhitting and hitting females and nonhitting and hitting males. (See Table A-10 in Appendix I.)

Male nonhitters, despite reporting that they had not beaten up another kid in the past year, still endorsed making someone give them something if they really wanted it, punching or hitting someone during an argument, fighting to defend friends, using threats, acting up in school if they didn't like their teacher, and damaging buildings and property as a way of getting even, at a significantly higher level than nonhitting females. It is especially noteworthy that 32% of nonhitting males agreed with the statement that "fighting is a good way to defend your friends," and 21.2% agreed with the statement that "it's OK to punch or hit someone when you're having an argument."

Significant differences emerged between nonhitting and hitting females and between nonhitting and hitting males. (See Tables A-11 and A-12 in Appendix I.) Hitters, whether male or female, endorsed violence to a significantly greater degree than their nonviolent counterparts. However, further examination of the data showed that despite these differences between hitters and nonhitters (whether male or female), such differences were not found when female hitters were compared with male nonhitters (see Table A-13 in Appendix I) and when female hitters were compared with male hitters (see Table A-14 in Appendix I).

Female hitters endorse five of the eight problems presented to a greater degree than male nonhitters (punching and hitting during an argument, using threats, acting up in school, right or wrong as a matter of personal opinion, and legalization of marijuana. Thus, female hitters differed significantly not only from their nonhitting female counterparts, but also from nonhitting males. Further, female hitters appear to have most in common with male hitters in that the only significant difference that distinguished female hitters from male hitters was the higher level of fighting in defense of friends reported by male hitters.

To summarize: For females especially, endorsement of moral judgments that sanction aggression and violence clearly distinguishes females who engage in violence from those who do not. This endorsement also distinguishes hitting females from nonhitting males. At the same time, where hitting females are concerned, interpersonal social values appear to play little or no role in providing a barrier to violence. This is different for males. With males (as with females), moral judgments play a key role in distinguishing those who hit others from those who do not, but (unlike females) interpersonal values also play an important role.

Self-concept

Because many educators and parents believe that negative behavior is connected to poor self-concept, we asked four questions that required students to describe themselves according to a four-point scale, where 1 = "Not very well at all," 2 = "Not very well," 3 = "Fairly well," and 4 = "Very well." Most students answered 3 = "Fairly well," or 4 = "Very well." (See Table A-15 in Appendix I.) However, males, whether hitters or nonhitters, reported significantly higher levels of agreement with the positive self-concept statements than females, whether they were hitters or nonhitters. Further, when students' scores for all four questions were summed, and means or averages were calculated and compared, three of the four items in the self-concept scale yielded statistically significant gender differences. Overall, males reported perceiving themselves as "good-looking" more often than females did; they also saw themselves as being able to "do most things well" and having "lots of confidence" to a significantly greater degree than females. This difference was not altered by membership in the hitter or nonhitter groups, thus suggesting that participation in violence is not particularly connected to self-concept as we conceptualized it in our survey. (See Table A-16 in Appendix I.)

Personal and social concerns

Respondents to the survey were asked to assess the seriousness of 16 social problems or issues facing Canadians today, identified first by Bibby and Posterski (1992): AIDS, child abuse, racial discrimination, teenage suicide, violence against women, the environment, the unequal treatment of women, violence in schools, drug abuse, alcohol abuse, youth gangs, native–white relations, the economy, global awareness, spirituality, and one's cultural group or heritage. What was notable in the responses was that most of the significant differences reported distinguished between males and females overall rather than between hitters and nonhitters. (See Table A-17 in Appendix I.) Females consistently reported higher levels of social concern than males in all areas, whether they were nonhitters or hitters.

For females, when comparing hitters and nonhitters, only three significant differences emerged. Hitting females reported higher levels of concern about the unequal treatment of women, and lower levels of concern with regard to violence in schools and global awareness, than did nonhitting females.

For males, four significant differences emerged. Nonhitting males reported higher levels of concern with regard to violence in schools, drug abuse, alcohol abuse, and youth gangs than hitting males, although these levels of concern were still lower than those reported by nonhitting females.

Also relevant to this category were those questions that asked survey respondents to comment on their ambitions, their monetary concerns, and certain aspects of their quality of life.

With regard to ambition, only one statistically significant difference emerged: Male hitters reported receiving more enjoyment from working than female hitters. (See Table A-18 in Appendix I.) They also reported enjoying working slightly, though not significantly, more than female and male nonhitters. Interestingly, although hitting males seemed to like having jobs, they (along with hitting females) appeared to place somewhat less (though not significantly less) importance upon working hard. Also, hitting males and hitting females reported having slightly (though not significantly) less confidence that "anyone who works hard will rise to the top." As well, given the percentage of students who responded that they experience "a great deal" of pressure to do well in school, hitting males and hitting females reported experiencing slightly (though not significantly) more pressure. Finally, it also appeared, from the percentage of students who reported that never having enough time bothers them "a great deal," that nonhitting males seemed less (though not significantly less) bothered by this than nonhitting females or hitting males and hitting females.

Questions related to students' monetary concerns revealed that fewer than half of all respondents worked during the school year. (See Table A-19 in Appendix I.) Of those who reported working, hitting boys reported having jobs most often, although they were not employed at statistically significant higher rates than others. Nonhitting males reported working fewer hours than hitting males and nonhitting or hitting females, although the number of hours they worked was not significantly lower than the rest. A significantly greater number of hitting males reported earning more than seven dollars an hour (the minimum wage in British Columbia) than either nonhitting males, hitting females, or nonhitting females, although a significant number of hitting females also reported earning more than seven dollars an hour when compared with nonhitting females. Finally, with regard to receiving an allowance, well over half of all respondents reported receiving one, with hitting females and hitting males reporting that they received the highest levels of allowance. Overall, hitters, whether male or female, reported having more money than nonhitters. Hitting males reported having the most money, although they also reported being significantly more bothered by a lack of money than did members of the other groups.

The quality-of-life questions asked students to state the importance of having a comfortable life, intelligence, humor, and good looks. Their answers showed that all groups (hitters and nonhitters, males and females) placed the same relative importance on these four variables, although male nonhitters seemed to place slightly more importance upon having a comfortable life and intelligence, while male hitters seemed to place slightly more importance on their looks. (See Table A-20 in Appendix I.) None of these slight differences proved to be statistically significant.

Support Systems

We asked respondents to answer a number of questions that identified to whom they would turn for help with specific problems. We also asked them two global questions, one which focused broadly on people and places to whom they could go for help, and one which asked how bothered they were at not being understood by their parents.

In answer to the first global question: "There are places and people I can go to if I need help" ("Strongly disagree," "Disagree," "Agree, "Strongly agree"), well over 80% of all students agreed that there were such people and places. At 92.2%, female nonhitters reported the highest levels of agreement with the statement, "There are places and people I can go to for help." Male nonhitters were next at 87.8%, then females hitters at 84.7%, followed by male hitters at 81.8%. Although some small differences in percentages were reported by these groups, *none of these differences are statistically significant.* This means that these are not actual differences, but merely artifacts of chance.

With regard to the second question, "How much does not being understood by your parents bother you?" ("A great deal," Quite a bit," "Some," "Little or none"), 47.9% of female hitters, 37.8% of male hitters, 37.7% of female nonhitters, and 25.5% of male nonhitters reported being bothered by not being understood by their parents "a great deal." Again, despite the fact that these numbers suggest real differences among groups, these are not statistically significant and must therefore be put down to chance.

Outlined below are the eight questions that probed some of the specifics regarding students' support systems. The data are reported here to allow the reader to see what the participants in the survey told us about their support systems, but have not been analyzed for statistically significant differences in the same way as the rest of the data reported here. This is because of the complexity of these comparisons. (See Tables A-21 to A-28 in Appendix I for raw-score data.)

1. Who are you most likely to turn to concerning spending money?
Overall, survey participants' responses indicated that most students (about 50% of nonhitting males and females and about 40% of hitting males and females) would turn to their parents.

2. Who are you most likely to turn to concerning relationships?
Overall, survey participants' responses indicated that most students would turn to their friends in this situation. Nonhitting females and hitting females indicate the highest levels of turning to friends (80.6% and 77.3%, respectively). Nonhitting males and hitting males also reported turning mostly to their friends for help with relationships, although they do this at somewhat lower rates than females. Further, nonhitting males report the lowest levels of turning to friends (59.6%), while at the same time reporting the highest levels of turning to no one (25.42%).

3. Who are you most likely to turn to concerning sex?
Hitting males and nonhitting females reported that they would turn to their friends at about the same rates (46.2% and 49.3%, respectively). Hitting females reported a higher rate (59.4%) of turning to friends; nonhitting males, however, reported a noticeably lower rate (34.2%)

than the other three groups. As well, as in question 2, nonhitting males, while reporting the lowest rates of turning to friends, also reported the highest rates of turning to no one (47.4%).

4. *Who are you most likely to turn to concerning having fun?*
Most survey participants, male or female, reported that they were most likely to turn to friends for fun. Females, especially hitting females, chose their friends over the other possibilities offered at rates that were about 10% higher than those for males. While all respondents gave low response rates when it came to choosing parents, hitting females chose parents at the lowest rate of all (0.7%). As well, respondents reported turning to no one at higher rates than those they reported for turning to parents. This is especially noticeable for males, who reported that they would turn to no one at the rate of about 14%, while their rates for turning to parents were about 4% to 5%.

5. *Who are you most likely to turn to concerning right and wrong?*
Nonhitting males and females reported turning most often to their parents (49.7% and 48.6%, respectively). Hitting males and females also report turning to their parents, but at lower rates (36% and 32.6%, respectively), with hitting females preferring friends over parents (38%). Nonhitting and hitting males report turning to no one at slightly higher rates than they report turning to friends (27.3% no one vs. 18.2% friends, for nonhitting males; and 29.6% no one vs. 25.8% friends, for hitting males).

6. *Who are you most likely to turn to concerning school?*
Nonhitting males and nonhitting females reported turning to their parents at higher rates than they reported turning to others (53.5% and 51.6%, respectively). Hitting males and females also reported turning to their parents more than to others, but their rates for doing this were lower than those of their nonhitting counterparts (39.1% and 37.5%, respectively). Further, hitting females reported turning to friends at almost the same rates that they reported turning to parents (36.0% vs. 37.5%). As well, although males' rates (both hitters and nonhitters) indicated that after parents, they would turn to friends, they also reported that they would turn to no one at nearly the same rates at which they reported turning to friends (16.8% vs. 18.8% for nonhitters, and 20.7% vs. 24.7% for hitters). School counselors were

chosen by some students as a source of help; but with the exception of hitting females, these rates were lower than those reported for turning to no one.

7. Who are you most likely to turn to concerning careers?
Most nonhitting males (65.7%) and females (60.0%) reported that they would turn to their parents. Hitting males followed suit, but at somewhat lower rates (52.0%), while hitting females once again reported the lowest rate of turning to their parents for help (44.9%). Respondents' second highest rates, with regard to whom to turn to, were those reported for turning to no one. For hitting males and non-hitting males, these were 24.4% and 16.4%, respectively, while for nonhitting females, the rate was 17.3%. Hitting females reported turning to friends at a slightly higher rate (21.0%) than they reported turning to no one (19.6%). With the exception of hitting females, who reported turning to school counselors at the rate of 10.9%, few students reported turning to school counselors for help with careers.

8. Who would you turn to concerning a major problem?
According to participants' self-reports, females (hitters and nonhitters alike) turned more to their friends than to their parents (48.0% and 51.2%, respectively). Nonhitting males turned more to their parents (52.9%), as did hitting males (37.9%), although they reported turning to friends almost as often as they did to parents (34.6%).

Overall, parents and friends were the two social support groups most respondents turned to most often. However, it is noteworthy that in the absence of turning to parents or friends, survey participants chose the category "no one" as their third option.

Sources of Enjoyment and Sources of Concern

Sources of enjoyment
We provided survey participants with 23 items intended to gauge their enjoyment from a variety of sources. These items were originally compiled by Bibby and Posterski (1992) as factors common to teenage life. We asked respondents to assess each item on a four-point scale: (4) "A great deal," (3) "Quite a bit," (2) "Some," and (1) "Little or none."

The items were then ranked in descending order according to the mean (overall average) score for enjoyment that respondents reported deriving from each. (See Table 2-1.)

According to Table 2-1, all respondents identified their friends as the number one source of enjoyment. High enjoyment ratings were also given to items generally associated with the adolescent subculture (e.g., music, parties, boyfriends/girlfriends and dates, sports, television, VCRs). In comparison, lower enjoyment ratings were accorded to various family members. As well, although friends were ranked number one by all respondents, females reported deriving significantly more enjoyment from their friends than males did. Also, although music was ranked number three overall, females reported significantly more enjoyment from music than males did. Lastly, although reading was ranked last by all respondents, females still reported deriving significantly more enjoyment from reading than males did. Conversely, males reported deriving significantly more enjoyment from sports, television, and VCRs than females did.

Despite these gender differences, males and females generated very similar rankings for most of the items. Further, those rankings that distinguished between hitters and nonhitters were few in number. Female and male hitters reported receiving significantly more enjoyment from parties and stereos than female and male nonhitters did. Also, male hitters reported receiving significantly more enjoyment from dating and from girlfriends than male nonhitters did. Finally, the reader should note that the difference between the highest- and lowest-ranked item was only 1.4 points. This suggests a cautious interpretation of the rankings, and indicates that all respondents derived at least some enjoyment from all the items offered.

Sources of concern

Survey participants were asked to rate how often they were bothered by various problems. The 12 problems were rated on a four-point scale from "little or none" to "a great deal." Table 2-2 (page 44) provides a ranking, in descending order, of the average level of "bothersomeness" elicited by each problem.

The adolescents in this sample tend to be bothered by all these problems to some degree. The most bothersome problems were the adolescents' perceptions of lack of time and money. To a lesser degree, the respondents were bothered by the uncertainty of what to do after

Table 2-1
SELF-REPORTED RATING OF ENJOYMENT THAT ADOLESCENTS RECEIVE FROM VARIOUS SOURCES AND ACTIVITIES (N=1,479)

Mean	Rank	Variable
3.550	1	Friends**
3.281	2	Car
3.277	3	Music**
3.273	4	*Girlfriend/Boyfriend*
3.260	5	Own room
3.220	**6**	**Stereo**
3.140	**7**	**Parties**
3.030	8	*Dates*
3.000	9	Being part of a group of kids/teens
2.980	10	Sports*
2.940	11	Pet
2.750	12	Mother
2.700	13	Television*
2.670	14	VCR
2.640	15	Father
2.540	16	Job
2.530	17	Grandparents
2.470	18	Self
2.400	19	City/Town you live in
2.330	20	Adult friend
2.224	21	Brothers and sisters
2.223	22	Reading**
2.140	23	School

Means are on a scale of 1 to 4, where:
1 = Little or no enjoyment   3= Quite a bit of enjoyment
2 = Some enjoyment   4 = A lot of enjoyment

* Denotes a gender difference ($p < .0001$), with males reporting more enjoyment.
** Denotes a gender difference ($p < .0001$), with females reporting more enjoyment.
Bold type denotes more enjoyment ($p < .0001$) for all hitters, male and female.
Italic type denotes more enjoyment ($p < .0001$) for hitting males.

graduation, and not having things to do. Adolescents were the least bothered by the fear of being attacked or beaten up, and by pressure to engage in sex.

As indicated in Table 2-2, three gender differences emerged in the respondents' ratings of bothersome problems. Females tended to report that they were more bothered by lack of parental understanding than

Table 2-2
Ratings of how often participants reported being bothered by various problems

Mean	Rank	Variable
2.958	1	Never seem to have enough time
2.828	2	Lack of money
2.788	3	Not understood by parents**
2.729	4	Pressure to do well in school
2.569	5	The way you look**
2.502	6	Losing friends**
2.462	7	What to do after finishing school
2.374	8	Not having things to do
2.181	9	*Not having a place to hang out*
2.146	10	Not having a girlfriend/boyfriend
1.180	11	Fear of being attacked or beaten up
1.630	12	*Pressure to engage in sex*

Means are on a scale of 1 to 4, where:
1 = Little or no bother   3 = Quite a bit of bother
2 = Some bother   4 = A lot of bother

**Denotes a gender difference ($p < .0001$), with females reporting being more bothered.
Italic type denotes a greater level of bother ($p < .0001$) reported by hitting males.

were males. Females were also more frequently bothered by the way they looked. In addition, females were significantly more bothered by the loss of friends. Also, hitting males reported that they felt significantly more bothered than nonhitting males and all females by not having a place to hang out and by feeling pressured to engage in sex.

Experience of Abuse and Victimization

All researchers who have inquired into violent behavior have noted that those who engage in violence are also victimized more often that those who do not engage in violence. We therefore asked survey participants to provide us with information about their experiences of victimization and abuse. We also asked them to answer questions about their perceptions and fears with regard to being victimized and abused.

Our findings followed the same patterns as those established by previous researchers in that hitters, both male and female, reported significantly greater rates of victimization and abuse. (See Flowers, 1990 and Chesney-Lind & Shelden, 1992 for in-depth discussions.)

Fear of being victimized or abused

Survey participants were asked to respond to seven questions about their fears of being victimized and/or abused. Of these seven questions, four yielded significant differences among groups. All significant differences reported are significant at $p < .0001$ (chi-square). Each of the seven questions is discussed in turn. (See Tables A-29 to A-40 in Appendix I.)

1. How often does the fear of being attacked or beaten up bother you?
According to all respondents (hitters and nonhitters), 20% to 25% of students are bothered by a general fear of being attacked or beaten up.

2. Are you afraid of being physically attacked at school?
As with question 1, no significant differences were found to distinguish among groups. Overall, roughly 20% of students reported feeling afraid that they might be attacked at school.

3. Are you afraid of being beaten up by a gang of kids?
Although there was some variation among groups in the number of respondents who answered "yes" to this question, this variation is not statistically significant, and is therefore a chance-based rather than a systematic variation. Thus, overall, approximately 20% of respondents reported being afraid of being beaten up by a gang of kids.

4. Have you ever stayed away from school because you were afraid?
Nonhitting males reported the lowest levels of this behavior. When their responses are compared with those of nonhitting and hitting females, the differences are statistically significant. This is not the case when a comparison is made between nonhitting and hitting males. At the same time, when comparing all females with hitting males, their rates of staying away from school were not statistically different. Thus, we may infer that nonhitting males stay away from school least often, and that females and hitting males stay way from school about 10% to 12% of the time.

5. Are you afraid that you might be physically abused at home?
As noted earlier in this chapter, nearly 20% of hitting females reported that they were afraid of being physically abused at home. This stands out in stark contrast to the level of fear reported by nonhitting

females (6.6%) and both nonhitting and hitting males (3.3% and 4.9%, respectively). The level of fear of being physically abused at home reported by hitting females is significantly higher than that reported by those in all other categories.

6. *Are you afraid that you might be sexually assaulted?*
Females (whether hitters or nonhitters) reported significantly higher levels of fear that they might be sexually assaulted. Hitting females reported the highest levels of fear (37.2%), levels that were significantly higher than those of nonhitting females (28.0%). Although some males reported fearing sexual assault, the vast majority (over 92%) reported having no such fear.

7. *Are you afraid that you might be talked into having sex with your boyfriend/girlfriend against your will?*
Females (both nonhitters and hitters) reported more fear than males of being talked into having sex against their will. Hitting females reported the highest levels of fear (33.4%). These were significantly higher than those reported by nonhitting females (14.3%), nonhitting males (2.8%), and hitting males (8.2%). As well, when compared with the level of fear reported by nonhitting males, the level of fear reported by all females (nonhitting and hitting) was significantly greater. However, the level of fear reported by nonhitting females was not significantly greater than that reported by hitting males; here, the level of fear was approximately the same, statistically speaking. Thus, nonhitting males appear to have the least fear with regard to being talked into sex against their will, while hitting females have the most fear, although the level of fear reported by nonhitting females is also substantial.

Experience of being victimized or abused
As well as asking about their fears, we had survey participants respond to five questions that explored their actual experiences of victimization and abuse. Each of these questions yielded significant differences among the four groups. All significant differences reported are significant at $p < .0001$ (chi-square).

1. *Have you ever been the victim of a gang of kids?*
Students' responses show two statistically significant differences, that between nonhitting females (4.1%) and hitting males (14.9%) and

that between nonhitting males (6.0%) and hitting males (14.9%). A comparison between hitting males and hitting females yielded no significant difference. Nor is there a significant difference between nonhitting males and nonhitting females. Thus, overall, nonhitters (whether female or male) experience the least amount of victimization at the hands of gangs of kids, while hitters (whether male or female) experience the most.

2. Have you ever been attacked on your way to or from school?
Significant differences were reported between hitting males (18.9%) and hitting females (5.4%), and between hitting males (18.9%) and nonhitting females (3.6%). Although the absolute values provided show a numerical difference between hitting males and nonhitting males, this difference is not statistically significant. Thus, overall, hitting males reported experiencing the highest rates of victimization on the way to or from school.

3. Have you ever been physically abused at home?
As noted earlier in this chapter, hitting females (19.9%) reported significantly higher rates of physical abuse at home than nonhitting females, nonhitting males, and hitting males. Also significant is the difference reported between hitting males (9.6%) and nonhitting males (3.0%). Nonhitting males (3.0%) and nonhitting females (6.3%) reported experiencing levels of abuse that are quite similar (i.e., they are not significantly different). Thus, of the four groups, hitting females reported the highest rates by far of victimization in the home, although hitting males also reported higher rates, at least in relation to their nonhitting male counterparts.

4. Have you ever been sexually abused?
Hitting females (23.5%) reported significantly higher rates of sexual abuse than nonhitting females (11.2%), nonhitting males (0.8%), and hitting males (4.5%). However, nonhitting females also reported significantly higher levels of sexual abuse than nonhitting males and hitting males. Overall, females reported greater rates of sexual abuse than males. Of the total number of participants, 96 females (13.6%) and 21 males (3%) reported that they had been sexually abused. According to the data provided by our respondents, females experienced sexual abuse at a ratio of 4.5:1 when compared with males.

5. Have you ever been talked into having sex with your boyfriend/girlfriend against your will?

Hitting females (13.7%) reported the highest levels of being talked into sex against their will. Their rates of experiencing this were significantly greater than those reported by nonhitting females (7.3%), non-hitting males (2.8%), and hitting males (7.1%). Hitting males and nonhitting females reported virtually the same rates of having been talked into having sex against their will. Nonhitting males reported the lowest levels of this of all the respondents. Where sexual abuse and forced sex is concerned, hitting females appeared to fare worst of all, while nonhitting males fared best.

PARTICIPATION IN DEVIANT BEHAVIOR

Beyond participating in violence (i.e., beating up another kid), students in the survey were asked to report on their involvement in a number of rule-breaking, deviant, and delinquent behaviors, as well as the misuse or illegal use of substances. These are summarized in Tables A-41a and A-41b (rule breaking, deviant/delinquent behaviors) and Table A-41c (misuse or illegal use of substances) in Appendix I.

Rule Breaking, deviant and delinquent behaviors

As noted earlier in this chapter, hitting females reported smoking without their parents' permission at significantly greater rates (38.4%) than nonhitting females (20.4%) and all males. As well, hitting females also reported lying, staying out all night without parents' permission, skipping classes or school, and stealing small items that didn't belong to them at significantly higher rates than nonhitting males and females, but not hitting males. Nonhitting females, while reporting lower rates of engagement in the six listed behaviors than hitting females, still reported higher levels of engagement in two of these — smoking without parents' permission and lying — than nonhitting males, who reported the lowest levels of all groups for these two behaviors. Hitting males reported higher levels of all six behaviors than non-hitting males, and statistically the same rates of behavior as hitting females, for staying out all night without parents' permission, skipping classes, skipping school, and stealing small items that didn't belong to them.

For the six behaviors listed in Table A-41b in Appendix I

(purposefully ruining parents' property after an argument, damaging others' property just for fun, taking something from a store without paying for it, breaking into a place just to look around, purposefully damaging school property, and carrying a weapon), hitting females reported significantly higher rates for all behaviors than nonhitting females and nonhitting males. Nonhitting females and males reported no statistically significant differences for any of the six behaviors listed. Hitting males, however, while also reporting significantly higher rates than nonhitting males and nonhitting females for all six behaviors, also reported significantly higher rates than hitting females for three of these: damaging others' property just for fun, breaking into a place just to look around, and carrying a weapon.

Misuse and illegal use of substances

As previously noted in this chapter, hitting females reported the highest rates (56.5%) of smoking cigarettes of all groups, while nonhitting males reported the lowest rates (9.9%). Nonhitting males also reported significantly lower rates of use of over-the-counter drugs (6.3%) than all other groups. With regard to the use of over-the-counter drugs, nonhitting females (10.6%), hitting females (15%), and hitting males (10.7%) reported similar rates which, when compared with those of nonhitting males, were all significantly higher. Hitting females also reported higher rates of drinking alcohol (26.9%), smoking marijuana (26.5%), and using other illegal drugs (17.9%) than both nonhitting females and nonhitting males. With respect to these last three behaviors, hitting females and hitting males reported virtually the same rates of misuse and illegal use. As well, nonhitting females and nonhitting males reported the same rates of use of these substances, rates that were significantly lower than those of their hitting counterparts. Finally, both nonhitting females and hitting females reported stopping themselves from eating (misuse of food as a substance) at rates that were significantly higher (10.9% and 13.8%, respectively) than those of either nonhitting or hitting males (1.7% and 3.3%, respectively). (See Table A-41c in Appendix I.)

The overall pattern that emerged from participants' self-reports suggests that with regard to rule-breaking, deviance, delinquency, and substance misuse, those who engage in beating up other people have far more in common with one another than they do with members of their own sex who do not engage in beating up other people. Hitters, whether female or male, reported statistically the same rates of behavior for 12 of the 18 behaviors listed.

A further pattern that emerged suggests that, overall, nonhitting males were least involved in rule-breaking, deviance, delinquency, and substance misuse, at least insofar as our survey was able to determine. Of the 18 surveyed behaviors, nonhitting males reported significantly lower rates than all others for four, and the same significantly lower rates as nonhitting females for 13 of the remaining 14 behaviors. They shared only one similarity in behavior with their hitting male counterparts: a significantly lower rate of misusing food. Their hitting male counterparts, however, outranked even hitting females on three of the 18 behaviors: damaging property, breaking and entering, and carrying weapons. Still, according to these data, similarity outweighs difference where hitters are concerned.

Who Is the Violent School Girl?

Having collected all the foregoing data, we next asked ourselves:

- Who is the violent school girl? How can we distinguish her from the nonviolent school girl?
- How does the violent school girl compare with the nonviolent school boy?
- How is the violent school girl similar to and different from the violent school boy?

The violent school girl: Similarities and differences

According to our data, the violent school girl comes from a family that at least superficially resembles the families of her nonviolent and violent counterparts, both male and female. In other words, differences in family configuration and living arrangements (two parents, including common-law and stepparents, or single parent), parental occupation, and parental education did not distinguish the violent school girl from the other groups considered.

Family dynamics did, however, provide a basis for identifying the violent school girl. She reported placing significantly less importance on family life than the nonviolent school girl did, although the level of importance she accorded the family was not statistically different from that reported by nonviolent and violent school boys. She also reported that enjoyment of her mother was significantly less applicable to her than did all other groups. Further, she feared being physically abused at home, and had been thus abused at a significantly greater rate than all other groups. As well, she smoked without parents' permission more than all other groups; lied to her parents more often than nonviolent school girls and nonviolent school boys (but at the same rate reported by violent school boys); stayed out all night and deliberately damaged her parents' property more than both nonviolent girls and nonviolent boys (and at the same rate as violent boys).

Belonging to a group or a gang such as the Rappers or Bangers was of great importance to both violent females and violent males, as was having the right clothes to fit in with the group or gang, and receiving enjoyment from parties. Where peer affiliation is concerned, the line of demarcation between groups did not run along gender lines, but rather along the violent/nonviolent distinction: that is, regardless of sex, those who engaged in violence reported more similarities than those who reported being nonviolent.

This violent/nonviolent distinction continued with regard to school: Violent students, whether female or male, reported significantly greater levels of acting up in school if they did not like their teachers, and significantly higher levels of damaging school property than their nonviolent counterparts.

The gender line was, however, clearly drawn with regard to interpersonal values and self-concept. Females, whether they were violent or nonviolent, reported that they saw themselves as less attractive, less capable, and less confident than the males (violent or nonviolent) reported themselves. At the same time, females, whether they were violent or nonviolent, reported a significantly higher rate of endorsement of friendship, being loved, concern for others, respect for others, forgiveness, honesty, politeness, generosity, and being respected, than males (violent or nonviolent). When violent school girls were compared with nonviolent girls, the only value that they endorsed at what approached a significantly lower level was honesty, which they endorsed at almost the same level as nonviolent school boys, a level significantly higher than that of violent boys.

The gender gap did not prevail where moral judgments were concerned. Although nonviolent school girls endorsed aggressive, violent, and illegal behavior at significantly lower rates than nonviolent and violent school boys, this was not the case with violent girls. Their rates of endorsement for such behavior were significantly higher than those reported by nonviolent girls. With regard to punching, using threats, acting up in school, the legalization of marijuana, and the notion that right and wrong is a matter of personal opinion, violent school girls' rates of endorsement were significantly higher than those reported by nonviolent school boys, and not significantly different from those reported by violent boys. Violent school girls differed from violent school boys on only one variable: fighting to defend one's friends, which violent boys endorsed at significantly higher rates than all other groups.

The gender gap did, however, prevail with regard to social and personal concerns. Here females, whether they were violent or nonviolent, consistently reported significantly higher levels of concern for all issues: AIDS, child abuse, racial discrimination, teenage suicide, violence against women, the environment, the unequal treatment of women, violence in schools, drug abuse, youth gangs, and native-white relations. In fact, violent girls reported higher levels of concern than all groups, including nonviolent girls, for the unequal treatment of women and for violence in schools. This pattern shifted only where alcohol abuse was concerned: Here, violent school girls and violent school boys reported the same levels of concern, levels that were significantly lower than those reported by both nonviolent girls and nonviolent boys.

Violent school girls and violent school boys also reported making more money than their nonviolent counterparts. Although violent boys reported earning higher hourly wages than members of all the other groups, violent girls reported higher wages than nonviolent girls and nonviolent boys. As well, violent school girls, along with violent school boys, reported significantly higher levels of allowance than nonviolent girls or boys, who reported very similar and lower levels of allowance.

With regard to sources of enjoyment, gender again prevailed, although for the most part, both sexes ranked the surveyed sources of enjoyment in the same order. Females, whether violent or nonviolent, placed more importance upon friends, music, and reading than males did; males, whether violent or nonviolent, placed more importance upon sports and television than females did. Although violent males placed more importance upon girlfriends and dating than all other groups, and violent females and males placed more value upon parties and their stereos than both nonviolent females and nonviolent males, violent students reported similarities with regard to only two out of 23 items, thus suggesting that gender determined preferences more often than involvement in violence did.

This pattern continued with regard to problems that were a source of bother to survey participants. On the whole, all participants ranked sources of bother in the same order, although females (violent and nonviolent) ranked not being understood by their parents, concerns about the way they looked, and losing friends as more bothersome than males (violent or nonviolent) did. Violent males ranked not having a place to hang out and experiencing pressure to engage in sex as more bothersome than all the other groups ranked these two items.

No significant gender or group differences were reported with regard to survey participants' sources of support. In general, all participants (violent and nonviolent) turned to their parents with concerns about money, right and wrong, school, careers, and major problems, and to their friends with regard to concerns about relationships, sex, and fun.

With regard to fears of victimization and abuse, two gender difference emerged: Females (violent and nonviolent) feared sexual assault and being talked into having sex against their will at significantly greater rates than males (violent and nonviolent). Violent school girls reported both these fears at rates that were significantly higher than those reported by all males, and significantly higher than those reported by nonviolent females. Otherwise, participants reported the same rates of fear of general attack, attack on the way to school, and being beaten by a gang. Violent school girls, nonviolent girls, and violent boys also reported the same rates for staying away from school because of fear, rates that were all significantly higher than those reported by nonviolent school boys.

Gender differences again emerged with regard to experiences with victimization. Females (violent and nonviolent) reported significantly higher rates of sexual abuse and being talked into sex against their will than males (violent and nonviolent). Further, as with levels of fear of these two experiences, violent females reported significantly higher rates of experience with victimization than those reported by nonviolent females.

Self-reports about other forms of victimization yielded some interesting connections. Violent school girls were victimized by gangs of kids as often as violent school boys were, although violent boys were more often attacked on their way to and from school. As well, violent girls were more often physically abused at home than any other group, including violent boys. Thus, violent girls reported more victimization in the form of physical abuse, sexual abuse, and attack by a gang of peers.

Finally, with regard to rule-breaking, deviance, and delinquency, the violent school girl was hard to distinguish from her violent male peers. She reported engaging in smoking without permission, lying to her parents, staying out all night without permission, skipping classes or school, stealing small items that didn't belong to her, stealing from stores, ruining her parents' property after an argument, and damaging school property at rates that were the same as those reported by violent school boys, rates that were significantly higher than those reported by both nonviolent boys and nonviolent girls. Violent school girls also reported breaking into places just to look around, damaging property just for fun, and carrying a weapon significantly more often than nonviolent girls and nonviolent boys, although these rates were not as high as those reported by violent boys. Further, violent school girls reported smoking more than members of all other groups, drinking alcohol, smoking marijuana, and using other illegal drugs significantly more often than nonviolent girls and nonviolent boys, and at the same rates reported by violent boys. Both violent and nonviolent girls stopped themselves from eating significantly more often than either violent or nonviolent boys.

SUMMARY: *The violent school girl*

According to our data, in many respects, the violent school girl looks much like the violent school boy: She misuses drugs and alcohol; engages in rule-breaking, deviance, and delinquency; endorses aggression. She enjoys similar pastimes, and she is affiliated with the same social groups.

She differs from the violent school boy in several key areas: She places greater importance on interpersonal values, and she is more concerned about social issues. She places more importance on friendship than both violent and nonviolent school boys do, and (like the violent school boy) she considers family of less importance than her nonviolent counterparts do. She places the least value of all the groups on her connection with her mother.

What stands out most clearly about the violent school girl is her greater fear of abuse, and actual experience of physical and sexual abuse, than all others who participated in the survey.

Moving Beyond Statistics

In the chapters that follow, the life-world and practices of the violent school girl are more clearly outlined and examined through case study accounts. These provide strong corroboration for the portrait of the violent school girl drawn with data from the *Survey of Student Life* (Artz & Riecken, 1994). They also provide insight into the perspectives that violent school girls bring to bear upon their own and others' behavior, and help the reader to understand that the girls' participation in violence is integral to a view of life in which violence makes sense.

Constructing an ethnography

My objective in using the case study approach was an ethnographic one: I was primarily concerned with understanding the lived experience of these girls. Ethnography, an approach to the study of human group life first used by anthropologists, has been variously defined as "written representation of culture[2] (or selected aspects of a culture)" (Van Maanen, 1988, p. 1), the inscription of social discourse (Geertz, 1973), the analytic description or reconstruction of cultural scenes and groups (Goetz & LeCompte, 1984), and "a type of writing, putting things to paper" (Geertz, 1988, p. 1) that addresses cultural questions through fieldwork or direct personal involvement with the subjects of one's study. According to Wolcott (1975),

> the term ethnography belongs to anthropology; ethnography provides the basic descriptive data on which cultural anthropology is founded. An ethnography is literally an anthropologist's picture of the way of life of some interacting human group. (p. 112)

Within the field of qualitative social research, ethnography is used not only by anthropologists, but also by sociologists (Dietz, Prus, & Shaffir, 1994), psychologists (Osborne, 1994), and educators (Wolcott, 1975). The focus of ethnographic research is, as Wolcott says, "the way of life of some interacting human group," whether that is a group living at a great distance or one that gathers down the street or next door.

Constructing an ethnography entails the gathering and interpretation of multiple kinds and forms of information concerning the group to be studied. This process is undertaken not at arm's length, but in the field. Ethnographers are participant-observers in the processes they study. They live and work among their subjects in order to understand how and why they behave as they do. Ethnographers use their own first-hand personal experiences with the study group to produce descriptive accounts that accurately reflect the characteristics and perceptions of that group. According to Wolcott (1975), an ethnographic account can be judged adequate if a person reading it

> could subsequently behave appropriately as a member of the society or social group about which he has been reading, or more modestly, whether he can anticipate and interpret what occurs in the group as appropriately as its own members. (p. 112)

Within the parameters of working towards a faithful documentation of the patterns and forms of the study group, the ethnographer enjoys what Wolcott describes as the freedom to "muddle about" and pursue hunches as she or he sees fit. Ethnographers discover patterns and problems. They do not test their data against predetermined hypotheses under the constraints of the experimental method, nor do they enter their inquiry with anything more than the foreknowledge gained from their previous experience as a guideline for action and interpretation.

Thus, for my study, I wanted to learn about "the ways in which [violent school girls] accomplish their activities on a day-to-day, moment-to-moment basis" with a view towards understanding "how [they] make sense of the situations they encounter in their daily routines and how they deal with these situations on an ongoing basis" (Dietz, Prus, & Shaffir, 1994, p. 2). Central to an understanding of violent school girls' meaning-making processes was an understanding of their "symbolic interactions." That is, I wanted to understand their violent behavior in terms of their internalization of the culturally produced sign systems generated and interpreted by their particular group or subculture.

The meaning of meaning
Blumer (1969), who coined the term "symbolic interactionism,"

suggested that the meaning we find in objects and experiences is neither intrinsic to those things, nor is it the product of accumulated psychological attributes brought to those experiences by the meaning maker. Instead, meaning is perspective-dependent. This means that we cannot expect to find only one meaning and one interpretation for each object in the sense that a chair is only and always a chair, a house is only and always a house, and a mother is only and always a woman. The perspective of the seer can transform a chair into a lion-tamer's training tool, the house into a valuable piece of real estate, and the mother into an agent that originates, engenders, or masterminds (as in, "necessity is the mother of invention").

Further, meaning is more than mere "psychical accretion brought to things by the person for whom the thing has meaning," that is, more than simply the "expression of constituent elements of a person's psyche, mind or psychological organization [that comes from] … such things as sensations, feelings, ideas, memories, motives and attitudes" (Blumer, 1969, p. 4). In symbolic interactionism, meanings arise "in the process of interaction between people … [and thus] as social products, as creations that are formed in and through the defining activities of people as they interact" (Blumer, 1969, pp. 4–5).

Thus described, meaning-making involves interactive interpretation. Interpretation, according to Blumer, requires two distinct steps. The first involves the human actor in communication with herself: She indicates to herself the objects towards which she is acting and the meanings that these have for her. The second step requires that she interprets and applies these meanings in the light of her situation and her actions.

Blumer (1969) emphasizes that the process of interaction with self is not merely premised on the interplay of the actor's psychological elements, but involves instead the internalizing of a social process which is the basis for the actor's communication with herself.

Social processes and participant-observation

In order to learn about the meaning-making processes of the violent school girls who participated in this study, I set out to understand the social processes in which they were immersed by becoming a participant-observer in their world. Participant-observation is described by Spradley (1979) as a research strategy that actively involves the researcher in the life-worlds of her participants in order to gain first-hand knowledge of their lived experience. Thus, the researcher becomes not merely an observer, but also an actor and an informant in the research process. The rationale for participant-observation is that

> it offers to those who are able and willing to assume the role of another in a more comprehensive sense, a unique and instructive form of data. ... Since it typically puts researchers in close, sustained contact with others, participant-observation generates further opportunities to gain insight into the viewpoints and practices of the other ... . (Prus, 1994, p. 21)

It is acknowledged that participant-observation is by definition a subjective approach to data gathering that places certain restrictions upon the interpretation of data. For example, a researcher would not seek to generalize from her data; rather, she would underscore the fact that her findings are personal and descriptive rather than empirical and analytic.[3] It is also acknowledged that the insights gained from first-hand experience allow a unique understanding of the phenomenon under study, moving the researcher beyond a search for psychological and sociological determinants of behavior into knowledge about

> the process of self-interaction through which the individual handles his world and constructs his action [and] the vital process of interpretation in which the individual notes and assesses what is presented to him and through which he maps out lines of overt behavior... . (Blumer, 1969, p. 15)

As the central thrust of my inquiry was to form an understanding of how adolescent school girls engaged in violence and made sense of this engagement, I believed that participant-observation would be a helpful and useful research methodology because it would bring me closer to the girls' lived experiences and to the lived experiences of others in their life-worlds.

My backgRound in the community

My status as a participant-observer in this inquiry was anchored in my four years of consulting with and training teachers and administrators in the school district in which I did my research.

I had worked with over 100 teachers (about 20 of whom were either principals, vice-principals, or board office personnel) in a series of workshops, each of which consisted of seven sessions spread over a period of three to four months. In these workshops, I helped teachers deal with their day-to-day problems in managing their most difficult students, and therefore had some understanding of the violence and aggression that they were encountering in their classrooms and schoolyards. The relationships I developed during this period lent me the credibility to be allowed to engage in the present inquiry; they also provided me with a basis from which to approach students, parents, and youth workers in the district. Further, as I visited the schools where I conducted my workshops, I began to develop an intuitive feel for the school-based life-world of my research participants, as I had the opportunity to see them in classrooms, on playgrounds, and on their way to and from school.

I also had other long-term participatory experience in this community. Having made my home there from 1975 until 1984, I knew it to be multifaceted and multidimensional. In part, it is a bedroom community that sprawls over a wide hinterland housing the people who work in the offices, shops, and businesses in the city. It is also an industrial community in which one finds small manufacturing businesses, heavy equipment yards, and unkempt strip malls interspersed with gas stations and doughnut shops. In some parts there is great affluence: architecturally designed homes housing well-paid professionals who prefer a quasi-rural lifestyle. In other parts one finds ramshackle buildings and rundown housing mixed with subsidized townhouse complexes occupied to a large extent by welfare recipients and the working poor. There are rural lanes, horse farms, and well-groomed subdivisions overlooking the ocean. There are also heavily traveled routes that pass by rusty car hulks and empty dump trucks parked in front of half-finished houses guarded by German shepherds on chains. Members from all social classes live together here, but the predominant flavor of the community is working class. It is a community that is always in the making, where enterprising developers continue to carve subdivisions out of forests and mountainsides. It is also a community that contains pockets of history reaching back to the earliest incursions of white settlements.

While living in this community, I was also employed there as a youth worker from 1981 to 1987. I still have collegial relationships with agency workers and the police which keep me current with local issues. I taught life skills to adult students at a local high school in 1988, and this experience gave me the opportunity to take part in some of the everyday life of a school.

Further, while living in this community, I fostered four special-care foster children (all girls aged 11 to 16) whose behavioral problems included acting out at school and (in two cases) participation in violence. This gave me first-hand parental experience in dealing with behavioral difficulties, hostility, aggression, and violence.

When I began this study, I made my status as researcher clear to all concerned. I was introduced to all participants as a researcher, and my role as researcher and theirs as voluntary informants in the research process were clearly outlined in the consent forms that were signed by the girls, their parents, and all adult participants. I also stated clearly to all involved that I entered into the research process in the spirit of understanding how it was that girls engaged in violence, and with the participants' help, hoped to apply that knowledge; that is, I viewed participants as partners who had much to contribute to the research process.

Thε sτudy
I gained access to the study participants in a variety of ways:

- Because it was known within the school district and the community that I was engaged in local research on youth violence, and because teachers and administrators saw it as useful for the district, I was given the opportunity to conduct a series of teachers' professional-development day workshops in which the focus was violence in schools. At these workshops, teachers and parents were invited to describe and discuss their first-hand experiences with violence in schools, thus providing me with descriptive data about the phenomenon. In all, three such workshops were conducted, in which over 50 people participated.

- My colleague, Ted Riecken, and I were invited to present a forum on youth violence to a parents' network, which we conducted as a workshop, again inviting parents to share their personal experiences. Two parent-network staff, four youth workers, and 12 parents attended the forum; all contributed their experiences and helped me to round out my description of the phenomenon of youth violence.

- As a result of these contacts in the community, several teachers, administrators, and parents volunteered to become further involved in the study by agreeing to be interviewed and by facilitating contact with their children or their students.

- The contacts that were made through these connections led to research relationships with six adolescent girls who had personal involvement with violence, and who became the key informants[4] in this study.

The key informants

Six key informants — all of whom had been involved in violent altercations — were identified by school and community agency counselors, by their classmates, and by the girls themselves, and agreed to participate in this inquiry. Five of the six were referred by their school counselors; one I approached myself. The names and any overtly identifying characteristics of all participants have been altered in order to preserve anonymity.

Informant 1: Sally. Sally, who volunteered for the study because she saw herself as a victim of violence, was 13 years old and in grade eight. She was known to the students in her school and to her teachers as a "tough" girl who intimidated both male and female classmates. Just before the interviews, she had been severely beaten by Marilee (Informant 2) and Marilee's best friend, Sarah. Since her beating, Sally had stopped attending school and was being schooled at home via correspondence. Since the age of six, Sally has been living with her mother and stepfather. She also has frequent contact with her father and his second wife of six years and their five-year-old daughter, Sally's half-sister. All four parents work, the women in offices, and the men at blue-collar jobs.

Informant 2: Marilee. Marilee (Sally's assailant) agreed to be part of the study at my request because she, like Sally, wanted to contribute her input as a self-described victim of violence. She was 16 and, like Sally, had given up attending school and was being educated at home via correspondence since sustaining a beating by a group of her fellow school girls two years previously. Marilee lives with her mother and father, who have been married for nearly 26 years. She has an older sister who is away at college. Both Marilee's parents work, her mother in an office, her father as a dispatcher for a taxi company.

Informant 3: Molly. Molly initially volunteered to participate in the study because, like Sally and Marilee, she had been beaten by a student at her school. Molly was no stranger to violence: She was known to use threats and intimidation and, on occasion, pushing, shoving, and banging into other people to let them know that she was in charge. She has an older brother who also has a reputation for toughness, and whom she relies upon to back her up if need be. Molly was 14 and in grade eight at the time of this study. She lives with her parents and three brothers (one older, two younger) in a small house in a modest part of the community. Molly's mother works in an office; her father is a carpenter. They have been married for 22 years.

Informant 4: Mary. Mary came to the study with the toughest of reputations because of her nearly constant involvement with fighting and other difficulties in school. She volunteered to participate because she had been attacked by another girl and now wanted to "do something about violence." Mary was 15 years old at the time of this study. She lives at home with her mother, father, and older brother, who (like Molly's brother) has a reputation for violence. Mary's father is a self-employed skilled tradesperson; her mother works in an office.

Informant 5: Linda. Linda volunteered for the study because, like Mary, she wanted "to do something about violence." She had been suspended from school on two occasions for fighting with Jenny (Informant 6), yet she saw her own involvement in violence as the result of victimization by Jenny. Linda was nearly 16 at the time of the study. Linda's parents have been married for 20 years. Her mother works as a clerk, her father as a mechanic.

Informant 6: Jenny. Jenny volunteered to participate in the study because she also saw herself as victimized by other girls, as well as by boys. Yet, previous to our interviews, Jenny had instigated three fights, each of which attracted large crowds of spectators (over 70 to 100 youths, and in one case over 300). Jenny is well known to other students in her school as a fighter (although Mary, who has known her since grade two, called her an "amateur"). Jenny was 14 and in grade eight at the time of this study. She lives with her parents and younger sister. Jenny's parents have been married for 16 years. Her mother manages a restaurant; her father works as a groundskeeper.

Over the course of just 15 months (from July 1993 to October 1994), I spent over 100 hours with the six key informants, approximately 15 hours with their parents, 50 hours with their educators, counselors, and law enforcement officers, and countless hours in their community observing everyday life.

Three of the key informants (Molly, Mary, and Linda) were friends, and often met with me as a group as well as individually. Also, Marilee knew Sally (and had helped her best friend Sarah beat Sally up); Molly, Mary, and Linda were well acquainted with Jenny, who attended school with them. These three disliked Jenny intensely and believed she deserved to be beaten, especially in view of Linda's having been suspended from school for hitting Jenny. Finally, Mary was close friends with Cathy, who had severely beaten Molly, a beating both Mary and Linda had witnessed.

The conversations I had with the key informants covered many aspects of their lives: their involvement in violence; their views of their parents, siblings, and other family members; their sense of self; their experiences of being female; their notions of friends and friendship; the social activities they pursue; their perspectives on their educators and their own educational performance; their ideas about right and wrong, and the origins of their moral stance.

All those involved in the study, including the informants who had participated in violence, saw themselves as contributors to an understanding of violence that would move us collectively closer to finding ways to prevent it. In that sense, we had a common purpose.

My discussions with the key informants and others who are part of their lives yielded over 1,400 pages of tape transcriptions and field notes. These pages became the basis for the next six chapters, which present the personal stories of each of the participants, and for Chapter Nine, which outlines my understanding of these young women. Chapter Ten, which concludes this book, outlines my suggestions for violence prevention and intervention.

Notes

1. The first four categories listed here, and the questions relating to them, were devised by Bibby and Posterski (1992) and are included with permission

2. "Culture" is a term that has been variously defined. Geertz (1973) lists

11 different definitions generated by noted anthropologist Clyde Kluckholm, as well as two more general descriptors used by other anthropologists; he also outlines his own. Accordingly, culture has been taken to mean: (1) "the total way of life of a people"; (2) "the social legacy the individual acquires from his group"; (3) "a way of thinking, feeling, and believing"; (4) "an abstraction from behavior"; (5) "a theory on the part of the anthropologist about the way in which a group of people in fact behave"; (6) a "storehouse of pooled learning"; (7) "a set of standardized orientations to recurrent problems"; (8) "learned behavior"; (9) "a mechanism for the normative regulation of behavior"; (10) "a set of techniques for adjusting both to the external environment and to other men"; (11) "a precipitate of history"; (12) a "sieve"; and (13) a "matrix." Geertz himself defines culture as a semiotic concept and notes that he believes, along with Max Weber, that "man is essentially an animal suspended in webs of significance he himself has spun." He therefore sees the analysis of culture "not as an experimental science in search of law but an interpretative one in search of meaning" (pp. 4–5). In this study, I will not use the term "culture" other than in the above references to definitions of ethnography. Instead, I will speak directly about behavior and meaning.

3. "Empirical and analytic" are terms assigned by Ted Aoki (1987) to the epistemological orientation that approaches understanding "in terms of informational knowledge (data, facts, generalizations, cause and effect laws, concepts, theories)" and attempts to link cause and effect through hypothetic-deductive reasoning. According to Aoki, the main focus of this orientation is prediction and control. Other researchers (Lather, 1991; Osborne, 1994) refer to this orientation as positivist and logical-empirical, and connect it, as does Aoki, to the practices of traditional natural science.

4. "Key informants" are those participants in an inquiry whose role it is to initiate and inform the researcher with regard to the phenomenon under study. It is their role to teach and to explain, to uncover and to demystify the processes that contribute to the creation and construction of the life-worlds and experiences in which they participate as "natives" (Spradley, 1979).

CHAPTER THREE

Sally's Story

The Daisy Chain

The daisy chain fits together as one,
Like a man and a woman they have lots of fun.
As the years go by they come apart and wither away
And there's no longer a sweet scent of love.
Hate takes over and it drives them both insane.
Hate take over and it drives them both insane.
Four years go by and they've both remarried,
But the love inside for each other still blossoms
Like the day the daisy chain was made,
Like the day the daisy chain was made.
(Song written by Sally)

Family dynamics

Sally has two families. She lives with her mother and stepfather, but she also has frequent contact with her father, stepmother, and their daughter, Sally's five-year-old half-sister.

Sally's parents split up when she was six years old and have been living with their new partners for over six years each. Sally's mother married her new partner; Sally's father lives common-law. As Sally sees it, her parents are better off with their present spouses; while they were together, they fought constantly, and both were unhappy.

At first, Sally was quite angry with both her parents for separating. She was angry with her mother for driving her father away, and with her father for leaving. But by the time she was eight, she had come to terms with what had happened. Things "fell into place," she said; she herself was now "fine" with regard to her parents' divorce.

Sally regards the family that consists of herself, her mother, and stepfather as an "all right family that has its bad times." The ups and downs center around how well she and her stepfather get along. During the "bad times," they fight and shout at each other, call each other names, and swear, sometimes loudly enough that neighbors have called the police.

According to Sally, the bad times happen because her stepfather "is not like a father unless he has to be." Instead, he "acts like a brother":

He listens to her music, talks the way Sally and her friends do (using such expressions as "dude"), and relates to everything she does much as she and her friends do. This leads to a kind of rivalry which Sally describes as "constantly fighting like brother and sister." Sally explains her stepfather's behavior as arising from the fact that he is nine years younger than Sally's mother, and that at 30 years of age, he still likes to "act like a kid." This situation creates problems for Sally because, as she puts it, "I do need him to act like a parent."

When Sally and her stepfather quarrel, Sally's mother "makes us talk about our problems instead of just yelling at each other … [She] gets really mad at us if we don't." Her mother also acts as an intermediary, approaching daughter and husband in turn to suggest better ways for them to relate to each other in the interests of domestic peace.

With regard to her other family, Sally hates her stepmother; during her visits there she prefers to spend time only with her father and half-sister, whom she feels able to control. Sally's hate for her stepmother stems from feeling continually criticized by her. Further, her stepmother has stated that Sally will not be included in her forthcoming wedding to Sally's father, because she wants no reminders there of his previous marriage. This exclusion leaves Sally feeling alone and angry.

Sally's general sense of her home life with her mother and stepfather is that "things are okay because mostly I'm never there." She finds her parents' rules fairly flexible — for example, curfews are negotiated to accommodate her activities. Sally compares her situation favorably with that of some of her friends, who "want to kill their parents" because they have too many rules. Most of Sally's closest friends have parents who have been divorced, and most think that family life is depressing.

Sally's mother

I learned more about the dynamics of Sally's family from her mother, whom I also interviewed. Sally's mother's main concern when I spoke to her was to break her own co-dependent patterns of interaction with those around her. That is, she wanted to stop controlling others by caring for them too much, and by trying to make them feel good. She had joined a co-dependents' group which she attends weekly, and which she says helps her. Yet, when it comes to Sally and Sally's stepfather, she continues to play the part of peacemaker. Often, this places her in a parental role in relationship to her husband.[1]

Sally's mother experiences further confusion with regard to co-dependency when she tries to take an authoritative or directive stance with Sally. For example, on the day of Sally's beating (when Sally was set up by her friend Adel to be beaten by Sarah and Marilee), her mother was reluctant to allow Sally to go to the store with Adel. However, she let her daughter go just so that she herself would "not act like a co-dependent." That is, she overruled her strongly suspicious hunch about Adel, and her own better judgment, because she did not wish to make Sally's decisions for her in the manner of a "co-dependent" mother.

In hindsight, she reflects that she might have questioned Adel, or encouraged Sally to do so, or refused permission, or diverted the girls' attention to keep them at home. Now, although she feels guilty for not acting on her hunch, she tries to suppress her negative feelings and thoughts about Sally's continuing friendship with Adel, because she does not want to influence or alienate Sally.

Sally's mother struggled with her co-dependency also when dealing with the police who investigated Sally's assault. On the one hand, she wanted the police to make Sally's case a priority and take action; on the other hand, she did not want to be "pushy." Thus, she forced herself to be patient with the police to the point that she found herself making excuses for them, in spite of feeling frustrated and angry with them for not returning her phone calls.

Sally's mother seems uncertain about what messages she should give to those around her: Should she be direct and clearly state her thoughts and feelings? Should she temper her message with understanding? Should she compromise without ever stating her ideas? This debate takes place only in Sally's mother's mind; those around her hear only messages so modified that they don't always grasp them.

Sally talked of her mother in generally positive terms but also described her as "co-dependent because she's always looking after other people" (a description that eerily echoes her mother's own description of herself). After the beating, Sally related, her mother followed through with the police and with the school, and obtained trauma counseling for Sally.

Sally's schooling

In the aftermath of the beating, Sally regressed, behaving in ways one might expect of a much younger child: She took to staying at home, dressed in flannel pajamas and a bathrobe; she sat in her mother's lap on the couch and would not let her mother out of her sight, even to go to the bathroom or have a shower.

Although Sally said her mother wanted her to face her fears and return to school, her mother herself expressed caution with regard to this. She had debated with both her husband and the police, and recalled fighting for the middle ground between Sally's father, who introduced the idea of correspondence schooling (and made arrangements with Sally to do this without first consulting Sally's mother), and Sally's stepfather, who had tried correspondence schooling himself and felt that Sally would do better to return to school immediately. In fact, Sally's mother had arranged with the school counselor for Sally to return gradually, with counseling support — but her idea somehow got lost in the flurry of family opinions.

A further debate regarding her return to school involved Sally and her stepmother, who warned that Sally would lose all her friends if she didn't go back. Sally disagreed, and set out to prove her stepmother wrong. She evidently didn't hear her mother's idea of a gradual return because the more immediate message — from her father as well as her stepmother — seemed to be, "go back to school at once."

In the end, the adults, who could not reach agreement among themselves, turned the decision over to Sally, who decided to stay home and do her lessons by correspondence.

Sally plans to stay with this arrangement until she enters grade 11. She is presently more successful at her school work than she was while attending school.

Peer relationships

Like most of the young people she knows, Sally looks to friends rather than family for feelings of connectedness, belonging, and protection. She and many of her friends are enthralled with the notion of gangs, which they seem to spend much time discussing.

Sally often spoke to me of her connections with gangs, particularly a gang called the "Bloods." Early in our conversations, she revealed that prior to being beaten up by Sarah and Marilee, she had cultivated a tough attitude and projected a threatening image. In fact, she felt it was ironic that she had been beaten, as she saw herself as "usually the tougher person who'd be like the one that people would have to back down against."

Conversations with Sally's fellow students revealed that this was not a spurious claim. However, both Sally and Adel (the "best friend" who helped lure Sally to the corner store where she was beaten up) also had reputations for toughness among their fellows, especially the younger ones. In fact, Sally's friendship with Adel was to some extent premised on toughness. As Sally described Adel's participation in her beating: "That's the kind of friendship we have, she wanted to see me get pushed around, and I would love to see her pushed around too."

Sally assured me that she isn't afraid of being beaten up again because "I have like tons of friends in gangs, and I'm not even scared." Although she briefly mentioned her injuries (which were considerable), and then discussed laying charges against Sarah, she was emphatic that she was unmoved because she felt protected by her affiliation with gang members.

When Sally talked about gangs, she became animated and excited. I followed her lead and asked her to tell me more about her connections with these gangs. She offered a detailed description of her notions of local gang life and her connections with people who carry guns and can arrange to kill people. For Sally, a gang is a group of people who

> go around killing people that bug them. Like the toughest guys and the toughest girls get together and then just form a gang and they go down and get guns and stuff.

When I asked whether these gangs actually killed people, Sally informed me that this

> depends. Okay, if they were to fight, they'd give the other gang the option, and if they wanted to use guns then they'd have gun fights and if they wanted to have fist fights, then they would do it. But they let them have the option. Like if I was to go to one of my friends and say, "Can you go and kill this person for me?" they would say, "How do you want them killed? When do you want it done?" and then they'd go and do it like a hit man.

Certainly, in Sally's eyes, these people are tough, but they are also "friendly people that would come up and talk to you," thus making it possible for Sally to get to know them. As she explained:

> There's a whole bunch of girls that I know that are in gangs, and they're pretty

nice, it's just staying off their bad side, 'cause they can do serious damage to you.

When I asked what might provoke girls in a gang to do serious damage to Sally or any other girl, she replied:

Anything. Like, okay, if you go to the club where they all hang out — and say you thought one of the guy Bloods was good-looking and you went up and started talking to him, if a girl Blood just didn't like the way you looked or didn't know why you were talking to her boyfriend, like you just wanted to ask him for a cigarette or something — that can provoke them, or if you were to call them names or give them a dirty look. Like, you just gotta be really careful around them, 'cause they could beat you up just for the way you look, or if they want your shoes, or if they don't like the shirt you're wearing or something.

Despite the personal risk involved, knowing people in gangs seemed very important to Sally. She told me rather proudly, "Did you hear about the drive-by shooting downtown, those two guys that did the drive-by shooting? Those were my friends."[2] Finally, she identified herself as a gang member in her own right:

I'm in a Skate gang — the Blue Snakes. Blue Snakes are not as extreme as Green Iguanas because we don't tattoo ourselves. I'm the only girl. It's rare to have girls as Skates ... .

When I asked her what it was like to be a Blue Snake, she answered:

It's perfect being a Skate because you, you've got your skateboard. That's something to do. You've got your skateboard, that also counts as weapon. And — there's not, like, but Skates don't get hassled a lot.

I asked her to explain to me how a skateboard could be used as a weapon and learned that

you pick it up and hit people. People only do this if they were gonna, like gonna get mugged or something. Usually, like, they yell, like they just kind of like, "Leave me alone!" I don't know, like my friend Allan, he used his skateboard to fight someone — a whole bunch of Rappers came up to him, stole his Walkman, stole his skateboard and he grabbed it back and hit them. So then they ran off, but they took his Walkman. Rappers and Skates fight each other. It's like Rappers think they're too good for Skates because that's all we hear on the news now is Rappers this and rap this and everything and Skaters, we are just calm and keep to ourselves. WE don't do anything. We like, our pastime is skateboarding. That's not hurting anybody.

When Sally talked about her connection with Skates and skateboarding, she premised her identity not on the individually oriented "I" but on the plural "we," and she had clear ideas about who constituted the "we" with whom she identified. As a Skate she is part of a group who pursue a certain activity. Skateboarding involves learning to do certain tricks, participating in skate-offs, and wearing certain clothes such as Airwalks, Doc Martens, and second-hand clothes bought at thrift stores. She was also clear that Skates are further distinguished by not being Rappers. For Sally, Rappers are people whose

> pastime is going around beating people up, fighting, everything. ... The Rappers, they go out and buy like, sixty dollar jeans. We go to Value Village and get ours for like five dollars. I mean there, there's like, that's what Skates are. They [Rappers] wear, they have baggy jeans, but we cut ours off at the bottom so it goes like straight down and they're pretty short, and then we wear like a big, big, big, oversized striped T-shirt, a toque, and there we go. They, they have to wear like a name brand hat, a name — like a labeled shirt, cross-colored jeans, like or whatever kind of shoes they're wearing now, and then start talking like the Rappers, start listening to their music and then they're slowly, slowly classified as one. And us, we go down to the thrift stores and — there we go. Rappers like to pick on Skates, nobody picks on Rappers.

To grasp the distinction between Skates and Rappers, I not only listened carefully to Sally, but also discussed this with other young people. I learned that Skates and Rappers do indeed have very different orientations, which are recognizable through differences in clothing styles and tastes in music (as outlined in Chapter Two). As Sally explained to me: Skates, Bangers, and Rappers all know one another; and Bangers are not as threatening to Skates as Rappers because

> like, there's no what's it called like, fighting, there's no fighting between the Bangers and the Skates. It's the Rappers, 'cause they like brand names and everything.

Sally appeared to feel strongly connected to her identity as a Skate, and traced her membership in a Skate gang back to her elementary school friendship with a boy who had initiated her into the world of skateboarding. Both the friendship and the affiliation to the sport have endured for a number of years, despite the fact that Sally has moved away from the neighborhood in which her Skater friend lives.

When I asked why she thought young people join gangs or groups such as the ones she described, she explained:

> Like, I think that people who go into one of those gangs, it's like they don't have a good family life, so they're using the gang as a family. Like, okay, well, if I'm in this gang, then the gang members are going to treat me like I'm there and they're gonna do this for me … so it's like having the comfort of like being somewhere where they belong, where like people are paying attention to you … .

According to Sally, some young women will go to great lengths to achieve a sense of belonging. They will submit to having sex with as many as 12 young men, hand-picked for them by the existing gang members, and/or endure being beaten without flinching for a specified number of minutes (where the beating consists of being kicked in the stomach, kicked in the head, and punched in the face) by the toughest girl in the gang. All this is considered the price of admission. Although Sally had never encountered such treatment herself, she seemed convinced that such things did take place.

For Sally, gang or group membership implied "being treated like I'm there," getting attention, and having a family. In our conversations, Sally gave me a great deal of information about her family, and several factors stand out in connection with "being treated like I'm there." During our second meeting, when I asked how things were going at home, she responded, "Fine, I'm never there." But when we talked about what Sally liked and wanted most from her family and from people in general, she revealed that she liked being listened to and getting attention. In other words, although she didn't spend much time with her family, she actually wanted their time and attention. Sally expressed all this clearly and simply: "I like it when people look at me … I like attention … I like people to recognize what I do and give me attention for it … ."

Sally does a number of things to get attention. She dyes her hair using unusual colors: greens, purples, odd shades of red. She tries out many different hairstyles, all of them deliberately "weird" and "original." She wears clothes that she describes as "weird," just like her hair, and in social settings she subscribes to behaviors that she hopes will make people notice her. When I first met with her, she had dyed her hair auburn, but unfortunately this was not bringing her the response from her parents that she was looking for:

> My dad didn't even notice, like he hasn't said anything and I've had it in for two weeks … . When I got home, my mom, she's like, "Get out of here." … I got in the house and she said, "Get out of my sight and don't come back until that's washed out."

Aside from getting attention from her parents, Sally likes to get reactions from other people, anyone who will look, anyone who will react:

> I wear like a really nice dress, that doesn't like, it's got like little tiny straps and then I'll wear a different patterned shirt and like, hifi socks that are striped. Then I'll wear my big Doc boots and I'll put my hair all in these weird positions and do little braids and everything and then when they [my parents] walk with me they go, "She's not with us, we don't know her," but I do it because I like it when people look at me, but I kind of like the glances, but not the stares — Then I feel different … . It's cool because there's no one else that's dressed like me … and people just look at me and some of them go, "Oh neat," and some of them go, "Oh my gosh," you know, but it's up to them. I like it. I like the attention … . And yes, I'd like to be on stage.

Music groups: The Beastie Boys (and beastie girls)

With regard to being on stage, Sally had much invested in someday being a performer. She and two of her friends have dreams of becoming musicians, performers just like their idols, the Beastie Boys, a punk music trio from New York. Sally was wearing a Beastie Boys T-shirt while telling me about her strong identification with these musicians:

> So, I'll play the bass and we're all going to be singers, we don't want to fight over who sings … . And Beverley is going to play drums and Lorraine's going to play electric guitar. … We're going to be just like the Beastie Boys, like I'm wearing this T-shirt here because MCA, he's my favorite, and he plays the bass, and Mike D., this is of course Beverley's favorite and he plays the drums, and King Ad-Rock, this is of course Lorraine's favorite and he plays the electric guitar, so we're a kind of like girl Beastie Boys kind of thing … . We want to be unique like that. We want to have a kind of weird sound that no one else has.

Rolling Stone Magazine describes the Beastie Boys as a band that offers a sly blending of the styles ... . *Ill Communication* [one of their albums] fuses jazz-laced hip-hop, crabby 1980-style punk thrash, aggressive, groove-heavy rap and the kind of infectiously sleazy instrumentals that can be heard playing in porn movies just after someone says, "Hey, you're not the regular cabana boy." (Mundy, 1994)

The Beastie Boys, whose dress style blends everything from thrift store finds to the latest in Skater gear (all of it several sizes too large), also blend language into word-association free-for-alls reminiscent of Joyce's *Finnegans Wake*. Thus, a Beastie Boy might describe another band he admires as, "Fly, fresh, dope and phat, they are ultimately the shit" (*Rolling Stone*, August 11, 1994) or perhaps respond to a reporter's question about whether or not he owns and uses exercise equipment with, "I have a uh, John Holmes penis pull. I have a basketball, a brand new Voit black streetball basketball. It's the best basketball I ever owned" (Mack, 1994). The group has become what Mundy (1994) terms "a leading cult" with an "original posture as cartoonish beer-swilling assholes" who are now considered "musical innovators, cultural pioneers and the kind of upstanding citizens [read, successful businessmen] that deserve to kick back and dig their bad selves" (p. 48).

Millions of young people like Sally and her friends identify with the Beastie Boys. Millions emulate their style of dress, their hair (which features wild colors and oddly angled razor cuts), their style of talking and their attitudes. For some, the identification goes beyond style and extends to life experiences.

Like Sally, Ad-Rock Horovitz's parents divorced when he was young (aged three), and he went to live with his mother. Like Sally, he discovered skateboarding early and still pursues this activity. Like Sally and her friends, who began to use marijuana, magic mushrooms, and acid (LSD) in grade six, and who have no trouble obtaining drugs and alcohol whenever they want, drugs and alcohol are part of Ad-Rock's everyday life and have been since at least grade four, when he first got caught for smoking pot. Ad-Rock's mother, whom he describes as "the coolest person ever" because she ran a hip thrift shop in New York City's West Village and liked to go to see rock bands and stumble down streets singing and laughing, died from alcoholism when he was in his teens.

Also like Sally, Ad-Rock is no stranger to violence. In a single year, he was charged with assault twice: once for throwing a full beer can at a female fan, and once for assaulting a television camera man who was trying to film him at a time when he did not wish to be filmed. The first charge was eventually dropped; the second brought him 200 hours of community work.

The other Beastie Boys, MCA Yauch and Mike D. Diamond (who lost his father at the age of 16), share Ad-Rock's history of early initiation into drug and alcohol misuse. And while all three grew up on New York's affluent upper west side among wealthy families, attended expensive liberal private schools, and were exposed to New York's intellectual and artistic elite, all three chose public acting out as a way of making their mark in the world. Credited with inventing the epidemic fad of ripping off hood ornaments from expensive European cars and the wearing of one's baseball cap back to front; known for being young, drunken, and bad, and for prancing about in clothes meant to shock, the Beastie Boys (all now well past the age of 30) have made a life's work of never growing up, at least in public. Instead, they have become trend setters whose greatest preoccupation is themselves, followed by sex, drugs, alcohol, and violence — as the lyrics from their songs demonstrate:

From "The New Style":
Father of many — married to none
And in case you're unaware I carry a gun
Stepped into the party — the place was overpacked
Saw the kid that dissed my honey and shot him in the back
I had to get a beeper because my phone is tapped
You better keep your mouth shut 'cause I'm feeling fully strapped
I got money in the bank — I can still get high
That's why your girlfriend thinks that I'm so fly
I've got money and juice — twin sisters in my bed
Their father had envy so I shot him in the head
If I played guitar I'd be Jimmy Page
The girlies I like are underage (check it!)
Girls with boyfriends are the kind I like
I'll steal your honey like I stole your bike
Your father — he's jealous 'cause I'm making that green
I've got the girlies' numbers from the places I have been[3]

From "No Sleep 'Til Brooklyn":
Another place — another train
Another bottle in the brain

Another girl — another fight
Another drive all night
Our manager's crazy — he always smokes dust
He's got his own room at the back of the bus
Tour 'round the world — you rock around the clock
Plane to hotel — girls on the jock
We're thrashing hotels like it's going out of style
Getting paid along the way 'cause it's worth your while
Four on the floor — Ad-Rock's out the door
MCA's in the back because he's skeezin' with some whore
We've got a safe in the trunk with money in a stack
With dice in the front and Brooklyn's in the back.[4]

Sally and her friends want to be girl Beastie Boys when they grow up, and in the meantime they are practicing for the role. For Sally, this includes overcoming shyness in order to be able to become a performer. Thus, she must change the way she behaves in social settings and must take risks that could get her into trouble:

Like, I'm really shy, but it's like if you get up there and act like an idiot people don't think you're shy, so even if I am shy, I can't do that … . If you don't act shy, people don't treat like you're shy, so I'm crazy now … . Like I'm totally over my shyness and everything, and last weekend, when we were downtown, I got Beverley's boyfriend in trouble. He's a Rapper, and he was really bugging me, so I go up to these big, big Rapper guys that look like they're real tough and I go, "See that guy over there? Well he thinks you're an idiot and he wants to fight with you." So he goes over and he's like, "What are you saying?" and he's like, "Nothing, I'm sure I didn't say nothing," and I'm just embarrassing myself going up to everyone and saying, "I think you're cool," and — everyone's like, "Stop it, stop it," and it was so much fun.

Practicing also includes doing drugs and believing that in her school of several hundred students "only about 12 kids don't smoke drugs and drop acid and they're all chess players." It means being a Skate and trying to be "original and different and like nobody else," while carefully emulating a music group that is the focal point for many other adolescents. It means wanting to live in a loft in New York City like the Beastie Boys did when they started out. It means talking the way the Beastie Boys talk, that is, juxtaposing insults with unusual word-associations meant to shock, amuse, and sometimes baffle the listener. It means talking about using drugs as if it were just something everyone did. Sally talks about getting drugs as if this were the most common of everyday experiences:

Uhm, there's about seven dealers at our school, you walk up to them and you say, "Can I get a gram or a hit?" And they say, "Okay," and you give them the money, and they give you the drugs, and you walk away. Or if they don't have any on them they say, "I can get it to you at lunch." They skip their class, their first class before lunch, and they go over to the high school and get it off a dealer at the high school and then come back to school.

Sally's assumption is simply that this is how it's done, and "we" (meaning everybody except maybe the odd chess player) all do it.

When I asked why the street groups she had described to me organized their identities around the music they listened to, Sally stated that for her, there was a direct connection between the music one listened to and the way one acted: "It's like the total biggest influence." When kids talk about what it is that makes them a Rapper or a Skate,

they're like, well, the music. It's just neat and it draws you to it and I like, I like to listen to it, I'm like, "Oh ya."

Further, Sally offered an explanation for why Rappers in particular are violent:

'Cause everyone's like, like it's like gangster music and everyone's like, "Oh ya, I gotta be tough. I gotta go kill people," like that and stuff … . 'Cause the lyrics in the rap music, it's like, "Ya, go out and kill your mom and then get the money and then go kill your dad" … . And then they say things like they're going to, they're going to get their gang after them and stuff … . Like, the reason why the kids wanna kill 'em is 'cause they have rules.

When I probed further into the actuality of such killings, Sally became vague but assured me that if someone wanted to get someone killed, it could be arranged. When I asked more questions as to the lives of kids whom she knows to engage in violence on a regular basis, she replied:

They're like always, they always need to either be drunk or like smoked up, and they always like have to be like doing something — like breaking into cars, houses, stuff like that.

In Sally's estimation, what lies beneath these behaviors is "a bad family life" and not enough personal attention, which together drives kids to seek out the connectedness and feeling of belonging found in groups and gangs. As a Rapper, a Banger or, in Sally's case, a Skate, a kid can be "somebody" with a ready-made and recognizable identity that is broadcast to others through music, dress, and the activities endemic to their group.

Sally expanded on the notion of a "bad family life" when she talked about her friends' families. With the exception of Lorraine, most of Sally's friends have experienced family break-ups that, like Sally's parents' break-up, followed several years of quarreling and fighting. But even Lorraine had not escaped experiencing difficulties at home and a "bad family life." As Sally described it, Lorraine was deeply unhappy with her family:

> Lorraine's parents are still together, and that's why she's so depressed. She hates her mother and she hates her father and wishes they would get divorced … . Her mother won't let her go and won't accept the fact that she's getting older and her dad's never there … . He goes away for months at a time to work, and she gets depressed … . She loves being depressed. She couldn't be happy, like her brother is such a goody goody, and she's just the opposite, and her mother's always going, "Why can't you be like Jim?" and people say, "You're Jim's little sister." That's like her name. Whenever she writes me a note she signs it "Jim's little sister," and she's really depressing. She's like so depressing, she makes Beverley and me want to cry whenever she goes on one of her depressing modes. She just sits there and her room's so dark, like a prisoner in jail … . She says, "Too many people are happy, what's there to be happy about? Trees are being cut down and people are dying. Who cares?" But she's really smart like me, and me and her are exactly alike, except I'm crazy and she's depressing.

It seems that only when the three girls get together and work at being "beastie girls" does Lorraine achieve some relief from her depression. When she engages with the other two in song writing, she begins to brighten up a little.

Growing up female

As Sally and I talked, besides being struck by the emotional abandonment she described, I also noticed that the sources from which she drew most of her inspiration and her identity were male and even degrading to women.

When I asked whether she wanted to be like any women she knew, Sally named four women. One was the 17-year-old daughter of a friend of her mother's whom she admires because "she's the nicest person and she's got a weight problem and she doesn't care," but whose real attraction is that she has a "gorgeous" brother. The second was Madonna, the world-famous pop-music sex idol. Sally's reason for looking up to Madonna is that "she can do anything she wants and not care what anybody thinks about her." (As well as being a lionized sex symbol, Madonna is a former battered wife whose marriage to Sean Penn — a Hollywood actor known for his tough, bad-boy image — floundered because Penn beat her during fits of drunken rage.)

The next woman she named was Marilyn Monroe, about whom she didn't have much to say except that she was dead. (As most people over 30 know, Marilyn Monroe died because she took an overdose of antidepressants combined with alcohol. Idolized by millions, romantically linked to John F. Kennedy, a veteran of four marriages and a survivor of sexual abuse in her younger years, Marilyn Monroe was never able to find peace.)

The last woman Sally named was Naomi Campbell, whom she described as "like a runway supermodel" whom she liked primarily because "she's got like a neat accent and she's really pretty."

Three of the four women Sally named are sex objects, highly paid and much adored for their bodies, their faces, and the images of narrowly defined female desirability that they project into the public mind in the service of the multibillion-dollar entertainment and fashion industries. At least two of them, Madonna and Marilyn Monroe, have suffered publicly for being the sex symbols their audiences pay them to be.

The very idols Sally chose (other than the daughter of her mother's friend) presented her with difficulties in being a girl. For her, the images provided for girls and women by the entertainment and fashion industries create expectations which all females must fulfill. Thus, Sally believes that most boys and a lot of other girls think that all young women must be "like Cindy Crawford, a supermodel, she's like underweight, like a perfect body, so pretty, like everything." And although Sally stated she didn't think she personally needed to conform to this image, she was well aware of it and constantly fighting against it.

In part, Sally finds refuge from the pressure to be thin and perfect by being the only girl in her Skate group. But here she faces a different kind of pressure and a different kind of discrimination. Here the boys tell her, "You, you gotta learn how to skate better, come on, you gotta alley a little bit higher." Although it's clear that she is welcome in the group largely because one of the good Skaters is her friend, she is not really contending as a Skate, who can enter skate-offs and find sponsorship through one of the local skate equipment suppliers, because she is a girl.

Because little encouragement is extended to girls to engage in skating for its own sake, there are few really good female Skaters to be found, especially in Sally's community. Therefore, Sally must often fight against the accusation that she is merely a "poser," someone who carries around a skateboard but can't really skate. As well, she faces harassment from other girls who accost her when they see her with a skateboard and yell out, "Oh yeah, what are you trying to be, a guy or something?" Often, such remarks provoke an aggressive reaction from Sally; and it is mostly under such circumstances that she has threatened other girls and faced them down.

The gender-based discrimination that Sally experiences with regard to her body and her participation in skateboarding reaches into other areas of her life as well. She gave me the following two examples. The first has to do with being prevented from taking part in an activity; the second has to do with being subjected to abuse as a result of the still deeply entrenched sexual double standard:

> A lot of Skater guys, they go snowboarding and then girls that want to go snowboarding, they get dumped on, and the guys go, "Stick to the ski slopes," you know, do the girls' thing and stuff. My friend Lorraine, her boyfriend's this big-time snowboarder, she wants to try it, but every time she asks her brother, her brother's like, "Don't, Lorraine, don't," he like tells her, "You're just going to get mocked and stuff," so she says, "Okay," and she just goes skiing.
>
> ***
>
> Uhm, it's like girls can be called sluts if they have sex, but guys are rewarded. If a girl's to go and do it with 50 guys, then they're called a slut or something, but if a guy's going to do it with 50 girls then like, it's "Right on!" ... Like, guys get rewarded and girls get beat up or pushed around or talked about, like rumors or something. I think it's really dumb because they're both doing the same thing.

Sally gave me a first-hand example of being the victim of the double standard she so abhors:

> My last boyfriend was a big-time Rapper and he was such a jerk, you can't explain it. There's something about him, I can't stand him now, I'd like to see

him die … . He called my friend a slut, and I do not like that name, slut is a word I hate, and he wouldn't stop calling her that and I told him to stop it … and he wouldn't let up with calling her that … . And there was a lot of stuff that he did that was, I don't know, low, like he set up his friend, who's a virgin and hated it, with Adel so she'd sleep with him, but somebody else told her it was a set-up so she said, "Okay, fine, you're dumped," but he still kept calling her a slut. And he well, used me, like we finally had sex and then as soon as that was over he's like, "Bye" … . And like, I'm so mad at myself for like actually letting him. We weren't going out for that long and stuff. I got so mad at myself for letting somebody do that to me, so, I don't know, I hate him so!

The fact that girls get "beat up or pushed around" and construed as "sluts" for showing an interest in sex led us back to discussing violence, because Sally's beating occurred under just such circumstances. Marilee, Sarah, and their friends had decided that Sally was a "slut" for showing interest in Sarah's boyfriend. The designation "slut" made Sally fair game for a beating, according to the rules as understood by Sally and by the girls in her social circle. (This insult is hurled at girls by other girls far more often than it is by boys, although boys also use it.)

Sally thinks the sexual double standard is "stupid" and says that she "just calls guys sluts too if they're going to call me and my friends that." But she also plays into the double standard by believing that being called a slut is "the biggest insult" — one that must be addressed, a direct attack worthy of an aggressive response:

Like, it'd be people taking me on, and then if someone was to pick on me, I'd turn around and do it right back. It's like this girl called Adel and me sluts, so I got really mad and I said, "You, you don't go around talking like that … and I'm like, "Who are you, like who are you to judge us?" and everything, and she's like, "Well I can if I want," so I pushed her and I said, "I don't wanna ever hear you calling anybody a slut, you can call them any other name, but like that one is just degrading." And she's like, "Fine!" So I just like pushed her again and walked away.

Thus, girls — even those who know that designating another girl a slut is simply buying into a "stupid" double standard — take such name calling seriously; they push each other around and beat each other up over it.

Despite her personal rejection of these standards, Sally knows them well. She knows also that these standards govern rules which, in the end, must be followed. As she explained earlier to me, if you were out somewhere and say you thought one of the [girls' boyfriends] was good-looking and you went up and started talking to him, if [she] didn't like the way you looked or didn't know why you were talking to her boyfriend, ... [she could] do serious damage to you.

Thus, when Sally showed an interest in Sarah's boyfriend and consequently got beaten up by Sarah and Marilee, she fell victim to the very double standard that she hates. It is a double standard that operates on many levels in Sally's life.

This became clear to me when Sally described how she likes to spend time with her little sister. Other than practicing to become a girl Beastie Boy, and being a Skate, Sally very much enjoys playing with Barbie dolls — not only with her little sister, but also with her friends, the same girls who want to be female Beastie Boys. Every afternoon,

> I do my school work and after, I play Barbies with my sister, and it's okay, as long as I get to be in charge of the game, and I love to put on Barbie's wedding dress and play them getting married ... . I have tons of Barbies myself and I keep them. I've got so much furniture. I've got three cars and a bathroom set and all this stuff so, and I'm not going to give it to my sister because when I have kids I want it. It's okay, sometimes I get sick of it because I take so long to get set up, like I have to have the house perfect and everything. Like I'm a perfectionist. I get it from my mom. After I'm set up, that takes an hour and then I only have half an hour to play with her because I leave at four-thirty ... . And I tell my friends that I play with Barbies and they go "Yeah, you're cool," some of them.
>
> Sibylle: How many of your friends do that?
> Sally: Lorraine, Beverley. Beverley is so crazy, she needs to go, she's like psycho, she loves Barbies, loves making them do things ... .

After our discussion, I read and reread the transcripts. I was reminded of the work of A.N. Leontyev (1981), a Russian psychologist who worked with and expanded on L.S. Vygotsky's theories on the development of self and mind. Leontyev suggests that, because it provides an arena in which children practice entering into an active relationship with self and others, play makes a strong contribution to the development of mind, self, and world. Within the serious practice (praxis) that is play, children try out and formulate their identities, and their understanding of how the world works. Given this, I considered what Barbie dolls might offer Sally.

Barbie dolls offer a version of womanliness premised on largely unattainable and very narrow standards of body image. They suggest that women ought to be long-limbed and thin, small-hipped and narrow-waisted, and above all else, large-breasted. They suggest that a woman's hair must be thick, long, and wavy, and preferably blond. They also suggest that women are and should be primarily preoccupied with how they look, with what they wear, and with their material possessions, particularly those that are useful to their domestic life. Barbie's primary focus is her wardrobe.

Barbie first appeared on the market in March 1959, as the embodiment of the perfect American teenage fashion model. According to a pamphlet enclosed in the package of the 35th anniversary reissue of the original Barbie, this doll was created by Ruth Handler, who describes Barbie (in an open letter to those who acquire the reissued doll) as "a role model for girls for over three decades ... [because] she allows girls from all around the world to live out their dreams and fantasies in spite of a real world that may seem too big" (manufacturer's pamphlet, Mattel toys, 1995).

The roles that Barbie offers — through her nearly 30 different guises — involve sunbathing, exercising, preparing for gala evenings on the town, singing in rock bands, dancing, and dressing glamorously in sexually alluring costumes. Some Barbies do seem to work for a living, but these are hard to find. I was able to locate one doctor Barbie, dressed in a white coat, a short skirt, and tight sweater, sporting a stethoscope and weighing a baby. She was also blond, buxom, and wearing a great deal of make-up on her "oh so coy ... delicately painted face" (manufacturer's pamphlet, Mattel Toys, 1995).

Since 1959, little has changed with regard to Barbie's underlying message about women's bodies and women's focal points. Barbie is still "a perfect blend of innocence and glamour, right down to ... her pretty pink polished fingertips," engaged primarily in achieving a "perfect look" (manufacturer's pamphlet, Mattel Toys, 1995). Over the years, Barbie has acquired a larger wardrobe and a greater range of accessories. She has acquired Ken as a playmate, as well as a house, a camper, and cars; but the underlying premise — that the ideal woman looks like a *Playboy Magazine* centerfold — has not altered.

For Sally, being like Barbie reinforces the notion of having to be thin and extends to getting married, playing the wedding game over and over again to perfectionist standards. Sally knows she should be thinner. She's clear that what is expected of a girl in the 1990s is "to be like Cindy Crawford," a thin and (according to Sally) "annoying" example of what "guys and other girls think girls should be like." She also knows that even though she wants to be a girl Beastie Boy and identifies herself as a Skate, the ultimate achievement for a woman is a wedding. Young women like Sally still understand (as did the women of my generation and generations of women before us) that no matter how else we occupy ourselves in the meantime, the greatest, most important goal is getting married. It is a goal that we can hope to achieve only by emulating, as closely as we can, the female templates provided for us by models like Cindy Crawford and that enduring sym-bol of ideal womanhood, Barbie.

Sally has "got the message" loud and clear. When I asked what she wanted to be when she grew up, she answered, "a model and a musi-cian." And Sally is not alone.

School

As Sally and I talked, I wondered how education fit into her life in the midst of all these other largely negative influences. I asked Sally about her experiences at school, and what they meant to her.

For Sally, school — when she did go there — was primarily a place to meet with other young people, and only secondarily a place where she went to receive an education. Mostly, she didn't go:

> Like I'd go to school, to get Adel, and then leave. So, we'd like walk, we'd have to walk to my house or her house, which takes about an hour, and like the principal kept calling our parents, and my mom just said that she knows that I don't like school, but she wants me to know that for her, school is a big deal, so she told me that I had to go.

When I asked her what school was like, Sally replied:

> Mmm ... I got a B in math once when I was in junior high. Everything else I failed, 'cause I was walking around and watching television.

When I probed further so that I could understand what she found dif-ficult about school, Sally explained:

> I don't like having people at school. Like, I like to keep to myself, unless, unless my friends from downtown, 'cause they're my loyal friends. And, I don't know, there's just no one there I like. 'Cause at school, you've always got

someone around you. You go to class with your friends and you get five-minute breaks with your friends, and then you get lunch. I just like being by myself ... .

Further discussion led us back to drugs and violence. According to Sally, school is where "fights happen almost every day" and where people are mean to one another. School is where Sally had to act tough. School is where she learned about drugs and sexual harassment. School is where she had a reputation to uphold, and where she made friends whom she defended when others called them sluts. School is where, in academic terms, she mostly failed. Sally hated school.

By contrast, Sally "loved" working on her correspondence courses at her father's house under his supervision:

Easy, I got an A in French. Then I got an E in French and I need to get tutoring, then I got a C+ in Science and I'm getting B's and A's in English and like, B's and A's in Math, and I haven't done any Guidance and Socials, I haven't sent anything in yet, but everything else is real easy, and it's better than school. It's like I can do whatever I want for as long as I want. It's just better than school. I don't like school ... . I'm going to stay on correspondence 'til grade 11.

In the end, the social demands of school were too much of a distraction for Sally; friends and drugs and sexual harassment and violence drove her out. She is far happier at home.

Each day Sally spends time with her father and sister and rides back and forth to the city with her mother. Each day she plays Barbies, and on weekends she meets her Skater friends and skates; or she gets together with Beverley and Lorraine and writes songs and practices being a girl Beastie Boy. When she wants excitement, she and the girl Beastie Boys go downtown, hang out with other kids, and create some diversion for themselves:

I just get this big bolt of energy and, okay, I'm in this hyper mood and when I get hyper, I am just like, if you don't want to be embarrassed, walk totally away from me because I'll just go up and talk to everyone. Like, "I think you're cool, but you need a haircut," like I'm so critical, it's really funny. And Beverley is exactly the same way only she's not so — she wouldn't go and do it, she mocks everybody behind their back, but I'm the person that goes up and says it. "You know what my friend just said about you?" and she goes, "You're an idiot," and stuff, and like, people just laugh, and we do it to have fun, for something to do ... .

Ultimately, Sally loves to do anything that will earn her some attention and a sense of belonging. She will dye her hair a multitude of colors and dress herself in weird and wonderful clothes. She will make friends with gang members. She will go to church socials with new acquaintances and sing religious songs on Friday nights when she has nothing else to do. She will take drugs and get into fights. She will go with her stepfather to the mall and pretend he's her older brother, and with her mother to Tupperware parties. And — although her mother "dragged" her there at first — she will go to see a counselor. Going for counseling is something that Sally really loves because it's

> uhm, really good, it's time ... a time to talk. (*Short laugh*) So you can talk about, like, all your problems and they can give you advice and stuff. 'Cause at first I said, "Well I won't go." And then when I met her [the counselor] and everything I'm like, "Okay. This isn't that bad." And now it's like, my mom has an hour-and-a-half appointment and she comes out to the car and I'll still be talking to my counselor, like we'll have a two-hour session. And my mom's like, "What kept you guys so long?" Tomorrow I'm going to bring in coffee and we're going to sit there and talk as long as we want ... .

This is where I left Sally: seeing her counselor on a weekly basis, and staying away from school.

Notes

1. The wife's assumption of a parental role with respect to her husband also features in other key informants' families. See, for example, "Mary's Story" (Chapter Six).
2. This information fits the facts. There was a drive-by shooting near a downtown park in which two youths from Sally's neighborhood drove by in a car and shot another youth in the leg. This shooting took place on November 22, 1993 and was reported in the *Victoria Times Colonist* on November 24, 1993.
3. Lyrics by M. Diamond, R. Rubin, A. Yauch and The King; music by R. Rubin and The King. Copyright © 1986 by Def Jam Music Inc. (ASCAP)/Brooklyn Dust Music (ASCAP). All rights reserved.
4. Lyrics by M. Diamond, A. Yauch, and The King; music by R. Rubin, A. Yauch, and The King. Copyright © 1986 by Def Jam Music Inc. (ASCAP)/Brooklyn Dust Music (ASCAP). All rights reserved.

CHAPTER FOUR

Marilee's Story

One time when my dad was drinking he kicked me out of the house, he hit me a couple of times, so I left that night and went to a friend's house. My dad regrets it, and he says he wouldn't do it again. He hit my mom too. He had her down on her knees right by the coffee table and he had her arm behind her back and he threatened to break it an' stuff and then she screamed. And I came down the stairs and she told me to phone the cops. So my dad left, and now they're back together and he's in counseling and it's better, but I'll never forgive him. Like inside, I'll never, ever forgive him, but I'll forgive him enough to keep my love for him and stuff. (*Excerpt from taped interview with Marilee*)

Family dynamics

Although Marilee described her family as basically good, there was much in what she told me that pointed to deep-seated and long-standing difficulties. Her parents have been together for nearly 26 years during which they have had many mini separations, short periods of time when one parent or the other left the family in order to cool off after a fight.

Fights occur frequently (as they did in Marilee's father's family when he was growing up). Everyone participates: Fights take place between mother and father, father and daughters, mother and daughters, or between the sisters. These altercations begin over small things and escalate into major confrontations. As Marilee described it:

All our fights start over stupid things, just little stupid things, and they always seem to happen on vacation or something like that. 'Cause Christmas time we'd always get in a fight, and the family would split up. My dad would go somewhere for a couple of days before Christmas, them come back. My sister and I got in a big huge fight on Valentine's Day, and I ran away ... .

The Valentine's Day fight was over who could wear a particular pair of shoes. Running away as a way of dealing with this fight was actually sanctioned or perhaps even suggested by Marilee's mother, who told her, "Okay, you can get out of the house, you know," and drove her to the house of a friend who had agreed to take her in.

According to Marilee, when her father is involved in the fighting he is usually drinking and listening to country music and feeling angry.

Furthermore, drinking together as a family and getting drunk is very much a part of any holiday and the celebration of birthdays and anniversaries. Marilee's parents purchase the alcohol for Marilee, her sister, and their friends, and sanction their drinking at home under their supervision. The trouble seems to be that the parents themselves drink right along with everyone else and set limits neither on their own nor on others' drinking.

As Marilee describes it, both parents "used to like to really party and stuff," but have lately cut back because "they figure they're getting too old for it." Drinking is still, however, Marilee's father's chosen form of recreation. It is his ritual to drink with the boys at the local bar every Friday, and while according to Marilee, he has cut back somewhat on the amount he drinks during the week, he "has to" drink on Fridays because he "needs his time to have fun," especially since his best drinking buddy has just "dropped dead" at age 50.

Most conflict in the family seems to be characterized by an "either/or" approach, that is, "either you do what I want you to do or I'll let you have it." "Letting you have it" begins with screaming, yelling and name calling, escalates to threats and, on occasion, physical violence, and usually ends in someone being told to "get out" or choosing to leave as a way of punishing his or her opponent.

People often leave, but they always come back. Ultimatums are frequently held over the heads of family members who are seen to be in the wrong. For example, at the time I spoke to her, Marilee's father was seen to be in the wrong because of hitting his wife. He was therefore given the ultimatum to "never do it again" or he's had it, "because he knows that if he makes one more mistake, he's gone!"

Marilee herself has a similar ultimatum hanging over her, although hers is not about her conduct during fights, but rather about her commitment to school. She knows that she has only one choice: "either do [schooling by] correspondence or get out." Marilee made it clear to me that she is no stranger to conflict and violence in her home.

Marilee's mother

As Marilee told me her story, I kept flashing back to my conversations with her mother, whom I had met when she addressed a parent network forum on youth violence which I attended.

Marilee's mother had expressed astonishment and dismay with regard to her daughter's involvement with violence. She talked at length about how shocked she was to learn of Marilee's participation in the beating of Sally.

In searching for an explanation, she and the other parents who participated in the forum focused on their children's peers as the culprits who had persuaded them to engage in violence. No one mentioned family violence. Everyone saw it as a "kids' problem" brought on by the need for status, which could be gained through intimidation of others.

Each parent in turn elaborated on this thesis, telling the others how their own children had never been violent and never experienced violence before they changed "180 degrees" when they "hit puberty" and started to hang around with their present friends. Several parents stated emphatically that since they had never even spanked their kids, there could be no connection between their children's violent behavior and anything they had experienced at home.

Marilee's mother said not a word about her husband, about the conflict in her family, about the violence each family member had both witnessed and experienced at the hands of other family members, and about the many times she or her husband had left the family temporarily because of fighting. She did not mention that her husband was currently in counseling under threat of being expelled from the family home if he stepped out of line. Instead, she talked about Marilee's need for anger management and about her own efforts to persuade Marilee to accept counseling. For Marilee's mother, and for the other parents who participated in this forum, youth violence is somehow derived from the state of being adolescent.

Marilee offered a different explanation. She saw her own violence as directly connected to her experiences with her family and to her deeply felt anger.

Peer relationships

Marilee agreed to talk to me only once because she was afraid of being labeled a "narc" (informer) by her peers for telling me what she knew about violence. Nevertheless, she was willing to enter into a lengthy discussion about many aspects of herself and her life.

Besides family, we talked about what most occupied Marilee, namely, "trying to become the person I'm supposed to be." When I asked who that person was, she answered: "Just the person I am right now, the person who doesn't do drugs."

It seemed that, since grade eight (Marilee was now completing grade ten by correspondence), she had not been the person she was "supposed" to be because she had become involved with "the scummy people," those who were "druggies and just didn't care," those who "did whatever they wanted."

As a self-described "scummy" person, Marilee had enjoyed herself by "basically living on the edge every second you were there." When I asked what living on the edge meant, I learned it meant defying one's parents primarily by taking drugs. When I asked what had induced her to become involved with drugs and "scummy" people, she told me:

> I met Rosie, a friend of mine, and she kind of, I never knew she was hangin' around with them, and I got pulled into them, and it just seemed like a good idea at the time. (*Laughs*) "Cause it was fun. It was exciting — rebelling against your parents, just being in control.

When I probed to find out why she was no longer "there," Marilee explained that her change of heart had occurred as a result of a "mishap" — that is, a narrowly averted beating at the hands of the very people she found so exciting to be around.

It seems that because she was a newcomer to this crowd, Marilee was also a target for suspicion. Thus, when a rumor circulated that the local police knew the members of this "scummy" crowd were smoking dope and had a list of their names, Marilee was targeted as a "narc" and singled out for a beating by some 40 people. She was to receive the beating at the hands of a number of girls who were threatening to "bash her face in."

These girls (whom Marilee had hitherto regarded as her friends) organized the beating, which was to take place just outside the same junior high school that Sally attended. The boys, who were also involved in targeting Marilee, were to be spectators. Their role was to watch and not to speak to Marilee, who was to receive her punishment at the hands of the girls.

Marilee avoided the beating by calling her mother and pleading with her to come to the school with her car and take Marilee home and out of harm's way.

She has been at home ever since. Like Sally, Marilee refuses to return to school, and is receiving the balance of her education by correspondence.

Goals and aspirations

While staying home and working on her correspondence course, Marilee began to consider what it meant to become the person she was "supposed" to be. When I spoke with her some two years after her threatened beating, she appeared to have reached some clarity about this.

At first, Marilee talked about herself in positive terms, and outlined her plans for the future: She would be a person who would not allow violence in her home. Her children would not experience the terror and the pain of being beaten or of watching their parents engage in violent quarrels, as she herself had.

Unlike her mother, Marilee would follow through on avoiding violence in her family, even if it meant divorcing her husband. She would not smoke in front of her children so that they would not pick up the habit from her, as she had picked it up from watching parents of friends smoke. She would marry as soon as she finished school.

Before that, perhaps when her boyfriend moved out of his family home and found an apartment, she would move in with him. She would "get out" (of her family home), get a job, "just a normal regular job, something to afford my car and my apartment, maybe pet grooming or daycare."

She would have children, a little boy and girl, for whom she had already picked names that her boyfriend also liked. She would build on her present situation:

> Everything's so good right now. You know, I've got a boyfriend, and he loves me, I love him, and my parents are fine. You know my sister's doing fine, and I've got my learner's [license]. You know I've finally turned 16, you know, so, and I've finally found friends and I finally realize that I don't have to find friends or boyfriends that everyone's gonna agree with. 'Cause I used to try and find, you know, find popular guys, good lookin' guys, but now, you know, Danny, and like all my friends, Rick and Tim and them, people think they're losers, other people consider them the losers. So they say, "Oh gross, don't hang out with them!" And it's like, "Excuse me, they're my friends, you know, they treat me good," and I'm tired of trying to find people that all my other friends are happy with. So I'll just be friends with who I'm friends with, and I'm fine.

Anger

As we talked and I tried to learn more about what "fine" looked like in the everyday sense, it turned out that things with Marilee were really not all that fine. In fact, most of the time, she struggles with feelings of anger, fear, insecurity, and grief. Despite her hopes of a rosy and secure future premised on marriage and children, she also suffers daily in a private world where the threat of violence is never very far away.

Marilee explained that violence occurs because kids have "attitudes." Citing herself and her friend Tanya as examples, she told me that

> most of my friends' parents hit them. It's like Tanya and her mom, it just happens. It's just like the kid has an attitude, and the parent gets fed up. I mean my mom told me, you know, from time to time, she wants to just punch me in the face. You know it's understandable why she does that. You know, I mean I can admit it, I get an attitude, it's just, you get an attitude … .

For Marilee, the feeling of anger is far more familiar than feeling "fine." As she describes it, everyday life is

> just like the commercials that are on now, the one uh, with the girl from "Sisters" on there, where she was saying how uhm, she was saying how kids look up to their mom and dad. You know, "Let's dress like mom, let's shave like dad." Uhm, and then they watch mom and dad yell and fight, you know and it's true enough. Kids grow up with violence, and — so I'm violent, and I'm a very angry person … . I can get very angry, and just, I don't always know why. Somehow, I mean something, just a little thing, triggers me off, and I'll just be like all angry. You know, I've grown up a very angry person … I'm that angry that I will deck someone, I'm just scared of the day that I end up punching a person when I shouldn't, 'cause I get so angry, I get so excited. I get angry and my adrenaline pumps up and I'm just like, "Ya, let's do it!" you know.

Thus, Marilee — in a condition that she describes as "pumped with anger" — had "decked" someone when she helped Sarah beat up Sally. Yet, she did not consider her involvement in that fight to be problematic. Indeed, she felt perfectly justified in pushing, shoving, and choking Sally and holding her for Sarah to beat up, because in her mind, Sally "deserved" such treatment for showing an interest in Sarah's boyfriend. Further, Marilee acknowledged that she hadn't actually hauled off and punched Sally although she wanted to, because she was afraid that if she did her parents would find out, and she wouldn't be able to get her learner's license.

Anger is a constant for Marilee. She is angry with her father for bringing violence into the home. Although she talked about things being "fine" with her sister, they often engage in what she describes as "huge fights over stupid little things." (For the moment there was peace between the sisters, likely because they were living several provinces apart.) On occasion, she is angry with Danny, her boyfriend, and fights with him just as she fights with her sister:

> It's like, somethin' little he'll say, I'll just start yelling at him, and then he'll start yelling back at me, and he'll start bringing somethin' else into it, and then I'll bring somethin' else into that and it's just like a big fight. Bang! and then it's like, "See ya!"

She also gets angry with her friends, the same friends she is so happy to have found, the "losers" whom she defends to other people and whom she describes as treating her "good." On the Saturday before I interviewed her, Marilee had become involved in a violent altercation with some of these very people:

> Me and my boyfriend, we were down at Seven-Eleven, and it was with the people that I was friends with at the time. Then, they just went against me so I got angry at them. So we were dr... I was drunk. Down at Seven-Eleven. I was fingering Rick and, you know, I was saying "Fuck you, man! Na na na ... " You know, stuff like that. And, just to joke around and Rick's was like, "'Kay let's go." I'm like "'Kay." 'Cause I was the only one saying it to him. You know, so, uhm, Danny took me and we walked, and then I got mad at Rick and I started walking ahead of them, for some reason, I don't know. So then, Mike and them drove by in the van and Danny's like "Fuck you!" and Rick hangs out the window and goes "What?," and Danny said "I said go fuck yourself!" So they stopped, and Mike come out. I just — try and stop Mike I'm like, "Don't touch him! Don't touch him!" Like, I'm "Don't touch my goddamn boyfriend!" He's like, "Oh, screw you!" So then he walks and I'm trying to stop Rick at the same time and I just turned around, and I just saw them fighting. I just walked off. I left. I was in tears. I was crying. I knew where I was going. I was gonna go straight to Tanya's but I just kept walking past Tanya's. I was just scared that I was gonna, you know, they're gonna come after me. The cops were gonna come up behind me saying "Danny's in — going to the hospital." "Danny's laying dead on the road." You know, "Danny's going to jail." You know, it's just, stuff was going through my head. I thought it was my fault. But Danny said it wasn't 'cause if he hadn't yelled anything out to them they wouldn't have stopped. 'Cause they were going right by us. But, I just thought it was stupid. So Sarah thinks that uh, Danny should charge Mike for it. 'Cause Mike's the one who started it.

Friendships with other girls

Marilee also gets angry with her girlfriends, even those she describes as her "best" friends — girls like Sarah, with whom she beat up Sally.

In the week before our interview, Marilee had decided "not to bother" with Sarah; she was angry with her for criticizing the amount of time Marilee spent with Danny. They had resumed speaking only because Sarah had gossip to share about the Saturday night Seven-Eleven fight, most particularly about Danny and the other boys, which Marilee wanted to hear.

Marilee's friendships with girls are tenuous and often premised on alliances against other girls, who are seen as "competition" for boys. For Marilee and her friends, boys are central to their sense of self-worth, largely because they have been abandoned physically or emotionally by their fathers. This was Marilee's explanation for Sarah's need to beat up Sally:

> It's her dad, I don't know what happened to him, but Sarah, I think, gets her anger from him. I can't remember the whole story, but I think her dad just basically left her, and so when guys leave Sarah, she can't handle it, because her dad did it to her. And when she was going out with Chris, she had an obsession with Mike, you know, she was fooling around with Mike when she was going out with Chris. And she just used to have an obsession with two guys all the time. And if one would try and leave her she would say, "Oh well, I'll be with you," to the other guy. So she gets lots of anger and depression from that, and so I think the fact that she might have thought that Chris might have left her, just because something could go wrong and Sally could have said something that Chris believed, or something like that, and Sarah got mad, right? Sally might try to take Chris away from her, and he was Sarah's, and nobody could touch Chris. Sarah could touch somebody else, but nobody could touch Chris.

As Marilee described it, she and other girls constantly look one another over in order to assess how much "competition" they might represent. As a consequence, she rarely forms alliances with those she views as giving her too much "competition." But with Sarah, she had made an exception:

> Sarah's very pretty. She's the only friend of mine that I have competition with, 'cause all my other friends I have no competition with, but she's the only one that I do … .

Violence, responsibility, and fear

Although she was one of the aggressors in their altercation, Marilee is still angry with Sally. She called Sally a bitch the last time she saw her because

> she had the snarkiest look on her face when we saw her the other day. It was like just two days ago, and I had the perfect chance just to go and punch her, but I go to my friend, I go, "Well let's just jerk her around and follow her … ."

As far as Marilee is concerned, Sally caused her own beating, and Sally is still in the wrong. Just after Sally's beating, Sarah, Marilee, and their boyfriends went to McDonald's and had something to eat. Except for making a few remarks such as, "Oh, that bitch broke my nail!" and "Oh, that bitch got blood on my sweater!" they didn't give Sally much thought. Their thoughts and feelings were focused on themselves.

The strongest emotion Marilee recalled feeling after the fight was justification. Marilee felt certain that she was right to help Sarah beat up Sally because

> I don't know how strong Sally is, and I don't know what she could have done to Sarah, so I basically saved Sarah if Sally had done damage to her.

Justification shifted to fear — another of Marilee's recurring emotions — when, during the course of their meal, a policeman walked into McDonald's. Marilee experienced a strong reaction, with her heart going "boom":

> 'Cause I, I think that's what scares me the most, is seeing the cop afterwards. It's like, he's gonna come up to me and say, "Hey, you're comin' with me," you know, it's just quite scary.

The policeman merely came over briefly and said hello to Marilee and her friends, bought his coffee, and left.

What Marilee had found so frightening about this encounter was the possibility of punishment: If she were caught, she might not be allowed to get her driver's license. She wasn't remorseful about what she had done; she was unconcerned about the effects of the beating on Sally's physical and emotional health. She demonstrated no empathy for Sally.

Indeed, during the fight, Sally's fear and Sally's blood served only to feed Marilee's aggression because she saw these as further wrongdoing on Sally's part. When Sally tried to escape, Marilee saw this as an act of defiance against Sarah. This prompted her to grab Sally, swing her around to face Sarah, and yell, "You stand there until she's done with you!" When Sally's blood spurted onto Sarah's sweater, the girls saw this as all the more reason to beat her up.

Fear of punishment was the sole factor that prevented Marilee from taking a more active role in Sally's beating:

> If there was no punishment at the time that Sarah was beating up Sally, I mean if there was nothing about going to Juvey [the local juvenile detention center], ... nothing about getting busted for it, I would have just killed her right there. Not like literally killed her, but I would have punched her as well.

Sarah, on the other hand, was not inhibited by fears of punishment. According to Marilee, Sarah's strongest reaction after the fight was a feeling of pride: "'Oh ya, wicked! I beat somebody up.' And [Sarah] got all this attention for it from everyone."

Marilee also got a lot of attention because of her involvement, attention she tried very hard to divert because

> that got me scared at the time, because everybody's thinkin' that I did it, so I'm thinkin' the word's gonna get around and then finally a parent was gonna get hold of the cops and say that I was the one who did it.

Interestingly, word did get around almost immediately to Marilee's mother, who did nothing. She talked with Marilee about the fight, asked her questions about what happened, but did not hold Marilee responsible (even though she had most of the details, which she later relayed to me). Ultimately, Marilee told me, her mother's only response was to suggest to Marilee that

> the only way I can fight is with her permission, if they've got me backed into a corner and I have no way out. You know if I have to fight that person to get myself out of there, then that's what I have to do.

For Marilee, the imperative to fight depends on how angry and how scared she is. It also depends on her commitment to what is, for her, an inviolable rule: that she must hate those whom her friends hate, and fight for her friends when called upon to do so.

Indeed, the need to fight for her friends further fuels Marilee's fear. As a consequence of her involvement with other girls and boys who fight, Marilee fears that she will be attacked or jumped from behind. This fear keeps her tied to "safe" parts of her neighborhood and prevents her from going to school. It also keeps her from going downtown, an area that she believes is rife with the threat of violence.

It is not only downtown that frightens Marilee; it is the whole world, which for Marilee is an altogether horrid place:

> I don't like the world right now, I think it's a piece of shit. It's filled with drugs and guns. I mean it's the guns that bother me. Because those kids, the ones that were by that park and the one that got shot, those were my friends [a claim that Sally also made]. All of them were my friends, the one guy that got shot in the leg was my friend and the guy that shot him was my friend too. So it was, I was involved with that.

It would seem, from Marilee's point of view, that guns are easy enough to get. The friend who was the shooter in the incident alluded to above sold his stereo and used the money to buy the gun through the illegal underground market. Marilee and her boyfriend have access to guns through the boyfriend's father, who takes them both into the countryside to shoot rifles. One of her closest girlfriend's mothers has a handgun which she keeps loaded and ready to hand because "her and Daniella's dad are getting divorced right now and her mom's so mad at her dad that she's ready to shoot him." Marilee herself (although she states emphatically that she hates guns and would never have one in the house or use one) also remarks that she would nevertheless use one if "like, I had to use one, like there was no other choice." Thus, Marilee lives with the ever-present threat of violence and death.

Death is already a very real part of Marilee's life. Two weeks before our interview, she lost two friends. One 14-year-old was killed when a 16-year-old he was driving with lost control of a sports car he had persuaded a salesman to let him test drive. The 16-year-old had just passed his driver's test and was inexperienced with fast cars. He attempted to negotiate a sharp curve in the road near his house at high speed, wrapped the demonstrator around a telephone pole, and killed his passenger.

The other friend, a 14-year-old girl, died of leukemia. As well, in the past year, Marilee's sister's boyfriend's best friend committed suicide by pulling his car into the family garage, attaching a hose to the exhaust system, and gassing himself. Marilee's explanation was:

Uhm, he was really screwed up mentally. Like not screwed up, screwed up, but he did a lot of drugs. And he didn't handle life. And people just thought of him as a party person, like, "Hey, there's party Chris." People never thought about Chris.

After telling me this story, Marilee noticed the time and abruptly ended our interview, because her boyfriend was coming over. I thanked her for allowing me to talk with her. As I sat on the steps by the door tying up my shoelaces, she said: "So, do you ever talk to girls about rape and molesting and that kind of thing?" I replied, "Well, sometimes they tell me about it when we're talking together; is there something you'd like to say to me about that?" She replied:

Well, only that when I was three I was molested by a baby sitter who put his fingers inside me, but just that, and when I was 14 and on summer vacation and visiting some friends, a 20-year-old guy got me drunk and raped me, and my mother knows and my counselor knows, and I still wake up every morning angry about it and hurt by it and wondering whether I should charge him.

On that note, Marilee left me standing in her driveway, got into her boyfriend's truck, and drove away.

CHAPTER FIVE

Molly's Story

My older brother molested me, he abused me up to about a year and a half ago, and I have these feelings, these flashbacks, it's like I can feel it happening all over again. When it happened, my mother didn't really believe me at first, but then my older brother went to live with my grandparents for six months and we all went for counseling, even him. And we talked a lot about what happened to my [younger] brother ... when he was little, when he got really sick, and the whole family got disrupted. We talked about this stuff [sexual abuse] too, but I don't like to bring it up because I get this feeling like they think I'm lying and everything, and then especially when it did everything to the family, I just don't want to talk about it. It's taken me forever to feel comfortable around my parents. With your parents, they love you so much and in your brother's case, they love him so much and they don't want to believe that he could do that to their daughter. They just want to try and block it out of their minds, they think it will just go away. My parents didn't really believe me until about uh, two weeks after I told them, I tried committing suicide by slitting my wrists and I tried taking an overdose of pills and all that, and that's when they finally believed me, and that really hurt. (*Excerpt from taped interview with Molly*)

Molly volunteered to participate in this study because she had been beaten by a schoolmate, Cathy. This was not, however, her first encounter with violence. Molly was well known at school for her threatening and aggressive behavior; she often pushed and shoved other students to let them know who was in charge. The school counselor, who introduced me to four of the six key informants in this study, seemed most concerned about Molly.

Family dynamics

Both Molly and her mother assured me that theirs was a "loving and close family" in which people really care about one another. But what does "loving and close" mean?

For Molly, close became too close, especially where her older brother was concerned. "Loving" requires clarification. Does "loving" mean you swallow your own experience and keep your mouth shut because you don't want trouble? Does it mean that, when you go for counseling to deal with sexual abuse in your family, you allow your brother's experience to become more important than your own so that you can put it all behind you and he can come home?

Two events stand out for Molly with regard to her family: The first, a traumatic illness involving Molly's second youngest brother, happened 10 years ago. The second event is her long-standing sexual abuse at the hands of her older brother, which began when she was about eight (and he was 10) and continued for nearly four years. In Molly's family lore, the first event explains the second, and the second event, according to Molly, has been subsumed by the first.

I pieced together my understanding of Molly's family climate from both Molly's and her mother's remarks. Molly's family is one in which "everyone feels everyone else's feelings," that is, Mother gauges the state of the family through the state of her own feelings. Thus, "if they're fine, chances are Mom's okay; if they're in distress, Mom is."

Family is also the source of their closest friendships. Parents and kids are intensely involved in one another's lives. Father and sons engage in physical combat, but that's "only natural." People yell and scream when they're angry, but that "happens in every family." Women make demands by yelling, but men hold sway. The family closes ranks against outsiders. Doors are left open, including doors to bedrooms; and Molly (despite advice from counselors given directly to her mother) still does not have a lock on her bedroom door.

Molly's family's central organizing story — the one they tell when they wish to illustrate the kind of family theirs is — was told to me as follows: While Molly's mother was pregnant with her fourth child, the third child, a boy, had a life-threatening episode as the result of being given a food substance to which he was allergic by an unwitting family member. This required major medical intervention, including an airlift from the small community in which they lived. The event caused much upset and turmoil, but the family pulled together and supported one another through it all.

This story is still central to the family's saga, even 10 years after the fact. It is the story they tell to show how everyone helped out, how everyone can forgive, how important it is to consider the second youngest brother's special food needs, and how this family can make it through anything.

This event also became central to the family's counseling experience in the wake of Molly's sexual abuse by her older brother. Somehow, the focus shifted from Molly's abuse to the early life trauma caused by her younger brother's near death, and the family's constant need for vigilance on his behalf. Somehow, this became the reason why the older brother molested his sister. Somehow, this became the reason why no one noticed.

Molly's MOTHER

When Molly's mother told me the family story, she didn't even mention her oldest son's sexual abuse of her daughter, although she knew that I had been told about it. Even when I provided openings in our conversation, Molly's mother side-stepped this issue.

It may indeed be true that Molly's family is close and tries to support its members. But it is also true that much that happens is denied, concealed, or overlooked, and that conflict arises frequently.

Molly's mother's acknowledges that her oldest son has often been in trouble. And while he and Molly participate in sports and play on school teams and work at part-time jobs, they also fight and get kicked out of school. Molly's father dominates the family (using physical force with the boys, angry silence and bad moods with his wife and daughter), and Molly's mother, while vocal in her opinions, ultimately defers to her husband.

I believe that if I had relied only upon Molly's mother to give me insight into her family and Molly's participation in violence, I would have heard only that kids get involved in violence because, as she explained to me,

> everybody starts to buck for their rank. It starts in grade six, when well, we're 11 years old and we're starting to develop and we're starting to look to who we're gonna be and some kids (like Molly) do very well, she's on every committee, she does extremely well in sports activities, she was "Miss Popularity" and all that. And those that aren't at that stage can either turn around and shoot you down to make themselves look better or to pull you down to their level. And then it's like, "I hate her," and she doesn't know how to handle it … and it all grows out of a kind of teenage rivalry … .

Molly's EXPERIENCE of violENCE

Molly's own version of herself and her involvement with violence was quite different from the analysis offered by her mother. At the time of our conversations, Molly was meeting with me in the context of a group that also included two other key informants, Mary (Chapter Six) and Linda (Chapter Seven). In these discussions, Molly was always the least vocal participant, who sometimes needed a little assistance from me to be heard. There were, however, two topics to which

Molly returned time and time again: that of having been beaten, and that of having been sexually abused.

At our first group meeting, I invited Molly to speak before the others because at that time, her beating at the hands of Mary's friend Cathy was still fresh and I wanted to give her the opportunity to say whatever was on her mind. She declined to say much until well into the first hour of our conversation. At that point, encouraged by promises of confidentiality, Molly began to describe her experience of having been beaten while 30 or 40 students stood by and watched.

She began by outlining the history of her interactions with Cathy. Like Sally, Molly made the mistake of showing interest in a boy who was already considered someone else's boyfriend, in this case Cathy's. The competition with Cathy for male attention began in September, right at the beginning of Molly's grade eight year, and culminated in a vicious beating the following January:

> It was like right in September, right, in my TAG[1] group, there was this guy I was talking to and Cathy came over and talked to us too. So later I told Jessica that Cathy was a real bitch. So Jessica told Cathy at lunch that I'd said she was a bitch, so I like, kinda apologized, like a lot, but she kept mouthing me off and she kept pushing me in the hallway wanting to fight, but that time a whole bunch of people stopped her. But another time, we were by the side of the school and there was this big rumor going around that I said that two guys molested me at a party or whatever and all that, and she walks up to me and goes, "What happened?" and I said, "Nothing fucking happened," and she goes, "Bullcrap!" and then she punched me and goes, "Hit me back!" and I was going to hit her, but then I wanted to get her in crap with the principal so I didn't hit her back. I know it's not good to rat on people, but I was mad. And then, like last week, I was talking about some guy that Cathy likes, and so a couple of days ago when I was walking home from school by the store, Cathy saw me and wanted me to fight her in front of a whole bunch of people, and she wouldn't stop, and started hitting me and she kept hitting me until Mr. Robertson came along in his car and made her stop and brought me home.

When I asked how she made sense of this event, Molly attributed Cathy's behavior to Cathy's hatred of her and her desire to "get" her:

> It's like, I don't know, the first time, you know like I don't know where it came from, but I did call her a bitch, but then there were a lot of other things that people told me that I said, that I didn't and I apologized to her like crazy and everything, and then after that she said like, "Okay," and everything, but then I heard that she just didn't like me like no matter what and if she could think

of a reason she'd use it against me. And so after a lot of incidents like pushing and calling me names, she just, I think that was like her chance by the store, and she took it.

When I asked whether Molly herself would beat up a schoolmate just because she disliked her, Mary jumped in and stated that while she probably would not do that, she might like to. When I asked what would stop her, Mary explained:

It's because I've got morals which I got from my mom, and there's certain rules, like, if they're older than me, if they're bigger than me, I would fight them, but if they're younger than me and smaller than me, there's no way that I would. I couldn't, I couldn't unless they were sitting there and just taunting me. If someone taunts me, then I get mad, and it's like it takes a lot to get me mad enough to fight. I don't like seeing it in myself, and I don't like being around it. And so when, if, and like if they taunt me and I get mad at them, there's no way in hell I'm gonna put up with it.

I turned again to Molly to ask for her perspective. She informed me that she had no real morals to speak of. Those she did have had come from her mother, and had mostly to do with sex because

… my mom didn't really have any morals until, uhm, like my brother had this big accident, and then I think after that she started to have all kinds of morals that she didn't show before, that she didn't really talk about. After that, everything came out, and after that she's like always letting us know how she's feeling. Like now she says, she sits me down and she goes, "You think sex is a game," and stuff, and she gives me this big lecture … . But when it comes to fighting, like if I get really mad, like with Jenny [another key informant; Chapter Eight] last night, I just felt like belting her 'cause she just kept coming up to me and bugging me and then saying she was sorry that she'd challenged me to a fight and "I hope we can be friends" and then following me around, and I was going, "Take a hike, Jenny, I'm not going to hit you or anything, but if you keep following me around, I'm going to fuckin' belt you."

Molly's remarks led to further discussions about fighting and how girls became embroiled in physical battles with each other. Again, Mary leaped in with her explanation before Molly had a chance to speak:

I don't know, I have this feeling, it's like instinct … . If someone does something wrong to you, there's a certain extent where you're gonna put up with it, and when that, when you stop putting up with it, that's when you get mad. And, and I usually give them another chance after I get mad, like if they make me mad, okay, okay, I'll let it boil for awhile. And if they piss me off again, then they're just gonna have to deal with it … .

When Mary finished her explanation, both Molly and Linda agreed that they fought physically with others whenever someone "made them mad." Thus, Molly wanted to "fuckin' belt" Jenny because Jenny was making her mad by following her around. Both Mary and Linda recalled several instances when they felt perfectly justified in hauling off and smashing someone because they were angry. Again, Mary supplied the words for all three:

> I hate being angry, 'cause it gets me in a bad mood. So I get rid of that anger and I take it out on something or someone, it gets rid of it.

That seemed clear enough to me, even though I could not agree with the sentiments expressed. What I still had trouble understanding was why those who were not angry and had no personal involvement in the fight would stand by and watch while someone else were being beaten. Here, Mary was again the quickest to supply the answer:

> Well, if there's a fight, everybody in the school just basically goes to watch it because it's different, entertainment sort of, a lot of people want to see somebody get their butt kicked in real life. It's kind of like TV, but only it's real life, and that's entertainment kind of, except if you're the one being beaten up.

When I still had trouble understanding how people could watch without intervening when someone was clearly being as badly hurt as Molly had been, Molly went on to tell me that,

> … the crowd was yelling to Cathy, "C'mon, hit her!" It wasn't the girls, it was the guys who did it, 'cause they want to see girls fight. It gets them pumped. It gets them excited, not in the physical, in the sexual … . Like this guy I was walking with when Cathy saw me said to me, "That's the chick who wants to beat you up," and then he waved at her and she started saying all these things to me and he just took off, and I felt like shit, but I'm fine now … .

Growing up female
Molly's reference to girls fighting as entertainment for boys that "got them excited, not in the physical, [but] in the sexual" sense of the word prompted me to ask what it was like to be a girl in this day and age. This time, Molly was the first to speak, and what she said was unquestioningly echoed by Linda and Mary. As Molly put it:

The guys here degrade you, they try to do that all the time. Like at the beginning of the year, there was like quite a bit of us that in my class, wore body suits and stuff and the guys would sit there staring at you, and you'd go, "What are you lookin' at?" and then they'd start saying all these things to you, stuff that made you feel really low. It was sort of sleazy, they'd say things like, "Oh, close your legs," like and "You smell like a fish," or whatever, and "Watch it, flies are comin' in," and "Flies are attacking," and "You smell like tuna."

When I asked how the girls made sense of the boys' behavior, they told me, "Oh, [the boys] think [such talk] is cool," and "It's their hormones and stuff."

Molly then spoke of feeling a great deal of pressure from boys, and also from certain girlfriends, to engage in sex:

I've noticed that there is pressure, like I've had people try to pressure me. Like more the pressure is from your boyfriend, or it's like from friends who are like, "Have you got laid yet?" And this is from the friends of the boyfriend, or it could be your friends. It's like with your friends, they sort of like when they're, when you're talking about it and you get into a conversation, they sort of get the hint that you have been or you haven't been by how you talk about it, but the guys, they're just like, "Oh, you're still a virgin," and they block their eyes and stuff. But if the guys do it, they're like big studs and stuff, and we're sluts. Like if they do it, they can be doin' it like many times and they think people consider them studs, and when we do it, we're sluts. Like, they dump you if you don't have sex with them, but when you break up with them and they've taken your virginity or whatever, he, he, he calls you a slut … . Guys, I think guys perceive us to be playing hard to get, and they perceive themselves as trying hard to get it constantly, and if we're just, if you're not playing hard to get then they think you're a slut.

I then asked whether the girls saw this as a double standard — one rule for the boys and one rule for the girls. They seemed confused by this question and required further explanation. After I gave it, to my great astonishment they told me that they didn't think it was a double standard; rather, "that's the way guys are."

It seemed to me that these girls had accepted the notion that they were sexual objects, an impression that was confirmed by the women they identified as female role models. Like Sally, they all chose Madonna as their number one favorite, followed by Marilyn Monroe and Cindy Crawford. They saw these women as role models because they had the power to "do whatever they want," that is, to direct their own lives.

While the girls admired this independence, they failed to see that any power these women had was directly related to their desirability as sexual objects. Thus, their power is male-dependent and male-controlled. But all the girls saw was that these women were wanted and worshiped because they were sexually desirable. Given that they had bought into the misconception that women's power is derived mainly from their sexual currency, the girls saw no way out, and endured harassment and abuse because "that's just the way it is."

Sexual harassment and abuse

At the end of one of our meetings, I had an opportunity to witness sexual harassment in action. This incident took place as Molly, Linda, and I were getting into my car so that I could drive them home. A group of boys were lined up at the top of some steps near the school entrance, apparently the better to ogle the girls as they went by. One boy called out, "Hey Melissa, nice bazongas [breasts]! You're doing a great job, keep growing them just like that." When I asked him to account for himself, he replied that he was "just a bad boy, I guess," and laughed while a chorus of admiring louts applauded.

Both Molly's and Linda's perception of this incident was that "that's just how it is; you put up with it because if you don't, it just gets worse." They told me that they didn't like such encounters and "really hated macho guys," but that "you gotta expect guys to be pigheaded; it's the way they are."

Our discussions about the difficulties of being young women in the late 20th century were not confined to talking about sexual harassment. Molly (and, it turned out, Linda) had both experienced sexual abuse before reaching puberty; Mary had experienced date rape. Molly had alluded to her sexual abuse in our first meeting when she referred to her mother's sense of "morals" vis-à-vis her older brother's "big accident." This "accident" later turned out to be his sexual abuse of her.

The girls' stories emerged in the context of a single discussion of sexual harassment generally, and what it means to be a young woman in the 1990s. The conversation ended with three disclosures of sexual abuse.

As suggested at the beginning of this chapter, Molly's parents had some difficulty accepting that Molly's brother had abused her; it took her suicide attempt for them to believe her. The fact of Molly's abuse came to be subsumed by the previous family trauma involving the youngest child's brush with death. This event focused both parents' attention on the younger boy, perhaps at the expense of their oldest son, who later acted out his need for attention by molesting his sister (or so the story goes).

That story had yet another dimension, one that was not immediately clear to me: namely, that Molly's mother also explained her son's abuse of his sister as an "accident." Further, this "accident" was caused not only by the boy's need for attention, but also (at least in part) by Molly's interest in sex as a game. As Molly explained:

> It all happened like that last year, like I was driving with her in the car and I told her about like what happened, and she was like, "Oh yeah," and she gave me a lecture on it and she said, "Well, did your brother do any of that to you?" and I felt so low, I felt so crummy. She was going back to work early. It was like the first time I told her what my brother did to me, and she gave me a lecture. She goes, "Did he have sex with you then?" It was really stupid. It was like she ended up giving me a lecture on sex for me to know what it is, and she said, "You think sex is a game." ... Like, I hate it when we're driving in the car and I mention something to my mom, and she goes, "Well, I don't need to give you this lecture, because you got it after everything your brother did to you," and then she starts giving me the lecture all over again. ... Then after that, after my brother's big accident [i.e. his sexual abuse of Molly], she had all these morals, these morals that she never had before, all to do with sex.

Disclosing her sexual abuse to her parents did not bring Molly much comfort, nor did engaging in a brief period of family counseling. Molly had found this experience embarrassing and wanted all discussion with family to end as quickly as possible. At the time of her disclosure to me, she was still a long way from resolving these issues, and apparently in need of more help. When I offered to facilitate this by finding her a counselor through a local agency, she rejected the idea. She knew that because of her age, her parents would have to be informed that she was receiving help, and she was unwilling to participate in anything that would put the subject of her sexual abuse back on the table. She said she did not wish to hurt her family.

But Molly had more to say on the subject of sex. Her experiences of sexual abuse did not end with being molested by her brother. About two months before our first meeting, she had been to a party where she and most of the other adolescents who attended got drunk.[2] At the time, Molly was taking medication to ease the pain of an injury sustained in gym class. In the course of the evening, she mixed pain killers with alcohol:

... I took 10 extra strength Tylenols and I just chugged back a bottle of rum and Coke and had a reaction, like I was really out of it, and I was like all over these guys. Like, people said I was acting like the biggest slut, but I didn't know what was going on. I was like really out of it, and I fell asleep in this chair, and everybody said that all these people were doing all this stuff to me, like these two guys were sitting at the party doing stuff to me ... .

This incident would fuel Cathy's justification, some weeks later, for challenging Molly to a fight. In Cathy's mind, Molly was a slut who deserved a beating.

School, sex, and violence

For Molly, Linda, and Mary, sex and female sexuality is fraught with difficulties. It has involved sexual harassment, sexual abuse, and date rape, as well as violence at the hands of other females just like themselves.

But the difficulties did not end there. They arose again in their sex education class, when the girls were presented with material on childbirth that frightened and disgusted them. What follows is a composite of all three girls' perceptions of sex education and childbirth:

We got this video all day yesterday, and one of the guys in the class passed out. It was so gross. I've never seen it in my life and I was just horrified. I'm never gonna have kids, it scared me big. It looked so painful. And the interviewer is sitting there and [the woman he was talking to] she goes, "I was pregnant," like she was talking about how the doctor put his things in to make the hole bigger and all this, and it hurt, but she didn't care, 'cause it would be for her own good and all this, 'cause he got some kind of gel and all this, but I would never do that. I think it's gross and scary, and it looks like it would hurt ... .

The lady giving birth just looked a mess, and I don't, I wouldn't want, like if I was a man, I don't know if I'd wanna be attracted to her anymore ... .

The labor that we watched, it lasted for something like 10 hours, and the lady would like, she'd go and have a shower and she was, while she was giving birth. And the girls in the class are just sittin' there going "ahh," and, and then as soon as she gave birth, and after, all that stuff came out after the baby, just as the bell rang and we just got up and "Uhm, gotta go." ... And I wouldn't want to do it, I wouldn't want to have a baby.

At the end of this lesson, the students had been left hanging. There had been no discussion, no time for debriefing, no time to deal with their feelings of fear and disgust.

In the end, for these young women, sex is for the most part a frightening, painful, and embarrassing fact of life, something that happens almost inevitably; it is certainly not viewed as a possible source of joy or pleasure. Mostly, sex is associated with confusion and a sense of alienation and humiliation.

Talking about sex education led to a discussion of the girls' experiences of being educated, of going to school and working with teachers.

Molly's experience of school mostly involved living down her older brother's reputation as a trouble-maker and struggling with the feeling that she was being "stereotyped," that is, categorized as being just like him. Of the eight teachers she had encountered in her first year in junior high, she picked only two that she liked and respected. She found she could like and respect a teacher, and work hard in class, if the teacher was

> laid back and understanding, and I can have some kind of relationship with them. Like most teachers don't remember what it's like to be a kid or whatever. I don't think we're supposed to be angels, but they want us to be angels. … If I like a teacher, I work harder in his class, and I get better marks if I like the teacher … .

When I inquired about marks, Molly described herself as a "C+, B student, but I'm not working to the max. If I wanted to I could get A's, but that would take work." For Molly, school wasn't so much about going to classes; rather, it was about navigating her complex social world. This included networking among friends and acquaintances, gossiping, defending her reputation, and finally, engaging in violence.

At the time of our meetings, Molly was spending much time out of class talking with the school counselor. She was also spending a great deal of time in class (and during her breaks) discussing other people and busying herself with the details of her own and others' private lives. At one point, all her teachers met in order to develop a strategy for dealing with Molly. It was decided that she would no longer be given permission to leave classes to go for counseling.

Molly's mother was consulted and she agreed with this approach. She believed that stopping counseling would somehow normalize Molly's behavior and help her get back on track. Molly's school counselor thought otherwise, but her opinion was overruled. In the counselor's estimation, much of Molly's behavior stemmed from unresolved issues relating to her sexual abuse, and to the aftermath of having been beaten. Without extensive therapy, the counselor believed, Molly would continue to experience difficulties, both at school and at home. Events proved her to be correct.

Molly returned to school a few days after being beaten by Cathy, and spent several weeks being treated as something of a sensation. She also became a target for attention from Jenny (Chapter Eight), who wanted to challenge Molly to a fight. Jenny thought it would enhance her own reputation if she were able to beat up a celebrity like Molly.

Molly didn't engage in fighting Jenny, but she did let it be known that if Jenny didn't leave her alone, she would beat her up with help from Mary and Linda. Jenny backed down, apologized, and then dogged Molly for days, trying to make friends. This infuriated Molly, who threatened to "belt" her.

Not only was Molly annoyed and frustrated at being dogged by Jenny; further, Jenny's behavior and Molly's lack of retaliation would eventually call Molly's social position into question, because Jenny was "hacking her down." The social rules that operate among these girls demanded that Molly stick up for herself. As they explained to me:

> If someone is hacking you down, they're making you look like an idiot, 'cause like, people look at you and mock you and they're thinking, "Oh, that person must be an idiot now." If you let somebody hack you down, and you don't do something about it and other people are watching you, they're going to think you're a goof, so you have to do it. You have to do it because you get angry and because you have to teach them a lesson.

Molly's problem with Jenny was solved for a time because Mary and Linda came to her aid. All three girls issued threats against Jenny. This brought action from Jenny's parents, who came to the school Christmas dance with the express purpose of keeping an eye on Linda, Mary, and Molly. At one point during the evening, Jenny's mother actually walked by Linda and gave her a push. This drew the girls' wrath, although they refrained from retaliating. What irked them most was their sense that Jenny's mother wasn't behaving as she should:

> Jenny's mother was being an immature little bitch. When you're an adult, you're supposed to be an adult, you're not supposed to be pushing around teenagers, I mean it's over and done with. You shouldn't be doing that. She was setting a bad example for her daughter ... .

After the Christmas dance episode, Mary and Linda rallied around Molly for some time. Mary, who had witnessed Cathy's beating of Molly, even offered to testify for the crown at Cathy's upcoming trial. And then Molly blew it all.

One day during a lull in one of her classes, Molly took it upon herself to tell four friends the details of Linda's sexual abuse, details that Linda had disclosed in our group meetings under strictest confidentiality. This information was passed along from person to person until Linda came to hear of it.

Molly was once again in danger of being beaten up, this time by Linda and Mary. But Linda and Mary thought better of it. Because of our discussions, they had begun to question violence as a means to an end. And although they felt justified about wanting to beat up Molly, they had also begun to entertain the notion that there were other ways to deal with problems.

This was a new and difficult way of thinking for these girls. Instead of ambushing Molly, they made an appointment with the school counselor, who arranged a meeting among the three. It was Mary and Linda's intention to confront Molly and give her an opportunity to account for herself. They also invited me to come to speak with them about what had happened.

Molly came to the meeting, but avoided even the smallest step towards taking responsibility for her actions. She excused herself by saying that she just couldn't hold in the things she knew about Linda anymore; the stress was such that she just had to tell someone. She had trouble apologizing to Linda, and sought instead to blame her actions on the situation.

Later, Molly lied to her mother and said that she had been scapegoated by the other two girls. She told her brother that she was being threatened, and he escorted her to and from school for several weeks. Her brother complained that he was receiving death threats by telephone, and Molly told her parents and her friends that these were coming from Mary. (The threats were real enough; they came not from Mary, however, but from an acquaintance of hers who took it upon himself to threaten Molly's brother.)

Fortunately, the school counselor intervened and gave Molly's mother the facts. Molly's mother had trouble acknowledging what her daughter had done, and instead put her behavior down to "school girl hysteria." She characterized Molly's indiscretion as an "accident" — a slip of the tongue.

Linda and Mary were shocked, hurt, and angered by Molly's behavior, but by this time they were committed to trying a non-violent approach. They met with the school counselor three more times, and I joined them once more.

We discussed the girls' feelings and continued to meet until Linda felt she had resolved the incident in a way that she could live with. They decided to exclude Molly from all their activities, school and social. They expressed the wish to continue meeting with me as a twosome. Further, they demanded an apology from Molly and a contract that she would stay away from them in the hallways and on the school grounds.

Molly complied with Mary and Linda's requests. She withdrew from contact with me, even though I offered to meet with her on her own. She made plans to change school districts in the coming year, and she stayed away from the counseling area for some time.

I saw Molly once more. She was getting into a car with her basketball teammates. She made eye contact with me but said nothing, and that's the last I saw of her.

Notes

1. TAG refers to Teacher Advisor Group, a mixed-grade group that students enter in their first year of junior high and in which they continue until graduation. The rationale is to offer students a chance to see, on a daily basis, at least one teacher in the capacity of advisor rather than classroom teacher. This personal relationship is intended to provide support and guidance. The idea behind having mixed grades in the same group is to broaden the students' social contacts. This is the ideal; the reality is not always so genial.

2. Molly started drinking alcohol in grade seven, at the age of 13. She began smoking cigarettes in grade eight. At the time of our meetings, she was also beginning to experiment with marijuana. All these substances were freely available to her through older friends. Molly's understanding of alcohol use is limited. When she drinks, she tends to drink large quantities. She said that the weekend before one of our meetings, she had drunk "a bottle of rum with Coke, but I've never drank it straight, and I can't drink whiskey unless it's mixed."

CHAPTER SIX

MARY'S STORY

Yeah, well, my dad's punched me a couple of times, and we've gotten into fist fights actually quite a few times. Usually that happens when there are other people around like my mom, but one time it happened when my mother wasn't around, then my brother jumped in and pulled him off me and started beating him up. And one time that I remember, this happened when I was about eight or nine years old, and this is just horrifying to me, but I want to talk about it. I remember my brother was locked in his room [as punishment for a misdemeanor] and my dad punched a hole through the door and then went into my brother's room and got on top of him and started hitting him and my mom grabbed a mirror, about the size of that calendar there [approximately 12" by 16"], and she grabbed it and had to smash it over my dad's head to make him stop. And I was just sitting in the kitchen just hollerin'. I didn't know what was going on. I was about ready to call the police. I was scared and I still get scared. (*Excerpt from taped interview with Mary*)

Family dynamics

Mary's family is characterized by violent behavior on all fronts. All family members engage in violence inside and outside the home. Mary's older brother often fights with other boys, and with Mary as well. Mary's father, a streetfighter since his youth, has lately begun to push around those young people whom he considers threatening to his children. Mary's mother admits to punching a postal worker in the nose during a recent postal strike.

Just before I began this study, Mary's father had an affair with Mary's mother's best friend while she was renting a room in their house. When Mary's mother discovered them in bed together, she was deeply upset, yet permitted her friend to remain. Tension in the household mounted until Mary's parents joined forces against the friend. They pushed her around, threatened her with violence, ordered her out of the house, and finally threw all her belongings from an upstairs window while Mary and her brother watched. Mary has been unable to forgive her father for his behavior, and cannot understand her mother's continued acceptance of him.

Mary's father is central to the in-home violence. When he fights physically with one of his children, either his wife or the other sibling may intervene to the point of counter-attacking him. Violent altercations take place in this family roughly once every three or four weeks.

At other times, everyone "tiptoes around in order not to upset Dad," but some minor irritation eventually escalates into physical combat between father and children. Mother then "reams Dad out" once again and "makes him smarten up," and the cycle begins anew. Father never hits Mother.

In spite of this climate of conflict, Mary's family expressed strong feelings of mutual affection and closeness. In particular, Mary spoke of loving her mother and loving yet hating her father; she also described her brother as her "best friend," one of the few people she felt she could rely on.

Mary's mother
Similarly, Mary's mother referred to her husband as her "best friend," and expressed her love for him very clearly. In our interviews, Mary's mother showed her feelings easily: She cried when things upset or moved her and showed a range of emotions from anger to joy, which she made no effort to conceal. As she described herself:

> I get emotional very easily; I'll cry in cartoons if they're sad … And I'm stubborn; … I won't back down, and I stand up for myself and demand the respect I deserve.

When I asked about standing up for herself, Mary's mother said she has to do this every day, especially with her husband, who strongly believes in traditional gender roles. That is, he demands that his wife take on all the domestic chores and cater to his feelings. If his wife is not available, he expects his daughter to jump into the breach.

While I talked with Mary's mother, her husband "hovered." Although we held our interview in the dining room of their home, well removed from the kitchen where Mary's father was working, Mary's father seemed to find it necessary to pass by the dining room frequently and look through the closed French doors. He also went up and down the stairs by the dining room a number of times. Once, he came bursting through the doors with a portable telephone in hand, insisting that the only plug that would work for the phone was in the dining room. At another point, he saw his wife crying, so he came into the room to comfort her and to question me. In reassuring his wife, he hugged her and brought her Kleenex, and told me with much feeling that he needed to know she was okay. As I observed these interactions, I was reminded of the kinds of behaviors that young children exhibit when their mother is talking with another adult or is engaged in an activity that takes her focus off the children.

When I asked Mary's mother what factors she thought might contribute to girls' violence, she suggested it was because "girls have always been repressed": Perhaps they were "ripping each other's faces off" because they were "frustrated that things are not equal." Other than that, she had "no idea where they get their ideas" and had no further insights into girls and violence.

Mary's Father

During my discussions with Mary and her mother, I learned that Mary's father left home when he was 15 years old because of continuing conflicts with his own father. (Mary's paternal grandfather is a life-long alcoholic who is not "allowed" to drink in his son's house, and chooses to make his visits to his son in a mobile home so that he can drink.)

After he left home, Mary's father lived on the street, taking shelter under a bridge. He worked as a janitor and then in the building trades, and saved enough money to buy a house by the time he was 19 years old. Mary's parents met when her father was 17 and her mother 15. They married four years later, and soon after had two children two years apart. According to Mary's mother, her husband has made it a daily crusade to be the center of her attention. She describes him as having

> a very controlling personality … . [Almost every day] I have to keep telling him he can't have complete control of everything … .

Mary describes her father as a "power-tripper" and an "asshole … who's got to have everything his way." Her feelings about him are strongly mixed:

> I love him for being my dad and I love him for all the things he has done for me, but I hate him for the things he's done to me and the family.

Mixed emotions were often apparent when Mary talked about her father. She recounted the good times she'd had with him, such as going skiing with him and her brother. At other times she was full of rage and hurt, such as when he declined her offer of help with his construction projects, or criticized her work, or refused to help her with chores, expecting instead that she serve him.

Mary discussed her continuing gender-related battles with her father with the same frustration, sadness, anger, and determination that I heard her mother express. Mary described it as follows:

> I think he should do more around the house. ... Half the stuff around this house is from him. I mean all this shit right here, all those papers there are his. ... Normally he's got a mess all over this table, like old statements and estimates and stuff. The computer room upstairs is a mess because he's just a slob and he walks into the house with his big work boots on and tracks dirt everywhere and it pisses me off ... and when I say, "Take your damn boots off your feet for the last time!" he goes, "I'm doing business, so get out of here."

On one occasion, I overheard a heated exchange between father and daughter that I found instructive. While I was visiting with Mary at her home, her father phoned. His truck had broken down, he was unable to pick up his wife and son from work, and he wanted Mary to find them and tell them what had happened. He also wanted Mary to tell her brother to find a ride home, then get in the family's second car which was parked in the driveway, and drive to where his father was in order to bring him home.

Mary lost her temper. She was angry with her father for being at a pub and calling from there to ask her to take care of his business. She told him to leave the pub, take a bus home, take the second car, and pick up the rest of the family himself. In fact, Mary's father appeared to have no idea how to find the bus. He preferred spending $20 to take a taxi if no one could pick him up. Mary got out a bus schedule and very carefully, albeit loudly and angrily, gave him detailed instructions for getting the bus home. When Mary's father simply refused to take a bus, she swore at him and told him how irresponsible he was.

I was struck by the role reversal that I was witnessing. To me, Mary sounded like an angry, out-of-control parent, while her father sounded like a lost and difficult child who did not want to take responsibility for his own actions. The language that flew back and forth was also instructive. Words like "fuck," "bitch," and "asshole" were used freely and frequently. After the exchange, Mary was visibly agitated, and talked at length about her father.

The family situation had not always been so volatile and difficult, she said, but much had changed in recent years. From the time she was "a little kid" until she turned 12 four years ago, her relationship with her father had been relatively happy. That year, however, her father had a number of anxiety attacks, which he attributed to stress over his children (particularly his son, who had begun stealing) and his work. He eventually took time off work and began taking Prozac (an antidepressant). The family saw a counselor, but Mary and her brother refused to cooperate, largely because they were angry with their father for blaming them for his emotional state. In any case, the approaches learned in counseling (such as family meetings) seemed to work best when the counselor was present, and less well when the family was on its own. Left to themselves, Mary's family returned to their old patterns of attack, blame, and defensiveness. Mary gave the following example of her father's behavior:

> Well, every time he got sick or something went wrong with him it was me and my brother's fault. … If he gets stressed out about something, it's usually because me and my brother were fighting, or we were fighting with him, or he was frustrated at us because we were being stupid or something like that. Like he'd pulled a muscle. He tore a muscle and he was having muscle spasms underneath his ribs when he was hooking up a trailer to our car so we could go motorbike riding, me and my dad and my brother. Because we used to motorbike all the time. And any way, he was hooking up the trailer for us to do that and [he pulled a muscle and had a muscle spasm] and he was on his back for about two weeks and he blamed it on us because he said we weren't helping enough.

When Mary's father blames Mary and her brother for his difficulties, Mary worries that her father may be right, that she or her brother may indeed be at fault. When I asked what she tells herself after her father has blamed her for something, she answered:

> I don't know … me and my brother both see it like it was something that we did wrong … Because he's fine with my mom. They get along great. She's the only reason why he hasn't left. All the times he's threatened to leave was because of me and my brother.

For Mary, the change in her father and in their relationship is "like he died or something, because it's not him anymore." And when she is not angry with him for being "such a jerk," she is deeply saddened by the absence of the father she once knew, whom she describes as someone who "would never do anything to hurt anybody … . He'd do anything he could to make us happy, and now he does anything possible to make us sad."

Mary's home has become a battleground. The battles are not constant; they are interspersed with good times. But she has learned to expect them — inside and outside the home.

School

For Mary, school was always problematic. Bullied as a child because of her weight and stereotyped (like Molly) as a "tough kid" because of her older brother, Mary soon found school to be a battleground not unlike home.

As with everything, Mary has strong opinions about school and her teachers. She believes that the teachers who "stereotype" her do so because of a particular vice-principal who

> will pick me and my friends out of a crowd and blame everything on us ... just for something to do, because we're his pet peeve. ... When I told him I didn't like being stereotyped, he told me if I didn't like it, then stop hanging around with my friends. Like we hang around at the corner, and he and the counselor told me I was with the wrong crowd. Not all the corner people are bad, like a lot of them have a good head on their shoulders ... . We like to hang out at the corner and I don't think we're different from anybody else, except for the fact we smoke. And some of the people out there do drugs and drink on weekends, but then again, I, the people in the school do drugs too. I mean you don't have to smoke to do drugs ... .

Being singled out and judged in this way made Mary angry and convinced her that the vice-principal was unfair in his approach to her and others like her. This was confirmed on two more occasions, which she described at length and with great feeling:

> I remember one time I was just totally mad at someone. ... These guys at the corner were kicking around a squirrel, and I went to the [vice-principal's] office and I was totally choked, like I was just furious. I wanted to beat the crap out of the guys for doing this and I poured my pop over these guys' heads and I told the vice-principal what happened and he said, "Well, you're at fault, you insulted those guys by pouring pop over their heads." And I'm going, "Oh my god, what an asshole!" I just wanted to totally deck him. I was sitting there going like this (*demonstrates*): my fists were clenched, I was so mad. ... I told my mom about it, and she gave me permission to give him the third degree on the last day of school, right after my last exam.

> I remember last year, I was so mad. Like because I had Mr. Jackson, it was the second year in a row, and he didn't like me because of my brother ... and I just

couldn't stand him. And it was getting to the end of the year and he just, we, he tried so hard with me but there's no, like, he treated us like children and I hated him. I'd do my work and I was getting good grades like B's and stuff and, Mr. Jackson, one day, we were, we were doin' our work and I was, Roberta was helping me because I was absent the day before. I finished all my work from the day before plus the work of that day. And he said that I was talking to Roberta and, uhm, he's like, and he goes, he's just checkin' everybody's work so to see if they can be dismissed, and I go, "I've done all my work," and he, he glanced at it and he looked away and he goes, "No you haven't, it's not all there," and I hadn't been able to flip over the page and I'd try, like, for about a half an hour I tried to tell him that I've done my work but it's all finished because I was finished five minutes before the end of class, and I was talking to Roberta because we were finished. And he was just like, and he, he said, "You have a detention," and I go, "Whatever!" and I just, I didn't want, I didn't want to swear and I didn't want to get totally choked so I sat there and he said, "You haven't done any work," and I go, "You haven't checked, I've done all my work," and he wouldn't check again. And he refused to. And so I said, "This is bull!" and I walked out of the classroom, and he's going, "Mary, get back here!" and I go, "Whatever!" and I kept walking. And then I went out for lunch and then next class was like, that was a Friday and the next class was on the next Tuesday, and I went into class and he's like he, he goes, "Hey, Mary, can you, can you come here for a sec?" and he called me up to his desk, and everybody's watching eh, and he goes, he has a big sheet and it's a behavior sheet, and it says "Mary talks constantly, Mary never, uhm, brings her books to class," which I always did, I, I tried hard. Well, I did talk, but only when I knew I could finish my work. And, "Mary, Mary, Mary obstructs the class," and all these different things and he'd circled the ones that I did, and I looked at him and I go, "You're full of shit!" and I slammed the paper down on his desk and he goes, "Get to the office!" and I go, and I go, "You're a waste of my time," and I kept on walking and I, I went, and I fff … . And then I walked. And I walked down to the office and then the vice-principal called me into the office and he goes, uhm, "What did you say to Mr., Mr. Johnson?" And I go, I told him, "You're full of shit," and he said, "Okay, pack your books up, you're out of here for four days." He didn't ask me why I said it, he didn't give me any chance to explain myself, and I was just, "This is bullshit." And my dad went in with me the, the next day, my dad is uhm, he's a businessman, so he knows how to conduct meetings, he, the vice-principal sat down, Mr. Johnson sat down, I sat down and my dad stood there and took a stand with his arms crossed. He wouldn't sit down, and the vice-principal says, "Would you like to have a seat?" and he said, "No," 'cause my dad likes to look down on people, especially the vice-principal, 'cause he doesn't like him. Uhm, and, he's, he's like, my dad's standing there going, "Well, you, you have no right to, uhm, to, like, limit my daughter's education just for an outburst in class which is caused by the teacher," and the vice-principal said, "No. She said the words. It came out of her lips. She has no excuse." And that was it. I mean, I, we tried. And he was gonna give me, something like, he didn't tell me that I was suspended when he said, "Go home," and he's just, he was a total, utter asshole over the whole deal. ... If you ask me, he's the most disgusting, disliked guy. He disrespects most every student in the school and he, he uhm, stereotypes the people who I want to hang out with.

Ultimately, what matters most to Mary, where teachers and school vice-principals are concerned, is respect. Mary defines respect as being listened to, being treated fairly, not being lied to, being treated with consideration, and being liked by the teacher. Whenever she did not encounter respect from teachers, she disliked them and engaged in battles with them that went on for years at a time. When I asked what it meant not to have respect, she responded:

> It's when they look down on us. Like, uhm, as a teacher sitting there and they're like, "I'm Mr. or Mrs. Whatever, and you are my student and you're a thing and you are supposed to learn." ... Like, school is for learning, but you can't learn from that. You can't learn if you're frustrated, you can't learn if you're upset. And when the teacher gets you upset, it's just like, "Go to hell!" ... When the teacher gets me upset I feel like hell inside and I can't learn. It's like Mr. Gray, He said something to me, we were just starting a test, and it was the first test of the year, right, and I asked him, "Well, does spelling count?" And he said, "Of course, are you stupid?" and he started putting me down, and I looked up and just gave him the dirtiest look, I go, "You are the biggest goof I've ever met in my entire life," and I went down and I wrote the test out, right, and I did, I failed the test 'cause I was so mad. I ended up breaking my pencil. And I wrote on the top before, like, just before I'd start yelling at him. I wrote on the top of my test, "You respect me and I'll respect you. Until then, I won't."

For Mary, being respected and liked by her teachers is vitally important. For one thing, this gives her incentive to work harder, even if she has difficulty with the subject matter. Mary described herself as an average student with marks ranging from C to C+, who occasionally gets D's in those classes which are taught by teachers whom she describes as "iffy." Despite her sometimes belligerent stance, Mary believes that teachers deserve respect, provided they show respect for their students:

> I don't know, I think you have to respect teachers, you know, if you get in their classes. I know that there's some I don't like, so I kinda act up or whatever, but I also got teachers I respect, so I'm good in their classes.

For Mary — as for Molly (Chapter Five) and Linda (Chapter Seven) — the lines are clearly drawn: If students don't like a teacher, he or she becomes fair game for acting-out, which includes a range of behaviors from talking in class to hurling insults, books, or other objects:

> One time I got kicked out of class for doing something I wasn't supposed to be doing, and he goes, "Get out," and I'm like, "You're wearing a hearing aid buddy, so you can't hear me whispering, right?" And he's like, "Just get out." And I'm like, "I wasn't talking," and he's like, "I heard you," and I go, "You, you have to wear a hearing aid, so how can you possibly have heard me?" And then he kicked me out and the next day the exact same thing happened. It was like a replay, so I just picked up my books and threw them at him (*laughs*) and I said, "Screw you!" and I walked out. Then the vice-principal had to teach me math for the rest of the term … . So when I get treated like that, I get mad, and when I get mad, I get the person back.

For Mary, being angry is sufficient justification for any kind of acting-out or violent behavior. At the time of our meetings, she firmly believed that she owed it to herself to discharge her anger at anyone who provoked her — in effect, that she must punish people for making her angry because if she didn't, she did harm to herself. Thus, lashing out both verbally and physically was acceptable to Mary:

> It lets you get in the last word, and it also gets your anger out at the same time, like you sort of go, "Ahh … It's over with."

Power imbalances and violence

Conditions that demanded a violent response from Mary generally involved some kind of power imbalance: an older, bigger person picking on a younger, smaller person; a teacher picking on a student; a parent picking on a child; anyone hurting an animal. Mary hates such "power-tripping." For her, the ultimate power-tripper is her school vice-principal, closely followed by her father:

> [The school vice-principal] is real power-tripper, and I hate power-trippers… . But you know, if there's somebody you really hate and they're in higher authority than you, you can't really say anything, and I can't do that, so the hatred just built and built … .

When she sees her father power-tripping, she usually takes him on — as, indeed, she does with anyone whom she believes is abusing their power over others. With fellow students, she also wades in:

My friend Cathy was going to beat up Sylvia Rivers, and I stepped in front of her and said, "Don't you touch her, she's my friend." And she goes, "Well, she called me a bitch," and I go, "I don't care if she called you a bitch, she's a hell of a lot smaller than you, and you're not touching her because if you do, I'll kick you back." And she's like, "Fine!" and she walked away. And then she tried to — as soon as I came out of the school and was walking over there and everybody's going, "There's a fight, there's a fight," and I said, "Who's fighting?" and they said, Cathy and Sylvia Rivers." And I'm like, "What the hell?!" So I run over there and jumped right in front of Cathy and I'm going, "What the hell is going on here?" And Cathy started telling me, "She's being a total bitch to me," and I just like stopped her. She would have had to fight me, so she didn't … .

Mary's intervention on Sylvia's behalf was also a move to help Cathy. At the time of our meetings, Mary was deeply concerned about Cathy, whom she saw as needing not just help with self-control, but help with the conditions of her life. Cathy lives with her mother, well known in the community as a "biker's moll." She is a heavy drinker and former drug addict who causes Cathy great concern. Cathy's stepfather, who lives in another city, is "not allowed" in Cathy's mother's house because he "treated Cathy like shit." Cathy's mother "threw him out" for beating up Cathy. He also beat up Cathy's mother.

According to Mary, "you have to tiptoe around this man much like you have to around my father, only he's much worse, he gets mad easier." Mary's reaction to Cathy's situation is to try to act as a counselor to her. She gives Cathy advice, and on many more occasions than the one described above, has tried to prevent Cathy from engaging in fights.

Mary also plays this role with other students, and is frequently called upon to act as a mediator. She even encouraged Molly to press charges against Cathy because Cathy "needs to be taught a lesson." Mary can always be drawn into a fight if she sees her engagement as one that upholds her stand against an imbalance of power.

Mary's well-publicized fight with a schoolmate, Andrea, also involved her in a power imbalance, in that Andrea was older and bigger than Mary. Mary thus felt perfectly justified in beating Andrea up:

I didn't start it. She's like 17, 18 and she's like six foot one and 200 pounds. All's I did was call a girl a bitch, and she got her older friends, 17-, 18-, 19-year-olds to come after me, and Andrea was one of them. She cursed at me, and I just laughed in her face. And she did it again the next night, and I laughed in her face again, and her friends wanted me to fight her, but I wouldn't because she was on drugs, and I don't fight people on drugs, 'cause … it doesn't hurt them as much and they can't feel things, so they don't know when they're hurt. But they kept spreading rumors about me, saying I was going to fight them all, so they showed up one night to fight me and they started swearin' at me, and I just laughed in their faces, I thought they were pathetic. And then Andrea grabbed me by the hair and started pulling me away from the lights into the dark, so I started to fight back. I kicked her in the stomach and pulled her coat over her head and won the fight. I caused her internal bleeding because she was on some kind of acid, and her stomach lining was really sensitive, only I didn't know that 'til later.

Mary has lived and breathed conflict for so long that she finds herself engaged in it wherever she goes. She takes on causes. She defends small animals against would-be torturers. She takes on teachers she believes are "acting like assholes." She stops older, bigger people from beating up younger, smaller people, and when pushed or insulted, she stands up for herself immediately.

Hierarchies and violence
Paradoxically, along with Mary's finely tuned appreciation for power imbalances, she also appreciates hierarchies and her place in them. While she abhors others "looking down" on her and rebels against anyone who suggests that she bow to their authority, she also dislikes it intensely when those whom she considers beneath her don't stay in their places. In Mary's eyes, such behavior calls for immediate redress. This is most apparent when younger girls from lower grades try to step out of line. For example, Mary was quite angry with Jenny (Chapter Eight) because

> she walks around acting like King Shit because she can fight, and you're not King Shit until you're in grade 10. While you're in grade eight, you're a nobody.

In Mary's eyes, Jenny is "a cocky little bitch" who has brought problems on herself not only because she doesn't know her place, but because she shows signs of being what Mary hates most — a power-tripper:

> I've had my run-ins with her. She's sort of a power tripper too. I mean, I can see when the grade 10s leave, Jenny will be the queen of the school, like sort of putting herself in a position of power, I don't know.

At this point, Mary shared a bit of insight into the behavior she most hated in Jenny:

> I think one reason why I haven't gotten really mad at her yet, is because she reminds me of me when I was in grade eight. I didn't fight like that, but I mouthed people off. I was really cocky. … When you're in grade eight, everybody tries to set up their own reputation. … That's why the grade eight boys are usually the cocky ones, because they want to set up a class-clown-type, cool-person reputation. And then there's the people in grade eight who are always trying to fit in somewhere because they haven't really got into a big school yet. They're like in a big sea and they're little fish instead of big fish, so they're trying to get a position where they're comfortable and sometimes they find the wrong position that they're in, like Jenny. I mean she's gotten so many people mad at her. She thinks that it's cool, and you have to mouth off a lot of people and get into a lot of fights to be cool.

It was around the notion of "cool" that Mary saw herself as different from Jenny. Mary did not enter into fights with people because she wanted to be cool, but only to redress perceived imbalances of power, to keep those who should be in their places in those places, and most importantly, to discharge her anger. In her mind, older and more mature and more righteous people like herself entered into fights because they were angry about an injustice, and that made a big difference.

Gender equity and violence
Mary had one further reason for engaging in confrontations and fights: equality with the males in her life. Mary believes that in order to achieve equality, she must prove to men (particularly her father) that she can handle herself:

> There's more equality now between girls and guys. And the guys think that if we're going to have equality, then we gotta be equal with them … . We were having this discussion in English class, and the guys think that girls are wimps because whenever they get in a fight they don't just duke it out, they just cry and about a month later they finally talk to each other, and then they cry again and they get all sappy and they're friends. Or they hate each other one day, and the next day they're friends. Guys are just like, "All we do is duke it out and then go for a beer."

Equality makes good sense to Mary, especially in view of her daily quest to get her father to acknowledge her, to help her with the chores, or even to take his shoes off when she has washed the floor. It also makes sense in view of Mary's mother's battles for equality with her husband. However, neither Molly nor Linda agreed with this explanation.

Linda believed that girls fight because "in some ways we're trying to be equal and in other ways, we're just doing what we want." Molly suggested that "I think it's more just kinda the image I want — like, don't mess with me!"

But — as our meetings revealed to me — the bottom line for Mary wasn't really equality; it was getting rid of her anger, an anger fueled by anything she perceived as unjust and unfair. With the view in mind that she wanted to be prepared to take on any physically threatening challenges, Mary had been taking karate lessons for some time, as had her mother and brother. Mary is truly proud that she can handle herself physically.

DATE RAPE

Indeed, much of Mary's talk focused on her ability to take people on, to take charge and be in control. Yet, despite her readiness to fight for herself and for those who are weaker, Mary did not fight on the night she was date-raped.

Mary's rape happened a year before she took part in this study, when for six months, owing to her continuing disagreements with her father, she took refuge at her grandmother's house. Mary rarely dates, but at that time she was "hanging around" with a 28-year-old man who supplied her with drugs and alcohol and drove her around in his car. On the night of her rape, she was completely confused:

> ... We were seeing each other for about, I guess a week or two weeks or whatever. I didn't want to have sex with him, but I never really told him that, because I was basically pissed out of my tree[1] and I didn't want to tell him because I, I felt really insecure because like I, I, it doesn't, I don't get very many chances to go out with people ... so I wasn't prepared, I wasn't like, I, I wasn't expecting it at all, and I just did it anyways. But I didn't want to and so ever since, I've just like — I broke up with him after. But I've like, you know, I didn't want to and I can't believe I did that.

The experience left Mary with lasting questions about herself because she blames herself for what happened. This sense of guilt and shame was further complicated by the reactions of her mother and grandmother, who found out about the rape by reading Mary's diary:

When my mom ... found out about this, this guy, she found out from my Gramma, ... and my Gramma read my diary, 'cause I left it there, but actually, 'cause you know I was like, "I don't mind," and it was underneath my bed and she read everything and that's when I was like heavily into drugs and I was heavily into alcohol ... . And my mom said to me, she said, "You," she started crying and then she told me that my Gramma, she said, "My mom invaded my trust by doing that when I was little [reading her diary]. I would have never done it to you, but she showed me the pages and I regret looking at them." She goes, "I'm not disappointed in you. I know everybody goes through it, and I just want you to know I'm there for you." But I didn't talk to my Gramma for about a year after that, even though she'd hound me, for that invading of trust.

Thus, in the aftermath, Mary's rape was sidelined. Instead, the issue had become betrayal of trust through the reading of her diary. Yet, the damaging betrayal of trust that is rape was never broached by Mary's mother and grandmother. It was buried along with all further references to Mary's construal of sexuality.

However, in our group meetings, Mary, Linda, Molly, and I talked a great deal about sex and sexuality, largely because the girls said talking made them feel better. The girls summed up sex in one word: "gross." They struggled with mixed feelings about whether or not they wanted to engage in sex, and had harsh things to say about girls who were sexually active.

For the most part, when these girls did engage in sex, they were usually drinking alcohol in large quantities. By the time they came to the point of intercourse, they were drunk and feeling ill from too much alcohol, and were not in control of their bodily functions. In the aftermath of taking part in sex under such conditions, they felt disgusted with themselves and with their partners. Similarly, whenever they heard of others engaging in sex, they felt righteously angry — particularly with the girls involved. They later used their knowledge and their anger as a justification to harass, threaten, and beat such girls.

Alcohol and drug use
Alcohol and drug use plays a large part in the girls' participation in sex and, on occasion, in violence. For Mary (as for Molly), alcohol use is synonymous with alcohol misuse. When they drink, these girls rarely stop at one or two drinks. Mary has been drunk to the point of being ill so many times that there are certain kinds of alcohol that she cannot even smell because she begins to feel sick:

Me and my friend shared a mickey of tequila shooters where you get the lemons and salt and water. ... That was harsh, we were on our butts soon, flat out. My cousins [who were with Mary and her friend in the family trailer, drinking on their own while their parents got drunk with Mary's parents up at the house], they were like mad at me, though, the next morning. They didn't tell my parents, and they were like, "We're cleaning up all your throw-up!" — there was throw-up from one end of the trailer to the other, it was so bad. And they're like, "We were thinking of getting your stomach pumped, 'cause you were starting to throw up blood and all that." And I can't even smell hard liquor any more. I can drink beer or coolers ... .

Sometimes when Mary gets drunk she "feels like punching people." Because of this, she prefers to drink only with those whom she feels she can trust. She gave an example of an experience she had while drinking around people whom she couldn't trust:

One of my friends, one of my ex — well he's never been my friend, we hang around the same crowd, his name is Grant. He is the most violent drunk I've ever met in my life. He was just brutal. He'd throw around his friends and beat the crap out of them when he was drunk. ... He was pissed one night, and I was drunk ... and we were all down at Taylor Lake and Grant's throwing around [my friend] Brent, just beating him up. I threw Grant off Brent and I go, "Don't you fucking touch him!" and I freaked out on Grant — he wanted to hit me, and Brent's like, "You hit this person, and I'll kill ya, literally." And Brent's not a violent drunk, like he'll run around and he'll fall and laugh 'cause he's falling ... and he'll tell you, "I'm a happy drunk, unless I'm pukin'." ...

After telling this story, Mary expressed a preference for drugs over alcohol, because

when you're smoking dope, you just break out laughing, you don't feel like punching people because it's just too hard. It takes too much ... . You're mellow ... . You just want to sit there and trip out on everybody ... . It's even good for school work. When I used to get stoned all the time last year, I remember, I used to sit in class and do my work because I didn't want the teacher to catch me, and this year I'm getting failing marks 'cause I'm not doing my work 'cause I'm never stoned.

Marijuana was not the only drug Mary used. In the past year, she had also used LSD regularly. She had a less favorable opinion of this drug because she had seen people "freaked out" while "doing acid." In her opinion, "people that are violent when they're on drugs are usually on acid or coke or something like that." She saw this as reason to stop using such drugs. But Mary had a further reason for quitting:

I used to use acid myself, and I quit completely because it was the type of drug, if you like it, you like it and if you don't you don't, and I liked it, and I quit because I liked it. ... It's not an addictive drug, but if you like it you want to do it again. And if you want it, you'll do it again and again. And okay, it got to the point where I was almost critically insane, like clinically, 'cause after a certain point of doing so much you can be clinically insane or — and I was just like, "There's no way!" ... I didn't want to be like Jeanette LeBlanc last year, who did acid so much that I like noticed a big change in her attitude — Like she got weird. She wore weird clothes and she was kind of a "low-life" and she was different. She, like, they get less brain cells; they lose their values. She got violent. She picked on smaller people.

In the end, despite her preference for marijuana and acid, Mary picked alcohol as her substance of choice because it didn't make her "weird," it was easy to get, and if she stayed home or near home to drink, her parents would give her permission to do so.

Mary's parents seem to make the abuse of alcohol relatively easy. They also seem to have encouraged Mary's use of tobacco. Mary has been smoking since age 10, as has her brother, who gave her her first cigarette. Everyone in Mary's home smokes, and her parents frequently pay her with cigarettes to do chores. Alternatively, they give her cash for extra chores so that she can buy her own cigarettes.

Much of Mary's social time revolves around cigarettes, alcohol, and drugs. She is a "corner person," that is, a smoker who hangs around the intersection nearest her school. This puts her in touch with other smokers, who on occasion also smoke marijuana both in and out if school, drop acid, and use cocaine when they can get it. On weekends especially, they drink large quantities of alcohol.

Mary pointed out that not all kids who smoke cigarettes automatically progress to drug and alcohol use and misuse. But the fact remains that their chances of coming into contact with kids who do are greater when they gather with other smokers at the corner.

For Mary, substance misuse is a part of life: All social occasions involve this. She spends much of her time hanging around spots where other kids congregate to "party." Near her house, there are several such haunts — an ocean beach, a lakefront, a wilderness trail — where young people regularly gather to drink and smoke. Partying when parents are away is also a favorite pastime:

When my parents went away this time it was really great, because we had a whole lot, we had about 20 to 30 people, we had an all-night party. Nothing got broken, nothing got stolen. There were no problems at all. Like, the music wasn't loud, 'cause we have renters. … Like, everybody helped us to clean up the pizza boxes and everything. It worked because I managed it, my brother didn't. He had all his friends over, and I, I was the one with the authority. I was the one who was, you know, looking after things and making sure nothing was going out of hand with his friends, that there was no fights or anything and he, he went to bed actually, and I, I stayed up until the next morning, then went to bed about one the next day.

Friendships

For Mary, such parties are wonderful times: times to spend in close company with others, times when she can shine, when she can be in charge and ensure that things run smoothly. Mary likes to have control in social situations. She likes to keep order and see that her form of justice prevails.

With both her male and her female friends, Mary likes to engage in sports such as riding and biking. She likes to compete and she likes to win. She also plays the role of peacebroker, protector/enforcer, and leader/guardian — roles that she backs up with physical threats when the friends she is trying to help step out of line:

With her friend Cathy:
Cathy's not tough. She's got this butch layout, but she's not tough, 'cause when we were best friends, I'd start wrestling with her on the trampoline or something in my front yard, and I'd hit her lighter than I'd hit my other friends and we were just joking around, we were just play fighting, and Cathy'd go, "Ow, that hurts," and it's just like, I didn't even swing hard. She doesn't know how to hit properly, she'd go something like this (*shows twisted arm*) when you're supposed to keep a straight fist and you should follow through like that (*demonstrates*). But now she's hanging out with this chick Eileen, she's wears these spiked rings, and ever since Cathy started hanging around with her, she thinks she's tough, and her and Eileen will go around looking for fights and … I just want to beat the crap out of Eileen and get her out of the picture so that Cathy can straighten up … .

With Jenny, when Jenny provoked Linda:
I was in the mall, and Jenny was there and I go, "Jenny, come here," and she broke down in tears. She was crying and she comes up to me and she goes, "I did not call you a bitch," and I go, "I'm talking to you right now, I never said I was gonna kick your ass, but other people said I was gonna kick your ass. I'm gonna ream you out right now, 'cause I'm pissed off at you. I'm gonna give you a second chance. You think you're King Shit of this school, you're not King Shit, me and Linda and all the other grade 10s are King Shit. … Don't mess

with us, 'cause we stick together, we're friends." And I go, "If you're not one of our friends and you piss us off, we stick together and we'll gang up on you." And she said, "Well, why haven't you, then?" And I go, "You know, you really got a mouth on your face, you know," and she goes, "Oh?" And I freaked out and I just started yelling at her again, and then I went on for another 15 minutes. I really know how to talk when I'm mad. … But she doesn't know when to quit. There's a point when you stop scowling at someone and calling them a bitch, like after they ream you out and threaten to beat the crap out of you, you should stop. Most people would stop, but Jenny doesn't.

Similarly, Mary persuaded her parents to allow her best friend Brent (who had moved out of province with his father, yet missed his friends and wanted to return) to come and live with them as a boarder. She organized the social life of her friends Tanya and Faye, and kept them involved in activities that she herself enjoyed pursuing. She takes control of her father's bad behavior. She supports her mother and acts as her confidante. She is defender and comrade-in-arms with her brother in the battle against their father.

In each of these relationships, Mary has definite expectations with regard to how her allies should behave. When they do not, she becomes first disappointed and hurt, then furiously angry.

When Brent moved back to town and struck up a relationship with Faye that sometimes excluded Mary, she was devastated and began to take exception to many of Brent's habits (drinking, misusing drugs, skipping school) that she had previously overlooked. (Eventually, she persuaded her parents to send him back to his family.) When Tanya disagreed with Mary's judgments about other people, Mary became frustrated and angry and wanted to beat Tanya up. When Faye became involved with Brent, Mary felt deserted and betrayed and stopped being friends with her. When her father "steps out of line," she "reams him out and gives him the third degree." When her mother is unavailable, she feels angry and abandoned. When her brother became mentally ill, she became irritated with the amount of time and attention he was receiving, then angry with her parents and her brother for failing to give her the attention she herself felt she needed.

Mostly, Mary believes that she benefits those whom she cares about. She acts as she does because she wants her friends to like her and spend time with her. She wants her brother to be healthy and happy so that she can continue to be his comrade. She wants her father to be easy-going and to acknowledge her contributions to the family.

She wants her mother to be less preoccupied with her father. And she wants other people to see her as a friendly person, someone who likes to have fun.

Abandonment and loneliness

In the end, Mary feels like an "outcasted little person," very much alone, somehow deprived of what she needs and what she feels she is entitled to.

For example, although she cooks the family's dinner, she frequently finds reasons not to eat with them in order to avoid the arguments that regularly occur at the table. Thus, she finds herself alone at a time when she might actually like some company. When she struggles with her chores or school work, she often seeks help from her parents or brother, but can rarely pin them down long enough to assist her.

> When I get home, well, I automatically stoke up the stove. That takes me about 15 minutes ... . Then when the house gets warmer, I sit down for about half an hour, then it's about 5:30, and then I get going outside and do the animals. I have to feed the chickens, do their water. if it's cold, I bring them water from the house because the pipes freeze and stuff. Sometimes I have to take the horse out of the barn. I usually have to tidy the kitchen before my mom gets home, and then I have to come in and cook the dinner ... .

The day before one of our interviews, Mary had actually received help from her mother and, after some urging, from her father:

> I've been sick the last couple of nights and I haven't done anything. Like yesterday I just helped my mom make dinner, ... and I didn't really do anything other than that. I've just been totally zonked. ... I was tired, I was grumpy and I was sick, and I was sitting in the family room, and my dad — when he's sick, he expects everybody to drop everything to do something for him. And I asked him to run to the store to get me some cough medicine, and he was sitting down watching TV ... and he said, "Ho, ho, give me a minute, you won't even let me sit down, raw, raw, raw." And I just freaked on him and I said, "Look, you asshole, you expect me to do everything when you're sick, and you won't even get off your lazy ass and go to the store to get me some cough syrup. Well, I'll tell you something, next time you're sick, I'm not going to do jack shit for you and you're gonna learn from that, 'cause then you're gonna have to get off your lazy ass and do something yourself!" And so he got up and went and got it for me, and that really fixed him for about two hours after that.

When I asked her where she learned to talk to people (especially her father!) in this manner, she was quick to answer: "Probably my dad; that's the way he talks to me all the time." In fact, every interaction between Mary and her father that I overheard rang exactly as described above.

Mary still holds out the hope that one day she will no longer feel lonely and abandoned in her own home, that her father will see the light and straighten himself out — preferably with direction from Mary — and that she can hang onto her dream of a family that is held together by love:

> I love my dad ... but I just don't like him. When I was a little girl, me and my dad were best friends, and now he doesn't even talk to me. [*Sobbing*] I don't know who he is any more ... Me and my brother both see it like it was something that we did wrong ... . All of this just makes me feel shitty about myself.

Ultimately, what Mary seeks is recognition and love, especially from her father, with whom she has built a pattern of interaction that neither of them seems able to break. When Mary talks about this, she first becomes angry and strident about "fixing" her father. Then she becomes quiet and sad and small, filling the room with a palpable loneliness mixed with the deepest sorrow.

NOTES

1. Mary has been drinking alcohol since about age 10, when she began sneaking drinks from the adults' glasses at her parents' parties. Both Mary's parents consume quite a bit of alcohol and combine most social events with heavy drinking. Mary appears to follow her parents' pattern of drinking. She does not like to travel far to parties because, after steady drinking, she does not wish to have to struggle to get home. Two examples of her drinking style:

> Last New Year's, I drank a bottle of Crown Royal whiskey straight — I chugged it back ... just kept going and going and going and there was just about one inch left out of the whole bottle and I was just like, "Oh this is fun, Happy New Year's!" — but after like a half an hour, I was in the bathroom throwing up. ... And about three or four weeks ago, I got drunk with some friends; we had a beach party and I drank two-thirds of a bottle of rye, another half of a two-liter [bottle], and I drank four maximum lights ... .

Linda's Story

My dad just doesn't trust me with guys, he thinks they'll just use me. One time when I got suspended from school for fighting, he said to me, "What do you think you are, a biker bitch? Why don't you go out and get filled up by the tit-ties and done up by the ass and stuff." ... It goes back to when I was younger, when uhm, I was uhm, molested for four years, by like a friend of the family, and my parents didn't believe me. Like I remember, I was like in grade three and they had this good feelings, good touches and bad touches program, and I told my teacher and she, like, told my principal and then my principal called my parents and my parents woke me up and I was in grade three, grade two or three, and they're like, "Well, what did he do to you?" uhm and I didn't, just, I didn't, I was scared to answer them so they like, "Did he do this, did he do that?" and I'm like, "Well ya," and they go, "Okay, well, we don't think he'd really do anything like that." And he kept coming over after that. He was my baby-sitter, and my parents kept having him over for dinner, and I remember one time when I was sitting at the table and there he was, this guy, he was just 17 and he used to help my dad build his car and stuff. And I remember sittin' at the table and I was just like, I felt embarrassed to be there in front of him, and I remember he had this headband on and I was just staring and my dad took me in the next room and told me I'd better stop acting rude and stuff. And later my dad made me watch a TV program on kids who, uhm, say they've been molested but have lied, and I just can't talk to my parents about sex or anything. (*Excerpt from taped interview with Linda*)

Family dynamics

Linda's description of her family focused primarily around her father's domination of her mother, her sister, and herself. Linda talked about her father often, and brought him up within the first 10 minutes of our first meeting with Mary and Molly (see "Molly's Story," Chapter Five). Like Mary, she describes herself as being unable to get along with her father because "he has to prove his authority all the time." Linda experiences her father as a man who doesn't listen to her, because "he never listens to anyone." This, according to Linda, makes him "like most guys, because guys never listen anyway."

Rather than listen, Linda's father "gives ultimatums and gets the belt." Not only does he use a belt; he also uses a martial arts exercise tool made up of two wooden batons joined by a chain, with which he hits his daughters across the legs. On occasion, being hit in this way has left the girls with bruises. In assessing her father's behavior, Linda suggested that he does what he does because she has a bad temper and therefore "I kind of like deserve what I get."

As well as using physical abuse, Linda's father makes frequent use of put-downs, lectures, and punitive gestures to straighten out his wife and daughters. For example, he wants his wife, a woman described by Linda as "all sweet and cute and quiet" and who manages her husband by "holding everything in until it hurts her," to change into a more outgoing person. To force her to do this, he has for the past three years refused to wear his wedding ring, because his wife is not behaving as he wants her to.

Linda seemed deeply troubled by her father's treatment of her mother, and expressed the wish that her mother would speak out more often:

> I don't want my mom to sit back and like hold everything in 'cause she'll just explode. And just like, I think it's better when she let's it out, 'cause it makes me feel better too. Like then she's like, not hurting herself. ... And when she wouldn't stick up for her rights, I don't know, we'd have some problems, like my mom and me, 'cause like, I'd just, I get mad at her and stuff, 'cause she wouldn't spend any time with me. And like it was my dad that told me about sex, 'cause she won't even talk about it, and I want her to talk about it 'cause when mothers talk to you it's comforting, and I can't talk to my mother about anything personal whatsoever. Some of my friends go home and ask their parents a question, and I don't want to ask my parents, and my friends are like, "Well, doesn't this girl have a mom?" Like, I just don't feel comfortable. Like, she doesn't feel comfortable talking about it, then it makes me feel uncomfortable talking to her.

Linda spends much of her time at home both craving contact with her parents and very carefully avoiding it. Although she wants desperately to be able to talk to her parents, particularly her mother, the risks are too great. Her father has often encouraged her to talk to him about "anything," but on the few occasions that she has actually approached him, he has greeted her openness with verbal and physical abuse. Her mother has never issued an invitation to talk, and has mostly kept her mouth tightly shut with regard to her private feelings on any subject. She has, however, joined her husband in denouncing Linda.

Not surprisingly, Linda spends as much time as possible by herself. This angers her parents, who believe she is being rude and secretive. In some ways, Linda's parents' perceptions that she has a secret life are accurate. According to Linda, they "don't have a clue" what she really does, and she does in fact take a number of precautions to keep her life completely separate from theirs.

Her chief allies in maintaining this secrecy are her best friend, a girl who has been suspended a number of times from school for fighting, and her best friend's mother. This mother "covers" for Linda by lying to Linda's parents about her whereabouts. She also occasionally joins Linda and her own daughter at parties with other adolescents and allows them to drink and use drugs in her presence. When Linda is out with her friends on weekends, she often drinks a great deal. Unlike her friend and her friend's mother, she doesn't engage in much sexual experimentation. She is too overcome with revulsion and often frightened by flashbacks from her own sexual abuse to allow herself much pleasure in sex.

School

Linda described herself as having a short temper and needing to prove that she has authority. By way of illustration, she talked extensively about school, where her main focus was engaging in fights with fellow students and power struggles with the vice-principal and some of her teachers.

She described the students she fights with as "cocky, little obnoxious kids who mouth you off and are trying to be cool and fit in, but they look like idiots." She described the vice-principal as someone who told her that she would be a "nobody" and who, just like her father, won't let anybody talk and won't listen.

Linda understood that she had an "anger problem" which manifested in her interactions with those who displeased her. Chief among those was her schoolmate Jenny (Chapter Eight), with whom she had several altercations. One of these culminated in Linda's suspension from school for backhanding Jenny across the face after Jenny told her to "kiss my god-damned ass."

Within the first half hour of our meeting, Linda had touched upon her propensity for anger, struggling with authority figures, and fighting with fellow students. These were her recurring themes; they came up in every meeting I had with her.

Anger and violence

Linda described herself as being capable of anger that can explode into violent rage. She also felt she had a deep capacity to hate. For Linda anger, rage, and hate come into play especially when she is confronted by someone she deems is treating her with disrespect. Jenny and the vice-principal have been most instrumental in triggering Linda's rage:

> I just got a lot of hatred for some people. … When I don't like somebody, say if somebody goes around, especially if they're, it really bothers me, 'cause it's that respect thing. If they're younger and they're calling me a bitch, I'll go up to them and confront them … and I'll say, "Look! Don't call me a bitch unless you're looking for a fight. Because I never did anything to you, so don't worry about it. You've got a problem here and you'll have even more of a problem if you keep your attitude up!" And like people, the crowd might see me, I can't really like, see myself when I'm doing it, I just know I got a lot of hatred. But when people like, see me they're like, "Calm down." I mean it's like they had a bet going with me that I can't go two days without saying a negative thing and all that, and I couldn't. … And there's one person [Jenny], and it just kinda happened after she mouthed me off, I was just like totally freaked with her and now I just want to slam her head into something. I wanna shoot her with a gun or something. I wanna kill her. … If I could I get away with it I'd kill her. I wouldn't necessarily kill her, but I'd get her good. I just want to teach her a lesson. I'd beat the crap out of her. She's pissed me off so badly, I just want to give her two black eyes. Then I'd be fine. I'd have gotten the last word in.

The vice-principal once triggered her rage by a telephone call he made to her home. The call was made after Linda took part in an incident in a school hallway in which one of her closest friends tripped a male student "by accident." The student reported this "accident" to the vice-principal, and later informed Linda and her friend that the vice-principal had told him he could press charges. To Linda, this was proof that the vice-principal was "out to get people," specifically herself and her friends.

Her anger grew when later that same day, the vice-principal called her at home to discuss her behavior with her. She was not home at the time, but her mother relayed the call to the home of the "best friend," whom Linda was then visiting. The call was received by Linda's friend's mother, who handed her the phone with the remark, "It's that asshole of the year!" This remark only served to solidify Linda's sense of having been wronged. By the time she took the phone, Linda was very angry, mostly because she found it intrusive and strange that she would be called first at home, then at a friend's home. When the vice-principal told her that he was calling because he wanted to discuss his impression of her and to let her know that several younger students had complained to him about her, Linda flew into a rage:

He didn't necessarily have to go and call me, he could have told me at the office. [When he called] I was so mad at the time, I was so mad. It just ruined my evening. I was just like, "Oh my god, I can't believe this! When I find out who did that [complained to the vice-principal] I'm going to kill them!" I was so mad!

This anger permeates Linda's life even when she actually knows better or has some understanding of an opponent's position. For example, even though she herself was picked on and bullied when she was younger, she finds herself picking on and bullying those students in her school who are picked on by others. Her reason for this is simple: "I've just got a lot of hatred."

The anger also emerges in her interactions with teachers, particularly those she has identified as "trying to be like your enemy." In Linda's mind, such teachers place themselves "above" their students and appear to convey dislike. With such a teacher, Linda goes out of her way to create disorder and distraction:

Miss Sangster, she doesn't like us. She just doesn't like anybody. She thinks that she's better than you. She struts around and points her finger. She, she's rude. The other day I walked out of her class 'cause I turned around and like, everybody was talking, and she doesn't like me, so I turned around like, I just turned around and laughed and she sent me to the back of the room. ... She's got no right to do that. She's very negative, she's got no right!

In an attempt to "get her teacher back," Linda purposefully set her up the next time she attended her class. She complained that she had a headache and asked her teacher for a Tylenol, knowing full well that her teacher could not comply because teachers cannot dispense medication to students. Linda repeated her request until a classmate offered to run across the street to her own home to get a pill for Linda. Miss Sangster refused the student permission. Linda then challenged her: "So this is the way you care for your students!" and was subsequently sent to the office.

At the office, she encountered her math teacher, who asked if she was being mouthy again, and her English teacher, with whom she had so far had a reasonably good relationship. The English teacher remarked that he "had now seen the other side" of Linda. This incident left Linda feeling angry and humiliated, but also fully justified in her behavior. Every aspect of it confirmed how wrong and bad teachers could be. Nothing that happened prompted her to revisit her own behavior because, in her mind, she was fully justified in everything that she did.

Unlike Mary, who prefers the direct-assault approach to teachers and anyone else who gets in her way, Linda chooses to undermine and undercut those teachers whom she dislikes. She saves direct attacks for fellow students, usually those who are younger and in a lower grade than herself. However, one of the four incidents she was involved in over one three-month period included an altercation between herself and the "best" friend who had "accidentally" tripped the male student in the hall. This friend was suspended for five days for fighting with a female student, as Linda was for hitting Jenny.

When Linda engages in a direct attack on another student, she usually feels justified because she does this only when she feels provoked. Provocation, for Linda, is being called names, either behind her back or to her face; this is enough to get her going. Here is how she described a typical incident:

> So I had this miff with a girl, actually a couple of days ago, and she, she ended up calling me a bitch and she would talk about me behind my back, and she's got a carrot stuck up her rear so far that she, it's true (*laughter*), she walks standing straight. No one likes her. That's just how bad she is. And she, she, you know, like, I gave her the chance in the first place, like I was friends with her and then she messed it up by calling me a bitch, like, in front of everybody. And I said, "Did you call me a bitch?" And it makes me so mad, especially when they're younger. My parents have always said, "Just walk away from it," but when other people walk away, I just get so mad, 'cause I think, "Oh, they're not gonna listen to me," so I just want to pound the crap out of them. So I wanted to beat the crap out of her. And I told her, and Mary told her too, that I could hit her. I mean I can take her, I mean I could just slam her down on the ground and that would be it. She's just a weakling, and she uses her snootiness to look down on people, and I don't like it. People like her shouldn't do that.

With Jenny, Linda was even more harsh:

> I told her she was in my face, she was calling me names and everything, like on the third day of school … and she's like giving me dirty looks and I'm like, whatever, okay, and then a couple of days later, I'm walking out and I hear this, "Fucking slut," and I turn around and say, "What the hell is that for?" and we kinda get in an argument and then I walked away. The next day it's, "There goes the bitch," and I'm, like, this is a grade eight talking to a grade 10.

And then at the dance she pushed me and I go, "Nice fucking outfit!" and then she went and told the vice-principal and then about a week went by and like I hadn't talked to her or anything and I was standing in the hall talking to my friend and I hear, "Kiss my ass!" so I said, "Say it to my face!" and so she did and then it was just like a reflex and I just went like that (*demonstrates a backhand smack*) and I backhanded her. I should have punched her. She pissed me off so badly.

For Linda, such provocation justified her own behavior of smacking Jenny across the face.

When we arrived at this point in the discussion, I told Linda (and Mary and Molly, who were also present) that I could understand her anger with Jenny but had a great deal of difficulty accepting that she or anyone could resort to a smack across the face merely because of being angry. She explained it to me this way:

Well, we've got to, because the teachers don't really help you, and there's not anything you can do to get them [people like Jenny] back. I mean if you go to a teacher, they don't really do anything. They just say, "Oh well, she's in grade eight, you should be able to handle it yourself. And it's just like, well, what can I do, I'm not allowed to hit her? And if you do hit her, it's like you get the message to her, "Don't mess with me again," basically, and you've got to get her back, 'cause we're older and they make us look like idiots by sitting and mouthing us off. And I definitely want to do it because I want to get her back.

Linda believed she had further justification for "getting Jenny back":

Jenny's a little liar. I even told her that. There is no way I'll ever resolve anything with her, and there's no way I'll ever be friends with her. ... She's a slut, she wears clothes that don't fit her, and we have every right to call her a slut. No offense [to me, the interviewer], but she's a slut. She slept with people at the beginning of the year, and then she was denying it, she's got a screw loose — and anyway, she really pisses me off right now because since she got in this one fight, she thinks she can beat up anybody. And that's, like, just so annoying. She fought that other chick just because she wanted to, she really didn't have any reason. ... Now she's running around saying that I couldn't fight worth a shit and that she's going to beat me up at the store and she's going to flatten me and stuff. And she goes to the elementary school where my sister goes and threatens grade sixes ... . And then she started giving my sister lip, so I turn around to her and I go, "Don't you even think about my sister, you don't even look at her, don't even walk by her!" I go, "Don't even think of her!"

Linda had no doubts at all that Jenny deserved a beating. In the final analysis, she had no doubts about what should happen whenever she was provoked. The rule was simple: When provoked, get them back! Neither Mary nor Molly offered a dissenting voice here. For all three, the choice was clear:

> You have to do it because if you don't you'll get angry, and that's just the way it is when you're a teenager. You don't really care if you get in trouble or whatever, There's not much maturity, I guess. And anyway, the trouble part isn't when you're hitting someone, because at least then you're not sittin' there fumin' anymore, the trouble part comes after that.

Drug and alcohol use

At this point in our conversation, the discussion moved from violence to the use of drugs. For Linda, drugs (marijuana and LSD) were a thing of the past, a past that began a few short weeks before our interviews. For the moment at least, Linda had "quit doing dope" because she had had enough for now. Having smoked pot nearly every day in grades eight and nine, and in the first two months of grade 10, she thought she would leave it alone. She offered no explanation for this decision other than to agree with Mary that maybe smoking dope and doing drugs such as LSD could become psychologically addictive, and might therefore pose problems. Linda had an image of a former friend in mind when she spoke about smoking dope:

> Melody, do you remember Melody, she smoked pot and she did acid, and she got really weird, like she'd dress weird and she did so much dope, like it made her violent sometimes, even when she wasn't violent, and she didn't really like people, I don't know … .

While Linda may have put marijuana and LSD aside, she had not done the same with alcohol. Like Molly and Mary, Linda drank regularly, especially on weekends, and she drank to get drunk. Linda had discovered alcohol when she was seven years old:

> When I was seven, I went to a wedding and me and my friends sat under a table drinking. It was like they [Linda's parents] didn't know, they were all up having a great time, and we just sat there drinking out of these little glasses. I got really out of it, and I was throwing up and they were all like, "Food poisoning!" Parents are so naive, like they couldn't imagine their seven-year-old daughter getting drunk, you know … .

Sexual Abuse

Linda, Molly, and Mary also talked about sex and morals. For Linda, what stood out was the extent to which she had been subjected to sexual abuse, and the clarity with which she could discuss her experiences of it. After disclosing her abuse (see "Molly's Story," Chapter Five), Linda described what it has been like for her to live with this experience:

> I just kept pushing it back and back and I, I even forgot about it. Like, that might sound weird, but uhm, uhm, I, I, I forgot it for a lot of years, and then last year it started coming back and I'd like seclude myself from my family, I'd just sit in my room. And, uhm, my parents would get mad like, 'cause I was, like I wasn't spending time with the family. And uhm, and then they'd, I just, I kept, I had like dreams, and this feeling that I kept having of how I felt like all the time that that happened. But now it gets more, I like get it more often. I, it's hard to, like, there's two different feelings, like one that like, if I hold something it will feel gross, and I like, just like, I let go of it. ... Like, it could be anything I'm holding onto, like I could be pulling my covers over me, and I just get grossed out like. ... And then there's this one [the other feeling] where it's in my head and I can hear something, but it's like a feeling but it's also what I'm hearing, and every time I hear it, I like kinda get — it's like something, something is being said to me and every time I hear it comes in more clearer, sort of. It's weird, I and uhm, now but, it's like I noticed like, over the years it's not like before when it was just a blur, now it's like I can almost hear what it says, but I can't. ... It's in my head ... and uhm it, it only like, it only, I can only have like, maybe not even five seconds to figure out what it is because once it goes away, then I just forget what it was like until it happens again, then it's like, "Oh ya." And then right after it happens it's like, I can't remember what it was like, but it's a voice ... .

Linda has experienced a number of difficulties in the aftermath of her abuse. As well as what she described above, she has experienced nightmares, flashbacks, and feelings of distrust for those around her:

> I'm not used to putting down on myself, but this made me really put down on myself. So when I put down on myself, I go into deep depression at home, and I won't talk to anybody and when I come to school I put on a fake smile and nobody can tell. And it's just like really stressful for me and for my friends when I tell them, and that's why I have a hard time. ... I just get really sensitive and a lot of people just, they don't know exactly why and it really hurts me more when my dad gets mad.

Linda's loneliness is poignantly clear. So far, only lying and "putting on a fake smile" has made it possible to cope with her parents.

As we continued to talk, Linda revealed more of the dimensions of the abuse she had been subjected to:

It's weird, 'cause I, last year I thought, "Well, I can handle this myself, right?" Like I'm going, "I don't need counseling for this." Like, I, in a way I sort of think that, but it just bugs me that not knowing what I'm feeling, and I certainly can't talk to my parents about anything. And my mom just kinda looks at me as if I was lying, so does my dad. And I remember, he [the abuser] used to get me and this little boy that lived down the road to do things with him, and he'd sit and watch ... uh, he'd like, he'd get me and him [the boy from down the road] to do something and we'd have to like do the same back to him [the abuser]. Uhm, I remember one time like I was only young, I was about five 'cause I was still in play school, I remember. And we were in the back of this car and we thought it was normal. Like we didn't think there was anything wrong, and I just feel so embarrassed. ... We, like I, we did just like normal people would have sex. That's sort of what happened, and my mom walked in and I was grounded for two weeks, I remember that. I was grounded, and I just feel so uncomfortable around my parents now. ... Another thing that really bugs me, uhm, like shortly after that was done, they, we — I didn't have many friends when I was little 'cause we lived in a small town and like — but, uhm, we had this tree house that we used to play on where, and we'd always play house and uhm, this guy would like always play house with us and stuff, and he, he like told us that the kids, the parents have to do such and such to the kids, that sort of thing. So, like, we're like playing the role, and then, me and this other boy, like we had to uhm, do stuff to him [the abuser] and, uhm, we had to do the same to this other little boy. Like, he got us to do it to another kid, like we molested him ... . Nobody wants to feel as bad as I do. ... I've always thought I was a bad person ... .

I asked Linda if she had ever had any help with her feelings as a result of being abused. In fact, she had approached the school-based child and family counselor for help, but was not at all happy with the outcome of this intervention:

[I don't want help] 'cause I remember, the family worker tried to go to Social Services[1] and then go to the cops and all that, and I was like really mad at her for that. I didn't, like it was done, over with, and I just wanted to, like, leave it at that, and just like, live with this sort of thing. Like, inside I kinda felt like when I found out that now these other people knew, it was like, well, I wonder — were they talking about me when they were discussing my business? ... It, it's never like, she's [the family worker] never gone through with it, it's like I was so mad I wouldn't even come out and talk to her or like do anything. It just made me feel worse, and I didn't, like, I couldn't concentrate in school ... .

Yet, Linda wished to speak of her sexual abuse almost every time we met. Talking about it seemed to help her feel better.

At the end of every meeting, before we parted, I asked each participant how she was feeling and what effect, if any, having told her story to the group had on her. Linda (and Molly and Mary, for that matter) replied each time that talking helped a great deal. For these girls, having the opportunity to talk — and most of all, to be listened to — was vitally important. As Linda put it:

> Ever since we started doing this, I kinda got everything out, so I kinda feel fine. ... I've learned a lot from it too, just sort of things that you know you have it, but you never recognized it before. Like it sort of brings you from the top [surface] to the inside. Like before [we met as a group], I thought it'd be spooky, that's basically what I thought, and I don't know, now I think you guys are totally smart, and when Mary and I went to the dance together and all those people were, like, interested and they're, like, it couldn't be [that we're actually doing something together], and they're like, Mary looks so nice and I'm like ... I feel a whole lot better. ... I feel better every time I talk about it.

In fact, talking about how she felt about her abuse prompted Linda to raise the issue one more time with her father:

> Remember when I told you guys about how my parents didn't believe and stuff [about being sexually abused]. Well, it was weird, 'cause about two weeks ago we were arguing and I've always had resentment towards my dad and he was like, "Why do you always treat me that way?" and stuff like that, and it took about two hours, but we kinda got down to it. And he asked me why I never go to him to talk to him. And I said, "'Cause I don't trust you," and he said "Why?" and I said, Because I don't." And he goes, "Why?" and I go, "Because you don't believe a thing I say." And he's like, "What, what, what?" getting all mad at me, and then I told him and he was like, "Well?" and I felt so ashamed about telling him, but he believed me this time. Then he said, he goes, "Yeah, well, all he did was show you his private parts and make you touch them." And I was like, "Well, that's not all," and I didn't want to tell him anything else, but he was like, "We, I can't believe that we didn't believe you, but it's just like you were a little kid at the time and we just thought you were getting ideas from something or whatever." He's like, "I'm sorry we didn't believe you," and then he was trying to make up, going, "Are you okay, blah, blah, blah?" They [both parents] were crying. ... But I wish now that I didn't tell them because they treat me like a kid. ... My dad's calling me his buddy, and then saying, "Oh, I better not call you that, 'cause that was the guy's [the abuser's] name," and he makes a big deal about it. ... It's like I wish I hadn't told him, I don't feel comfortable. ... And I told him that I went to counseling, and he

was like, "Well, it's water under the bridge, you shouldn't let it get you," and he told me to quit seeing a counselor … .

Thus, while Linda did eventually feel better because now she was at least believed by her parents, she still felt uncomfortable and uneasy with their intimate knowledge of her sexuality. As well, she felt unsure what to do with those feelings. Her parents frowned upon counseling, since it involved seeking help outside the family. Further, Linda still had a great deal of unresolved anger over how the school-based social worker had dealt with her request for help. When I suggested a different counselor, one who would make herself available merely to talk and to listen, Linda, Mary, and Molly all declined because

> we just don't want to tell our parents about this, and we've kind of resolved this in our families and we don't want to go to Social Services again, 'cause I've [Linda] already had it happen twice [meaning the social worker had contacted her family on two occasions]. And if that's any of the things [we have to do], I'm totally against it, 'cause that worker tried to press charges against him, and I'm like, well … . She called my parents the day after I told her and she questioned my parents about everything. My parents said it was true, and that's when it got brought up again, and she, like, went to Social Services and all that was really ahhh … . And I was so mad at her 'cause I didn't even want to bring it up and she went to the police and stuff … .

What Linda wanted was to be able to talk freely about her sexual abuse without anyone but herself taking action. She wanted to be heard, and she wanted to hear what had happened to other people. She expressly did not want me or anyone else to proceed upon the information she had shared. Most of all, she did not want her parents involved in what for her was a deeply painful and embarrassing experience.

Given that she had already talked with another counselor who had satisfied the requirements of the law about sexual abuse disclosure (i.e., by alerting Social Services and the police), I was able to do as Linda wished. I listened, as did the other two members of our small group. This seemed to help.

It helped until Molly broke her commitment to the group's confidentiality. One day, during an interlude in one of her classes, Molly told some fellow students about Linda's sexual abuse (see "Molly's Story," Chapter Five), despite her own first-hand experience with the shame and embarrassment of having others know.

Even with the continuing support of the school counselor and myself, this latest betrayal sent Linda a clear message: There is no really safe place anywhere. And while Linda continued to meet with Mary and me after Molly's betrayal, I believe the experience of being violated yet again only served to confirm for Linda that the world is a hostile place.

Notes

1. Any adult who hears a disclosure of sexual abuse from a youth under the age of 19 is obliged by law to report this to a ministry social worker.

CHAPTER EIGHT

Jenny's Story

We're a very close family, and they always back me up whenever I want them to. And I stand up for my sister. I learned to stand up for myself from my uncle. He didn't have the same problems like I did with kids picking on him, but he did get called out for a fight and he beat the guy up and broke his nose, so he tells me how to box because he had to take boxing when he was younger. So he showed me, he said, "You've got to do this," and he'd push me over, and he's always play fighting. He always says, "Don't let anybody push you around." So he pushes me and I push him back. He's bigger than me, and he showed me how to defend myself. So did my grandfather. He's got eight guns. He told me, "Don't let anybody push you around," too, and so did my grandmother. My grandparents don't like it when I get pushed around, and my parents don't either. When another kid tied to push me around at the mall my dad went over and said "You better watch it," and started yelling at her. And my grandfather wanted to run over these girls that wanted to beat me up. I've seen him when he's mad. He throws things and breaks them. Like, if he's got a glass he'll just throw it up and like smash it on a table. He's been in fights like at weddings like with some of my cousins, when they were all drunk. And my dad, he's been in lots of fights, like, when he lived on the streets. He sort of lived on the streets and at home, because his parents were alcoholics and they died. His mom died when he was 13 or 14, and his dad when I was five, but they were alcoholics so they beat him, so he didn't live at home and he couldn't go to school. He doesn't hit people anymore though, he doesn't believe in it unless it's another guy. But when he gets mad he calls me horrible names and that makes me mad and it makes me cry. And when I'm mad I punch, I'm so used to punching I punch everything. I punch my sister, and when I'm mad at school, I punch the lockers, but it doesn't hurt. (*Excerpt from taped interview with Jenny*)

Family dynamics

Jenny's family, like Molly's, is "close," not just emotionally, but geographically: Jenny's parents, her sister, her grandmother and grandfather, and her maternal uncle all live together in two houses set about 100 feet apart on a piece of country property. Mother and grandmother work together, and the family spends most of its social and recreational time together.

This family togetherness has some limits, which are dictated by rigid family rules. For example, several of Jenny's mother's siblings and their children are excluded from all family activities because Jenny's grandparents strongly disapprove of their lifestyle (they live on social assistance). These relatives are not spoken to and are never invited to family gatherings; should they appear, they are fair game for a beating.

Family exclusion also extends to Jenny's father's brothers, mostly because of minor infractions, such as not returning tools that they have borrowed. At the time of my meeting with Jenny, one such brother-to-brother fight had evolved into a court battle and a family rift that caused Jenny to "hate" her cousins and not speak to them at school.

"Closeness" is also withheld from other members of Jenny's extended family, specifically Jenny's father's son, who was born to a woman he had a relationship with before he became involved with Jenny's mother some 16 years ago. Jenny's father had never acknowledged this son, who was now 18 years old; the boy had often been trouble with the law and was currently in jail.

In this family, "closeness" also entailed a high degree of emotional reactivity to one another's actions. For example, when Jenny became involved with a boy who did not meet with the family's approval, her parents and grandparents became very angry with her, and demanded that she stop seeing him. Jenny, however, was adamant about not giving her boyfriend up, and frequently lied about being with him. This conflict escalated into a six-week-long battle during which family members yelled and screamed at one another. Jenny's father frequently referred to her as a "bitch," a "tramp," and a "whore." In the midst of it all, Jenny's mother became ill with migraines and stomach pains, symptoms similar to those she had experienced when she had stomach cancer nine years earlier. Jenny's grandmother told Jenny she was the cause of her mother's illness, because she was the source of her mother's stress.

Jenny then became the center of a family storm in which everyone came down hard on her for upsetting her mother. Finally, Jenny's father told her, "If you can't live by my rules, you can't live here at all!" and kicked her out of the house. Her mother then began to cry and asked Jenny if she really wanted to leave the family. Jenny retorted: "If you can't stand my fighting with you, why don't you just sign me over to a group home!" Jenny's mother then pleaded with her to stay.

Jenny's father relented, and she was allowed to remain. Promises of better behavior were then extracted from her. Jenny made these promises willingly enough, but continued to lie about her whereabouts and to see her boyfriend (until he broke up with her because he found a girl he liked better).

In general, conflicts in Jenny's family quickly become extremely emotionally charged. When any two people clash, all the others choose sides:

> When we get mad in my family, we just yell and scream. So if I get mad at my sister and I push her, she'll yell at me and I'll get back at her. Then I'll go to my room and turn on the music. I hate my sister, and my mom gets mad at me. … If my mom gets mad she'll hit me in the back of the head, and she tells me to ignore my sister but I can't. She comes right up to me and yells in my face and I get mad, so I hit her or push her, and it happens every day. … We don't get along because we're totally different people. Like, I take after my dad and she takes after my mom. My dad wants everybody to like him. He gets 30 people in a room and he talks to everybody, and I do the same thing. I like people to like me, and I don't like people hating me. And my mom, she's got a bad temper, and my sister does. So if I do something wrong, my mom will get mad and my dad will get mad at her, so I don't get grounded. But if my dad gets mad at my sister, then my mom yells at my dad.

Taking sides is a common practice and, during extended periods of family conflict, hate and anger prevail between opposing sides. However, if any member is attacked by someone from outside the family, this hate is temporarily suspended, and the family closes ranks. Thus, while Jenny "hates" her sister, she nevertheless threatens any of her sister's schoolmates who give her trouble. At the time when Jenny was threatened with expulsion from the household, her parents nevertheless attended a school Christmas dance in order to "keep an eye on" her schoolmate Linda (Chapter Seven), who had been suspended for hitting Jenny but had returned to school in time to attend the dance.

I found Linda's description of Jenny's parents' behavior illustrative of the family's style:

> Jenny got her mom and dad to go to the dance because she said we [Linda, Mary, and Molly] were going to beat her up or something, and her mom came up to me and pushed me. It happened when Jenny was pointing me out to her mom and all that and she was walking one way and I was walking the other way and she just kinda of pushed me. And her dad's a total asshole. He's like at the dance the whole time. He's like eyeing us all and all that, he's just an idiot.

The family's style, and their stance towards those whom they consider adversaries, is perhaps best summed up by the bumper sticker displayed on the family camper: *A boss is like a diaper: full of shit and always on your ass.*

Jenny's mother

Jenny's mother is baffled by what she describes as a "180 degree" personality change in her daughter, who until junior high had been a quiet and "perfect" child who didn't require much attention. Jenny's mother appears not to grasp the connection between her family's aggressive and combative stance and Jenny's involvement in fighting outside the home. She described her own and her husband's involvement in Jenny's outside conflicts very matter-of-factly as "talking to" people. She cannot fathom how Jenny may have learned to fight, because in her mind, nothing that happens at home could possibly be connected to Jenny's behavior at school and on the street.

Jenny's mother thinks Jenny's aggression springs from (a) her moving from elementary school to junior secondary school, with a consequent change in friends, and (b) the fact that "nowadays, girls compete to be equal because you don't have to be a wallflower, you sort of have to do what the boys do to be accepted as an equal."

For Jenny's mother, Jenny's new friends (male and female) provided the central influence in Jenny's progression to violence, because many of them came from homes that were in constant turmoil, where children and parents battle frequently and strife is commonplace. She could not see, however, that her own home was not all that different. Rather, she considered it a place where people care about one another, a factor she saw as being absent in the homes of Jenny's friends.

Interestingly enough, Mary — who attended grade school with Jenny and had known her and her relatives for seven years — had no difficulty in seeing a connection between Jenny's behavior and that of Jenny's family. She recounted frequently seeing them in the midst of some altercation or other, either in the schoolyard, on the street, or in the mall. Jenny's mother, however, like Molly's, can see only her family's closeness.

Self-image

Unlike her mother, Jenny herself likes her "180 degree" personality reversal. She feels her life has changed for the better since she began to engage in fights, and often spoke to me about her involvement in, and her attachment to, fighting. Being known as a fighter had become a vitally important part of her self-image.

Jenny knew she had a great deal invested in acting "tough" and being seen by others as a force to be reckoned with. At 5'3" and weighing about 107 pounds, she described herself to me this way:

> Kids are scared of me, because I can look really tough, especially when I'm mad. It's because I'm built big. My parents even say that. I've got big shoulders compared to my mom, and when I'm big, everyone tells me, "You're going to be scary," and I stand up and I look down on them and I always give them a dirty look, and everyone's sure I'm going to get them. And if I get mad, I don't yell, I get mad and I hit.

When I asked Jenny what she thought about herself when she behaved in this manner she answered, "I don't think I like myself. I don't think I'm pretty, and I think I'm fat." She then disclosed that hating herself and being hated by others hearkened back to earlier experiences of being bullied and scapegoated in school, and to her eventual evolution into a fighter, a "tough girl" with an image to protect.

When Jenny started school years ago she was "shy and quiet, and the teacher didn't think I understood well, so I was put back into grade two." From what Jenny and her mother both told me, Jenny was so quiet that her teachers were concerned that she might be developmentally delayed. Jenny had her first experiences with being bullied shortly after being held back a grade. She was picked on and ridiculed by her fellow students, first for being slow, and as time went on, also for being fat. This continued for several years until, in grade five, Jenny decided to take action:

> … I stood up for myself. I was getting tired of being pushed around by everybody saying I was fat and I didn't like that … . In grade six, I was so tired of being told I was so fat, I started going on a diet. … I went right down to 80 pounds, I didn't eat for two weeks. … I won't do that again, I felt terrible, but in a way I felt good because I was getting thinner and I had to get new clothes. But then I got so sick [Jenny developed shingles at age 13], so I just watch what I eat now.

Since that time, Jenny has worked hard to stay thin and to cultivate her reputation as a fighter who will take on all comers.

Dieting and being thin brought Jenny immediate attention from many people:

> I didn't eat and I got sick … and my doctor, he was just telling me that I shouldn't do that because you can get sick and you can die, so I started eating

again. ... I can't eat cookies or cake, I get sick, I think because I'm not used to eating sugar now — or chocolate. ... Sometimes I skip breakfast, and I don't really eat lunch. I eat very little for supper ... I watch my weight all the time. I weigh myself every day, but sometimes I don't look. ... Nobody ever thinks I'm fat. Everybody tells me to eat. They all tell me to eat, like my best friend. She was over the other night and I'll give her a cookie, but I won't eat any. Then she'll get mad until I at least have one. My friends want me to eat, because sometimes I go the whole day without eating. ... My mom doesn't like it. That's why I started eating, because she got upset. She told the doctor and phoned the school to make sure I ate my lunch. She kept me home a couple of days and told me to eat. ... The doctor phones once in a while to see how I am. ... There was a time when I got shingles. He said that I was run down from not eating. My doctor said it was strange for a 13-year-old girl to have it. ... I got it when I wasn't eating and I'd go out and then I went to a concert and I didn't have anything to eat ... and I collapsed a couple of times at the concert. I had like lots of money to buy food, but I'd already bought a T-shirt instead, so my friends bought me something to drink ... .

Thus, while Jenny has suffered from not eating, she has also received a great deal of caring attention — something she did not get when she was a "perfect," shy, and very quiet kid.

Fighting also has brought Jenny a number of rewards: Almost as soon as she began to stand up for herself, the amount of bullying and ridicule she was subjected to declined, and her fellow students began to see her in different light. Some saw her as someone to turn to when they needed protection. Others saw her as someone who could provide them with entertainment, because she could so easily be goaded into fighting. Overall, Jenny was no longer alone, and rarely without some form of attention.

In the end, Jenny's "rep" provides her with a far better role to play than the one she was originally assigned by those who bullied her. In fact, Jenny's investment in fighting has become so central to her sense of self that it is now "just something I do," and something she would find extremely difficult to stop:

I could only stop fighting if I get arrested, 'cause I haven't got arrested yet, and if I was taken out of school or put in an alternative [school], then I'd try to stop, or if it's hurting my parents really bad. I'd stop if I really got into trouble for it. Like, I would never stab anybody because I don't believe in using weapons [except rings in lieu of knuckle dusters], but I don't know, if I really got in trouble because I really hurt them, like if I broke their nose and I was getting charged for that or I hit them first and I got arrested for it, then I'd try not to fight because I wouldn't want that to happen again because I don't really like getting in trouble with the police. But I can't stop myself, because it's just because everybody I know is so used to me fighting that, "Oh, this person's bugging me," and half my friends can't take care of themselves and I say, "Fine, I'll take care of it." And I guess too, if like, I got beaten up really bad, I'd definitely learn to walk away — beaten up like in the hospital beaten up. Like if I get a black eye or a broken nose, that wouldn't stop me, because that can happen to anybody. But mostly there's no other way I can think of [to stop] 'cause everybody, everybody, like I've got people at both [junior and secondary] schools knowing me as a fighter, and it would be just kind of awkward like, "Now there's going to be a fight, do you want to go?" I'll probably go. I'd still go 'cause everybody's just used to me going, "Yeah, sure, I'll go," and I'll be the first one there. And all my friends, a lot of people said, "Well, if you want to stop, go ahead. Like we're not going to stop being your friend or anything," but in a way, I might lose a couple of my friends, and a lot of people won't like me after a while, and I like having a lot of friends.

Peer relationships

Friends are the most important thing in Jenny's life, especially in view of her years of suffering as a friendless scapegoat. Peer relationships are usually important to adolescents (Bibby & Posterski, 1992; Artz & Riecken, 1994). But with Jenny, there is an added level of intensity to how firmly she grasps onto her friendships, largely because she never again wants to be bullied and alone:

> Right now, my friends — I don't really think my family's not important — but I'd rather spend most of my time with my friends because my family is so boring and right now my friends are the most important thing.

However, some of Jenny's friendships are difficult and fraught with contradictions, as friends turn into enemies and then back again into friends:

> Janet Williams, she was my friend and we were enemies first and she didn't like my friends, so she'd always get me into trouble. Like, there was a new girl who came and we said this and that about each other and we got mad at each other, so we hated each other for two years and then the new girl left, and we found out what she did, that she said things about each other to us, so we apologized for everything, so we were friends, but then she didn't like that I liked Todd, and she didn't like my clothes, so she called me out, and that's how we had a big fight [which was watched by over 100 spectators].

In order to keep the attention of her friends and maintain her image as a fighter and defender, Jenny engages in fights more or less constantly. (If she hasn't had a fight for some time, she will systematically work her way through the people she knows, or knows about, until she finds someone she can provoke into fighting.) She also diets continually so that she will never again be fat. And she spends as much money as possible on clothes.

Jenny is primarily interested in forming friendships with boys. Her greatest source of joy is the knowledge that she can attract positive attention from males. She attributes this directly to having lost weight. As a child, however, her tormentors were mostly boys:

> It started in about grade three, all the boys used to pick on me. They used to go around calling me fat and ugly. ... It bothered me, and after a while, even my good friends started doing that, so I couldn't take it anymore. So I started pushing them or yell back and they stopped bugging me. It didn't matter how big they were ... .

Things are different now, and although Jenny still believes that she is "fat and ugly" and still hates herself, she feels good when she is getting attention from boys. Her best day of the year was her first day of junior high school: On that day, she got 15 phone calls from 15 different boys. At times like that, Jenny likes herself at least momentarily because

> it's really important to have a guy ask you out. I thought it was neat [when they all called me]. And I like myself when all the guys I hang out with don't think I'm fat and ugly. They like me, and my friend, she doesn't really get that many boyfriends because of her weight. She doesn't like if she's around me and I get a guy asking me out, and a couple of hours later someone else asked me out. ... I feel good about myself, I have a boyfriend.

Dynamics of violence

While Jenny enjoys having a boyfriend and tries hard never to be without one, she also likes having other male friends. On occasion, she will fight with males as well as with females. When Jenny fights with males, her reasons for fighting are different from those she gives for fighting with females.

With females, Jenny engages in fights for male attention. These fights are usually triggered by a dispute about who has the right to look at or talk to a particular boy, or who has the right to wear a particular style or article of clothing — clothing that is meant to attract boys.

Jenny will also try to provoke fights with girls whose attitudes she doesn't like. She will fight girls who appear to threaten her friends. In the last analysis, she will fight anyone (male or female) with a reputation for being tough, in order to uphold and increase her own reputation as a fighter. Here is how Jenny described a fight with a female opponent:

> I got in a fight with a girl at school because she didn't like the way I wear my clothes. It got started when, umm, I was going out with this boy from another school, and she was mad, she liked him and she didn't like the fact I was going out with him so she picked on me about my clothes and my attitude and I just kept ignoring her 'til the point where she called a fight. She said. "You probably are scared to have a fight," so I went [to the place where the fight had been called] but I wasn't scared [just] 'cause she's in grade nine, but she was [scared]. I found out where she was hiding and I said, "If you want to fight," I said, "Come on, let's go!" Okay, so well, we ended up fighting and we haven't seen each other since. ... She pulled my hair and slapped my face, and I punched her in the face. I cut her right by the eye [with my rings] and I scratched her and she backed off and left. ... There were about 50 people watching.

With male opponents, the dynamics are somewhat different. Jenny will engage in fights with males either because of derogatory (usually sexual) comments they have made about Jenny or her friends, or because they have challenged her for intimidating or hurting their girlfriends. The dynamics also involve a desire on Jenny's part to be considered equal to males.

Jenny's fight with Marty was typical of her fights with males. Marty had shown an interest in Jenny, but she rejected him. This made him angry, and he began to express a dislike for her. At the same time, he also found another girlfriend. When Jenny and another friend began phoning Marty, his new girlfriend objected. Jenny and her friend replied that they could call anyone they wanted to. This angered Marty, who told some of Jenny's friends: "Yeah, I'll get Jenny, and I'll jump her from behind and I'll stab her!" (As Jenny understood it: "He was going to kill me with a knife, a machete.") This prompted Jenny to enlist several friends, male and female, to set up Marty by inviting him to the movies with the express understanding that Jenny would not be there. Of course she was there, along with two male friends, who began to beat up Marty for her:

> First Jim [her boyfriend] started punching Marty in the face, Jim and Ted did. Then Derek Holmes came and said, "What's going on?" and they told Derek

that Marty wanted to beat me up, so Derek took Marty and slammed his head into a wall. And then he started punching him, and then Marty's dad came around the corner to pick up Marty, so he got in the truck, and then his dad said, "You want to fight? All of you come down to the house!" So at the time when I got there, there was about 75 kids there on my side, but only about 20 of us went down to the house because people couldn't stay because they were getting picked up. ... So 20 of us went down, and Marty wouldn't come out of the house until I got off the property, because I went right up to the door and said, "Come on outside! You wanted to fight!" and he says, "I ain't coming out till Jenny's off the property!" So I got dragged off by Jim and Matt and Andy. They had to drag me off because I was really mad. And then Marty came out-side and it was going to be a one-on-one fight with Derek, and like Derek didn't even know about it till that night, so they started fighting. Derek was fighting because he was afraid I'd really get hurt and because it wasn't right for a girl to fight a guy, he didn't think. And I'm like, "I want to get in there!" ... because it wasn't fair that Derek was doing it for me. But then it stopped and the dad, he was there, yelling at me, and I was yelling and screaming, "Yeah, well, your oldest son tried running me over, he tried hitting me with his car!" — But he didn't hit me because I got pulled out of the way by Carey Henderson. ... I fell, but I was okay... And then I was yelling and Derek and Marty stopped and Marty yelled, "Come on, you wanted to hit me, so hit me!" And he spat in my face. I got really mad. I took off my coat, I had a leather coat, and dropped it and grabbed him by his hair and he turned around and hit me ... so I punched him in the face. I cut him and then he got mad and he sort of punched me in the face ... and Derek was busy talking to the dad and yelling at the dad. The dad was telling us, "Leave! The fight's over!" But then I sort of attacked his son and then the dad came over, and I tripped and fell. Marty pushed me into his brother's car and I dented the door with my shoulder and my head, so I had big bruises. Jim came and he's yelling, "Get off her, get off her!" He's kicking Marty, trying to get him away, and Derek came over to try and get Marty away from me. Marty's dad came over and took Derek and punched him in the jaw and held him on the ground and so Marty jumped off me and I got up and walked away, and he started kicking Derek in the face. So the dad let go, and Derek was like, "Oh my jaw, oh my jaw!" He thought he broke it, and we all took off and the dad got in his truck and started it, so he thought he was going to chase us. And we all took off and he got out of his truck, so we all went back and then the police showed up and took down all our names ... .

That ended the fight for the time being, but it continued the follow-ing day:

The next day like, when I was walking with my friend down the road, he [Marty's dad] saw me and I'm like, "Whatever!" and I gave him a dirty look and he drove by so he stopped just like dead in the middle of the road, turned around and started chasing me. I'm running down the road towards the mall and Jim and about 15 guys I know from school came around the corner and I'm screaming. They came over and got all around me. The dad pulled in the parking lot and was yelling at me, so they're all yelling at him and he went to leave and he stopped and came out because this boy, Carey Henderson, was yelling at him. He came out and just started strangling Carey. He picked him up and strangled him and put him down and then like left. And then we left and the dad followed us for the rest of the day. … And then I went home, and I felt really bad because I don't know what the dad was going to do because he's so mental, so I told my parents and they got mad, but then we were going to press charges but we didn't because I would have got in the most trouble if anybody pressed charges because it was because of me. But so then everything cooled down after that … .

When I asked Jenny how she felt about all this, she had a great deal to say:

I was mad for Derek because of what happened to him, and if he didn't know [about Marty wanting to stab me] it would never have happened. … And I felt bad in the fight because I wanted to fight Marty. I wanted to fight him to see if he would hit me or not, because if he did and hurt me, I had 19 other people behind me. They would have all jumped in. … They were all trying to hold me back because I was really wanting to get in. I didn't even think about anything, I was just so mad. After a while, I didn't even know where I was, I was so mad. … I didn't want Derek fighting, I wanted to do it. But Derek did fight, so I gave him hugs for that. I was hugging him because his jaw was all sore and he got bit. Marty bit him, so we were trying to make him laugh, and then after a while, he got so mad and he just wanted to fight again. … I was so mad, I wasn't scared [even though] Marty told everyone he has a gun. … He really has a gun because he lives with his dad and his older brother and they don't have a mom. So his dad has a gun for hunting. So Marty has a gun and he was gonna use it on me if he saw me going down the road. I heard he was gonna, but I didn't think he would because he knows if he did anything he wouldn't live. And he's not gonna use it anymore because I talked to the dad, and the dad didn't know anything about it. He thought it just started that Friday night. And I told him, "Your effing son this and your son that, he was going to use his gun on me and he was going to stab me and hit me." And he's going, "Yeah, well, I gave him permission to hit you, but I promise he will not use any weapons on you." I said, "Well just make sure of that, because if he uses any weapons on me, you'll have weapons used on you." My dad would use weapons on him, he was really mad. My grandfather's a hunter. He has eight guns. So if like, I got shot, my grandfather would.

Jenny felt emphatically that, all in all, fighting was a good thing:

I like fighting. It's exciting. I like the power of being able to beat up people. Like, if I fight them, and I'm winning, I feel good about myself, and I think of myself as tough. ... I'm not scared of anybody, so that feels good. My friends are scared of a lot of people, and I go, "Oh yeah, but I'm not scared of them." Some of my friends, like this one girl from the other junior high school, admire me. ... It's getting on my nerves because she phones me 15 times a night, it's boring. ... She admires me because like, if someone's picking on her, I said, "Well, tell them I'll have a talk with them." And I did, and she told all her friends and they're all scared of me now and they don't even know me. (*Chuckle*) All these people in grade eight at that junior high are scared of me, they don't even know me, and they're scared of me. It makes me feel powerful.

In fact, Jenny has come to like this feeling of power so well that she finds fights wherever she can: in her own school, at the other junior high school in the district, and even in the elementary school her sister attends. On occasion, Jenny threatens and bullies students in grades five and six.

When I suggested that her behavior sounded quite a bit like that of those who had once bullied her, she assured me that what she was doing was different. In her mind, she was keeping order and threatening only those who appeared to be intimidating or otherwise irritating to her friends. To Jenny, this meant she was doing the right thing.

Gangs

Jenny revealed that she was interested in knowing people in gangs. Like Sally (Chapter Three), she was enamored of the "Bloods" because

like, they're always there for you. ... Like, I watched this show "Geraldo." There's like six of them, girls that belong to gangs and mom says, "You admire them, don't you?" I go, "Yeah, I do." Like, they're always there for you, like if you need something. ... They're tough. They're all pretty, too. Everybody's scared of them. ... I like it when people are scared of me. It just makes me feel good. I feel like, "Oh, finally someone's scared of me."

Jenny believed that if she were to join a gang, she would be forever safe from attack. Then, she would not only have herself to depend upon, she would have the gang. The attraction was not so much the gang itself, but rather the safety she thought the gang would provide. However, Jenny was clear that if joining a gang meant either upsetting or losing her friends, she would forgo seeking out a gang to join.

I asked about her attraction to the six gang girls displayed on the talk show she had seen. I wondered if Jenny wanted to be like them. Her answer was illuminating:

> I admired them, but I didn't really like them ... because they were bad, and they were all dumb. There was this one girl, she was 13. I'm older than her and she looked like she was 17 and ... it seemed like she could only say three words, "Fuck you, you're a fucking bitch," like three or four words, and she couldn't say anything else. And none of them were in school. But this one girl, I admire out of them all because she was getting out of the gang. She's got a baby. She's 15 and her boyfriend is in the gang as well. He's leaving and they're in school so they can get a job. It's like I want an education. I want a good job, I just don't know what I want to be ... .

Goals and aspirations

Although friends, fighting, and being tough and powerful were most important to Jenny, she also placed some value upon school. She stated that she didn't think that she would drop out of school before completing grade 12, despite the fact that she dislikes school. But Jenny's main focus with regard to the future is not on further training or education; it is on getting married:

> I wanted to be an airline stewardess, but that changed. I don't want to do that because I love traveling, but I got to thinking that if I have to travel, I can't have a husband and kids. I plan to have a husband and have kids and get a job, a good paying job. ... I want to get married when I'm 20 and have two kids, a boy and a girl, and I plan to stay with all my friends that I have now. ... I don't want to go to university. I don't like school that much, I wouldn't be able to take it. ... Some teachers told me I could be a cop because I've already experienced everything so I'd understand, but I don't like police at all. ... I won't be able to be a teacher ... , it's just I don't like kids, 'cause like I have a bad temper sometimes, but I can be a counselor, 'cause of this fighting and everything, I'll be able to help other kids that's fighting. ... I'd probably be against it later on, but right now, I like it ... .

Thus, although Jenny envisions a very traditional future, for the moment, fighting and its associated perquisites take precedence over anything else.

Death

Along with her interest in gangs and fighting, Jenny also has a fascination for death. When I asked about the violence associated with most gangs, she told me that violence wasn't an issue:

[It] doesn't bother me, like my mother thinks there's something wrong with me 'cause I'm so into death. I'm very much into death. When we're moving into my grandma's house, she goes, "What color do you want your room?" I go, "Black, what other color?" She goes, "Fine." So I got black walls, carpet, absolutely everything I own is black. I'm getting rid of all my stuff that's not black. I sit and draw crosses that are black and I draw so that they're bleeding. Like I sit in class and I write about death. Once in a while, I'll have the devil's star. I don't worship the devil, but like, I like believing in the devil more than I believe in God because there's something evil, I don't know. ... I know about this stuff because I read a book called *Michelle Remembers* [a psychiatrist's account of ritual abuse], and it was all about the devil and what really got me is my uncle's ex-girlfriend lived in the house where all this stuff happened to [Michelle] when she was five. ... I like knowing what happened. ... I didn't like [the people who abused Michelle] but I like the devil himself. ... I don't know. ... What I don't like about it is if you get possessed, like I watched *The Exorcist* and I go, "Oh my god, I don't want to be possessed by the devil!" I don't know, I just admire death. ... I like the devil. He's evil. He's powerful. He likes killing people. I don't like killing people, but I like death.

When I asked Jenny to tell me what it was about death that interested her, she replied:

It's hard to say, I like it, it's just black, black and someone being dead. You know, like watching TV, like I like horror movies. Sometimes I like the way people die in the movies, like in *The Exorcist*, when she got possessed, she was able to throw people out the windows, so that's what she did. ... It's just I like the devil and evil. ... I don't like God. I don't go to church. It's boring. ... If I was possessed I could sit here and this glass would explode. And I can make just anything happen. Like I admire that. ... I like death and the color black, but I don't like watching "live" someone who is really dying. I cry when someone in my family dies ... .

I was somewhat relieved to hear that Jenny did not want to see an actual death, but I probed further to assure myself that her fascination did not carry with it a plan to harm either herself or someone else. Jenny was clear that she did not want to kill anyone. She was also clear that she herself did not want to die, but she had considered suicide:

I don't want to go, it makes me sad, but I did. Like, I don't know, like I thought about ways I could and I know that if I ever wanted to I know how to do it. But I don't like pain. I wouldn't be able to stab myself or like shoot myself, I wouldn't be able to stand the pain. I was thinking about doing that last year. My friend and I were sitting and talking about ways that we could kill ourselves. Like she was really into it. She still is. She's like one of those people who, "Oh yeah, I'll slit my wrist and my throat." I'm like, Oh, I wouldn't be able to stand the pain. ... She's weird. She's unhappy. She doesn't like herself. ... She's overweight. ... She thinks she's ugly because she's fat. She doesn't really like herself, and she has weird ways of doing things.

Ways of belonging

Jenny's reflections on death and suicide prompted me to check again to see how she felt about herself. Again, she told me that she was ugly and fat, but that she felt good about herself for now because she has a boyfriend and is getting a great deal of attention from boys. When I asked Jenny about how she felt about being a girl, she replied,

> It's hard, just because everybody's fighting, so like if you don't fight, you're going to get beaten up. Like we [girls] can't do most things. ... I can't box because only guys are allowed to. ... There's so many things you have to do, like watch who you are. If you're not a fighter, and there's a gang, and they don't like you, you can get hurt, so you have to watch your back. Like, I have to watch my back all the time. ... It's hard too because everybody wants to have friends and wants to be cool and if you're not, if you're some sort of geek [it's hard]. And right now, I'm not considered as a geek. If you're not a geek, you can have hundreds of friends, but you have to do a lot to keep them ... .

When I asked Jenny what things she "has to do" to keep friends, she gave as examples the fact that she drinks alcohol to the point of throwing up, and aspires to the current fashion of body piercing and tattooing. Her best friend wants to have her eyebrow, belly button, and nose pierced, while Jenny wants to begin with having only her belly button pierced. Part of the girls' attraction to body piercing is that doing this would be a direct rebellion against their mothers, and therefore a statement of autonomy and power.

Similarly, both girls wanted to get a tattoo. Jenny envisioned "a black panther that's walking on my shoulder; since I like black, it's going to be black." When I asked Jenny where she got the idea for this tattoo, she told me,

> My dad. He's got a black panther and an eagle, and I admire my dad. He's like, I don't know. ... Like he's very tough. He's not a wimp. If someone's bugging me, he'll go and beat him up.

Thus, getting a tattoo not only signals kinship with her friend; it also signals a connection to her father and to his image of toughness.

In order to identify with a group she can call her own, Jenny calls herself a "Rapper." She embraces rap music and Rapper fashions, as well as the concomitant values of antagonism and hostility towards outsiders. For Jenny, being a Rapper means hanging out primarily with boys, wearing baggy clothes, and listening to music that Jenny describes as

> heavy, with lots of swearing, and some of them say bad things about girls and women like they should be told when they should have a baby and stuff, but some of them don't, and I always listen to that. ... Women are equal. ... I think that women being equal is fair. I don't think it's fair that they can't do certain things. Like I don't think it's fair, there's this boxing club that I'm sup- posed to join, but they won't let me in because I'm a girl ... . [When they said I couldn't join] I was mad. My uncle's friends with the guy [who runs the box- ing club], so he's gonna come out to my house every night... . I'm gonna learn to box ... .

REfLECTiNG ON violENCE

Throughout our conversations, Jenny returned again and again to the importance of being able to fight, and seemed unable to see fighting in anything but a positive light. At one point we were discussing this while sitting in the food court of a local mall. Sitting near us was a man with a five- or six-year-old boy. They were laughing and talking, and appeared to be enjoying each other's company. I pointed them out to Jenny just after she had finished telling me about yet another fight she had been in that had made her feel "good" because she won, and because the other person had sustained worse injuries than she had.

I asked Jenny what she saw when she looked at the man and boy sitting at the next table. She saw them as a father and son who were out having a good time together. I asked her next what it might be like if the boy were to be beaten up by someone and had to go home to his father with his face all beaten and bruised, and then I asked how she thought the father might feel upon seeing his son in that state. Suddenly, Jenny dropped her face into her hands. She ran both hands over her face and into her hair, and groaned. Then she looked at me and said:

> Don't ask me to think about that. If you ask me to think about that, I'll have to stop what I'm doing, and I don't want to stop what I'm doing.

Jenny, at the time of our meetings, was unprepared to stop fighting of her own volition.

The last time I saw Jenny she was at her home. She had been suspended from school for participating in two fights in one day. The "main event," a planned battle with a girl who was sometimes her "good" friend, was called by both girls as a way of deciding which of the two had the right to wear certain clothes and go out with a certain boy.

This fight was held in front of a crowd of over 300 students. It was broken up by the principal of Jenny's school with assistance from a male counselor. The two men had driven to the fight as soon as they heard what was going on, and put an end to it as quickly as they could.

The "warm-up" before the main event took place as Jenny made her way to the fight. As she walked along the road to the corner store that was the designated "arena," a car pulled up and another girl, also a rival for the attention of a boy, jumped out and attacked Jenny from behind. Jenny managed to best her and continued on her way in order to fight the agreed-upon battle.

Both Jenny and her opponents were battered and bruised. No charges were laid because it was difficult to decide who was the victim and who was the assailant. Jenny was proud of herself, but she was grounded. Her mother took time off work and stayed home to supervise Jenny. She also went to Jenny's school and returned with a stack of books and homework. When Jenny was finished, she went back for more.

Jenny's mother had decided to take action. She intended to do everything in her power to prevent Jenny from participating in any more fights, and was receiving backing from the school. I gave Jenny and her mother the name of a violence counselor at a local social services agency, along with that of a youth group leader who works with young people who, like Jenny, are moving rapidly towards involvement with the juvenile justice system.

When I left them, Jenny and her mother were making phone calls to the people I suggested. Eventually, Jenny joined the youth group and saw the counselor. While she may still value fighting and toughness, she has not been engaged in a major physical battle since that time.

CHAPTER NINE

Making Sense

> [Young] women, the focus of this [work], develop into social beings in the following sequence. Initially copying other's gestures, the infant girl progresses through play and game stages until she forms a *mind* with the rational ability to understand symbolic gestures. This mind allows her to become an object to herself with the capacity to make moral judgments and decisions on courses of action. Each woman develops in this way a *self* that is reflective and capable of viewing actions from both her own point of view and that of *others*. She is historically located in the community through this learning process, called socialization. (Mead, 1934, cited in Deegan, 1987)

In this chapter, I summarize the key informants' perspectives on themselves and their worlds. I also offer my own analysis of their experience, and outline what I have come to understand about violent girls as a result of this study.

Family Dynamics of the Key Informants

Larson, Goltz, and Hobart state that "Whatever the form, and wherever it is found, the family is the primary source of meaningful relationships from birth to death" (p. 3). The authors offer three basic assumptions that speak to the depth and endurance of familial experience:

1. The family is primarily responsible for the reproduction and nurturant care of children.
2. The family is primarily responsible for the establishment of an individual's social identity, social role and social status.
3. The family is the primary source of intimacy and need fulfillment for the individual throughout the life span. (pp. 3–6)

If we accept these assumptions, the family is the primary matrix for the internalization of social processes, in that the family mediates and interprets the larger social context to its members, particularly its children. The internalization of social processes (noted by Vygotsky, 1978, and Blumer, 1969) is, of course, not limited to the family. But in looking to the family, one may uncover the core social and interpersonal processes by which individuals draw meaning and create a foundation for their perspectives of self, others, and the world.

Through the *Survey of Student Life* (Artz & Riecken, 1994), my colleague and I learned that we could expect violent school girls to live in two-parent families at very much the same rates as non-violent school girls, and that their parents were likely to have about the same level of education and occupation. These findings were borne out by the six key informants, all of whom lived in two-parent families in which both parents worked, and for whom material poverty was not a factor. We also learned that we could expect violent school girls to place less importance on family life than non-violent girls, and that enjoyment of their mothers was less applicable to them than to other students. After hearing my informants' stories, I was able to understand some of the reasons why violent girls may have responded in this way.

In the course of our discussions, my six key informants frequently talked about family. Within the first five minutes of meeting with Molly, Mary, and Linda, they had brought parents, brothers, and sisters into the discussion. Throughout our time together, these girls continued to ponder their own actions and feelings in the light of their experiences with their families. Sally, Marilee, and Jenny also mentioned family members each time we met to talk. Many times, the girls used their parents' behaviors and viewpoints as reference points for their own. Although each girl had her own unique family story to tell, all six had in common an experience of family that included strife and disruption, deep pain and sorrow.

Often, after meeting with the six girls and their parents, I would drive home in a state of grief. At times I was overwhelmed by the conditions of the lives these girls were revealing to me. Despite my 18 years of front-line child and youth care work, and my four years of working with adult women survivors of abuse, and despite the fact that I know well that children are used and abused by their family members and others on a daily basis, the raw immediacy of the stories I was hearing hit me hard.

There was something in the matter-of-fact way in which they recounted their experiences that particularly bothered me, for while they did not shy away from expressing their anger and frustration, they also took it for granted that this is simply the way life is. Basically, they saw their own families as "okay," although they saw the families of others who lived similar lives as "bad." Both the girls and their parents appeared to be looking through a glass darkly and not seeing their own reflections.

The PARENTS

The mothers seemed unable to make the connection between life as lived within the family and their daughters' involvement in violence. They welcomed me into their homes, gave freely of their time, made me cups of coffee, met me for lunch, attended parent forums, chatted with me on the telephone, and told me details about their private lives that in some cases, they had not shared with anyone else. They wanted to help me to "do something" about youth violence, and I believe they were sincere in that desire. They were committed to the project, as were their daughters, but what they seemed unable to do was to look inward for the answers.

Perhaps the greatest source of my grief was that I saw families in deep trouble, families with multiple and serious problems, who were constructing life worlds and ways of dealing with life that transmitted to their daughters ways of being and doing that did not and could not serve them well. And while these families were engaging in this sad and sorry game of "pass it on," they were also looking around for someone to blame and punish for youth violence. The Young Offenders Act, the Ministry of Social Services, the schools, adolescence itself and hormones, other families — all were candidates for the role of chief culprit. And while they looked elsewhere, I looked to them, not so much as culprits, but as the place to start the work. And as I looked to them, I wondered where one could begin.

My answer to myself was, "Begin at the beginning." The beginning, as I saw it, was the parents' families of origin. In this respect, I have data from Marilee, Mary, and Jenny that are quite similar. They each have fathers who come from families who threw them out at an early age after subjecting them to physical abuse and other effects of parental alcoholism. These three men spent time living on the streets, surviving by dint of hard physical labor and the willingness to use their fists. They got married early in life, around the age of 20 or 21, to women as young as themselves or younger. The women they married (or who married them) also share similar backgrounds.

Two of these women (Mary's and Jenny's mothers) understood that they themselves had been silenced and undervalued as they grew up. Mary's mother describes her father, an educated man with a PhD, as a domineering individual who gave her very clear messages about the unimportance of women and women's ideas and who, to this day, believes that women should be led by the men they are there to serve.

Mary's mother articulated her experiences:

> When it came to getting a college or a university education, my dad just said things like, "You can't" and "Girls can't do this" and messages like, "Look after your man"-type messages instead of "Look after yourself"-type messages... . And I had a hard time talking because I was always scared of people judging me and giving me a hard time. I guess my parents are very judgmental people. You know, whatever you say, you get judged on, instead of being okay.

Jenny's mother described herself as feeling unhappy and invisible as she grew up:

> I was the one daughter, middle child, with an older brother and a younger brother. And my parents were geared towards sports, men's sports, hunting, and I'm not. I didn't really have much to contribute to any conversation. My brothers and my dad, they worked the same type of job, so they had all those things in common. So when I was growing up, I always felt I had nothing to contribute, so I didn't need to say anything. I didn't need to be in the same room ... . I always felt out of place because I'm different; I think I'm different from my family.

The silencing and devaluing at the hands of, and in the name of, men that these women describe is not unlike Linda's account of her mother's experience: "holding everything in until it hurts her" in order to avoid her husband's wrath. It also ties in with Sally's mother's struggle with what she calls her co-dependency, that is, her well-ingrained habit of putting others' (particularly men's) feelings and needs before her own, and her propensity to arrange her life and that of her family to satisfy the demands of her partner (witness her battle with her husband and ex-husband over Sally's school plans). Consistent with the survey findings cited in Chapter Two, namely, that violent girls reported the highest levels of concern about the unequal treatment of women, the key informants were worried about their mothers.

The fathers in each of these families behave in ways that destroy family harmony. Sally's stepfather enters into a sibling rivalry with her out of which come shouting matches that cause the neighbors to call the police. Marilee's father drinks, gets angry, and hits his wife and daughters. Molly's father uses physical force to control his sons, and his sons live out the dominance message in a number of ways, including sexual abuse. Mary's father regularly physically abuses his children. Linda's father rules his household with intimidation and physical abuse. Jenny's grandfather and uncle engage in physical violence, while her father models intimidation in his approach to Jenny's rivals in the community.

In some cases, the mothers fight back. Mary's mother engages in daily battles with her husband over her rights and the rights of her children. Sometimes she uses physical force to restrain her husband's violence; sometimes she uses it to make her point outside the family. Jenny's mother is no longer silent, and where her husband and her daughters are concerned, expresses her views loudly and clearly, as do Molly's and Marilee's mothers. Jenny's mother also engages in verbal battles and even pushing-and-shoving matches with Jenny's friends. Sally's mother does what she can to "make" her husband and her daughter fight less. Sometimes she accomplishes this by yelling and screaming at them. And while the mothers may yell and scream, the effect of this is only momentary, especially where their husbands are concerned. With their husbands, the mothers of the key informants appear to be committed to fighting the same battles over and over again. Linda's mother still maintains a guarded silence, and has been willing to do this for many years.

All these couples, with the exception of Sally's parents, have been married for between 16 and 26 years. All profess a strong commitment to marriage and family, for while Sally's mother and father have been divorced, they have each sought out other partners with whom they intend to remain. When I discussed this with the mothers, they let me know that they were proud of having stayed married for so many years. They interpreted the fact that they had not divorced as a strong indicator that their families were good families. In fact, several mothers told me that they were mystified by their daughter's behavior because after all, mom and dad were still together.

Typically, these women act as both wife and mother to their husbands. In the role of wife, they remain subordinate even while attempting to fight for equality because, despite their considerable efforts, nothing really changes. In the role of mother-to-their-husbands, they admonish and lecture and attempt to teach, they make rules and give ultimatums, and they punish. They also demand that their children behave in ways that won't upset their oldest "man-child." For while they fight for equality on the one hand, they help to maintain their subordinate positions on the other, by assuming responsibility for the family's climate of feeling, specifically the emotional states of their husbands.

Sally's mother's struggle with her "co-dependency" is a good example of this. Although she fights to get free of mothering her husband by managing his emotional world for him, she is unable to understand her own experiences without reference to her "co-dependent" label. Thus encumbered, she is unsure of just how to respond to the inequities around her. Each move she makes must be second-guessed in the light of her "co-dependent" problems: whether to counsel her daughter, even when she intuitively senses trouble on the horizon; whether to entreat her husband and daughter to avoid antagonizing each other; whether to hold the police accountable for following through on the charges laid against her daughter's assailant. Everything she does is colored by the possibility that she may be doing it solely because she is "co-dependent." Thus, wavering and inaction keep her tied to precisely the behavior she is working so hard to change.

The meaning of intimacy

Despite the obvious tension and conflict apparent in all these families, both the mothers of the key informants and their daughters believe they have good families because all family members are "close." In the course of our interviews, I came to recognize that, in the life-worlds of the key informants, being "close" means being deeply emotionally enmeshed, especially in a destructive way. That is, the more family members felt one another's feelings, took on one another's battles, engaged in knowing one another's business, told one another what to do, and attempted to exert control over one another's behavior, the "closer" they were.

In these families, one mark of "closeness" is knowing something about a family member that no one else knows. Thus, to share a secret, or to know the latest family gossip and to team up in an effort to control another's life, makes two people "close." Further, being "close" is often equated with having the right to place demands or expectations on one another. For example, when Mary described herself as close to her brother, she meant she had special privileges with regard to him that gave her first call on his time and attention; in other words, she owned a part of him.

Closeness also extends to exerting strong influence over others' mental, physical, and emotional states. Thus, Jenny's parents and grandparents believe that Jenny made her mother physically ill; Mary's father believes that his children are responsible for his stress, and sees them as the cause of injuries that he suffers while doing things for them; and Molly's mother measures her family's emotional health according to the state of her own feelings. Finally, being close in these families does *not* mean understanding and accepting family members on their own terms, while making an effort to respect and value their unique contributions. Closeness does *not* extend to attempting to understand why people do what they do. Instead, it means that one expects other people to be as much like oneself as possible.

In fact, the state of being close (which is really the state of being the-same-as) is strongly connected to the state of being right and good. Individual differences are not applauded; they are seen as threats to connectedness and goodness. When differences exist, closeness is withheld; family members are rejected, ejected, and excluded, sometimes for many years. A refined individuation of self and other is largely absent here. Closeness is not based in an understanding of individual differences, nor is it based on an acceptance of the kind of mutual independence that ultimately leads to secure notions of relatedness and the possibility of truly loving others for themselves. Instead, it is based on rigid notions of self and others that demand conformity.

Conflict and its resolution

Often, violation of the expectations that arise out of closeness lead to conflict. Conflict very quickly becomes vehement and ugly, and frequently includes physical as well as emotional violence, largely because the perspective in which righteous action is grounded is one that endorses the use of power over others and construes others as the source and cause of one's feelings.

Power in these families is anchored in two things: (a) physical might, and (b) the right to determine and enforce rigidly held rules (and one's own point of view). This right is usually tied to one's role in the family. Roles are hierarchically arranged with fathers at the top, mothers a distant second, and children at the bottom, in descending order according to age.

Fathers can delegate disciplinary duties within the household to mothers, which is the case in both Jenny's and Sally's families. So, for example, when Jenny's mother struggles with Jenny, she engages on the following grounds: (a) because she believes that when she is frustrated with Jenny it is because of something Jenny has done to her (emotional enmeshment); and (b) because she sees it as her job to enforce the household rules, which Jenny is violating. These rules are largely premised on absolute and hierarchical notions of power, such as: "I'm your mother; therefore you do what I say," or, "as long as you're under my roof, I'll call the shots." Therefore, if Jenny does not uphold the rules (behavior that always somehow hurts or offends the rule maker), Jenny is wrong and bad, and deserves to be punished.

In Jenny's family, given the personalizing of all offenses, punishment involves personal rejection which, in its ultimate form, means getting thrown out — out of the house or, in some cases, out of the family. Mary's father proceeds in a similar fashion. If his children displease him, he sees them as the source of his frustration and anger and believes himself to be perfectly justified in yelling at them and pushing them around or beating them if they dare to answer back. When his anger reaches its pinnacle, he threatens to desert his family, or to eject the designated offender, as he did his son. If Molly's mother feels angry or frustrated, she takes this as a signal that something is wrong in the family and goes looking for the source of her frustration among her children. In Marilee's family, the rules are well known: One either upholds them or gets out. Linda's father takes for himself the right to decide what is right and wrong and who deserves punishment, and enforces his views with the aid of belts and sticks. Sally's stepfather yells and screams to make his point. Sally's mother, while somewhat milder than the rest, uses her anger to make her family members behave. All this enforcement involves the use of rough and foul language. People call one another assholes, jerks, and idiots. Girls and women are whores and sluts. Family members tell one another that they are stupid and worthless. The general tone created by the use of such crude language is punitive and judgmental in the extreme.

When conflict arises, resolution is achieved by first establishing the identity of the offender. The offender is relatively easy to find; she is usually the one who has broken the rules and "made" the offended person feel frustrated and angry. When the identity of the culprit has been established, she is then judged and blamed, and held responsible for the offended person's feelings and those of anyone else who has taken the offended person's part. This makes the offender fair game for punishment at the hands of the offended person and his or her allies.

Punishment involves calling the offender names, screaming at her, and (if the offended person is not yet satisfied) pushing the offender around or punching her. The type of punishment and its duration is decided upon by the offended person, and is directly tied to that individual's personal sense of satisfaction. When the offended person is satisfied that punishment has been carried out, order has been restored, and the problem is — for the moment — resolved.

The use of physical and emotional violence is justified on instrumental grounds: Violence is used as a means to stop or control those who are upsetting the person who applies it. Nothing has changed, however, because source and problem have been collapsed into one. The source of the problematic behavior has been punished, but the problem itself (usually a behavior) has not been addressed. No new approaches or strategies have been discussed, negotiated, or modeled. No distinction is made between person and behavior. The message being delivered loudly and clearly is that the offender behaves badly because she *is* bad.

This person-based badness makes the offender deserving of punishment which is specifically aimed at her personhood, that is, punishment that is purposefully designed to hurt and degrade the offender. Acts are overlooked because the focus is on actors. Behavioral alternatives are not considered, because only differences in states of feeling are entertained. Thus, people are not asked to consider different courses of action; they are asked to *be* different people. In the end, people don't really change what they do; they just get better at hiding it and, most of all, at hiding themselves.

Messages conveyed
What, then, do these families offer their daughters as a base for forming interpretations of self and world? What has been conveyed to these girls about men and women, power, relationships, attachment, feelings, conflict, rules, punishment, and most of all, themselves?

They have seen that men are far more important and more powerful than women, and that men's importance is not connected to the contributions they make to the greater good. Rather, it is bound up in their being stronger and more forceful than women. Thus, they have seen that power resides for the most part in physical force, that right is tied to might, and that rules have their source in those who have the power to impose them.

Where relationships are concerned, they have seen that pride is taken in the duration of relationships rather than in their quality, and that relationships are based upon roles rather than the development of mutual understanding. Thus, one stays married simply because one is a wife; one loves one's child simply because she is one's daughter. In this way, these girls have seen their parents partake of relationships that last for many years, yet bring with them continuous cycles of abuse and pain, and in which role-bound behavior never shifts. They have seen that being "close" means having no personal boundaries, that closeness demands sameness and does not tolerate deviation from the narrow confines of being like the person to whom one is close. Further, this closeness also demands the ability to anticipate the needs and wants of others and the ability to feel another's feelings.

They have seen that feelings are caused by forces outside themselves and arise because of what others do; thus, feelings must be controlled through controlling others. They have seen that conflict arises out of creating destructive feelings in others, feelings' for which the offending person is solely responsible, and which justify the offended person's wrath. They have seen that when wrath has been aroused, punishment must follow, a punishment that is administered in a fit of rage and is designed to maximize the pain of the offending person.

As indicated by the self-report data generated by the *Survey of Student Life* (Artz & Riecken, 1994), violent girls reported the highest rates of fear of, and experience with, physical abuse. Physical and emotional abuse were certainly facts of life for the key informants. All had been beaten at home, and had witnessed the beating of other family members. The implicit message conveyed to them here is that when someone behaves badly, it is because he or she is bad.

This sense of badness is intensified by the shared language of these interactions. The message that speaks to the badness of the offender is delivered with tones of voice and gestures that underline the worthlessness of the offender, while the labels and judgments that are being hurled at her make clear exactly how she is being construed. "Look what you've done to your mother, you fucking little whore!" leaves little room for doubt.

How are these interactions translated into notions of self and world?

Experiences of Self

Each of the key informants left me with a unique impression of how she saw herself. Sally presented herself as a "Skate," a member of a recognizable street group, and as an individual enamored with being "weird, original, and different," someone who loves attention and enjoys provoking shocked reactions in other people. Marilee presented herself as one very much involved in trying to be "the person she is supposed to be," someone who plans to break the cycle of family violence through creating a traditional and harmonious, "white-picket fence" future for herself. Molly described herself mostly as confused and stressed by her experiences with abuse. Mary saw herself as the champion of just causes and defender of the underdog, a person who takes charge and takes people on. Linda saw herself as struggling to overcome her experiences with sexual abuse. Jenny presented herself as a person who loves to fight and is intrigued by death.

Although each girl's self-image was unique, each of the six had a great deal in common with the other five, whether they happened to be opponents or allies. Each had come forward as a participant in the study first of all because she had identified herself as a victim of female-to-female violence. After some discussion, each participant also emerged as a perpetrator, an individual as experienced with threatening, intimidating, and beating others as she was with being attacked. The key informants' self-reports with regard to participation in violence and victimization fit with the data generated by the *Survey of Student Life* (Artz & Riecken, 1994) in that they, like the violent girls who participated in the survey, were both perpetrators and victims.

Anger

As a group, the key informants presented themselves as tough and street-wise, knowledgeable about and connected with most aspects of youth violence in their community, and willing to take on those who dared to question their carefully crafted images of power. They also shared a deeply felt anger which at times turned into rage, even hate; and they shared a painful sense of loneliness and abandonment.

As the girls discussed their anger, I saw a strong connection with the physical and emotional abuse they suffered at home, and in Jenny's case, also with the bullying and degradation she experienced while in elementary school. I also saw a strong connection with the sexual abuse that five of the six suffered at the hands of someone they knew and trusted. Their loneliness and abandonment — exemplified through Sally's and Jenny's search for connectedness and belonging in groups like the Skates and the Rappers, Mary's notion of herself as "an outcasted little person," Linda's isolation from her family, Molly's unfulfilled need to be safe and understood in her own home, and Marilee's view of the world as a "piece of shit" — seem to be tied, in large part, to the same experiences that engender the key informants' anger. Having been violated physically, emotionally, and in some cases also sexually, the key informants seemed to have little hope that they could trust even those closest to them.

Fear

Even when the girls thought that they could depend upon their families (as Jenny did when she expressed the belief that her father and grandfather would protect and defend her, or take retaliatory action if someone hurt her), they seemed unable to let their guard down for any length of time. Her family's support did not exempt Jenny from feeling that she must always "watch her back," and from hoping to find refuge in a local gang.

The notion of having to "watch one's back" was one that also affected the other informants: Marilee feared leaving her own neighborhood to go downtown or to school; she feared being exposed as a "narc" because she had talked to me. Similar fear showed itself in Mary's offensive and belligerent approach to adult authority figures. It also came out in the generally defensive way in which all six girls positioned themselves in relation to those around them.

Self-worth

Despite describing themselves as tough and powerful, the key informants also saw themselves as lacking worth in their own eyes and in the eyes of others.

Jenny described herself as "fat and ugly"; Marilee felt herself to be one of the "scummy" people who aligned herself with "losers." Linda, in the aftermath of her sexual abuse, thought of herself as a "bad person," bad-tempered and deserving of the abuse she received at the hands of her father. Mary felt she was not liked by her teachers and was stereotyped as a "bad kid" by the vice-principal of her school. Though she sometimes felt responsible for her father's problems, she was also keenly aware that he considered her less important and less able because she is a girl.

Sally, in her persona as a Skate, saw herself as a member of a group of outcasts, people who are generally singled out by others, especially

Rappers, as targets for aggression. She also felt ignored by her parents and rejected and disliked by her stepmother. Molly, who struggled with the designation of "slut" after being sexually abused while drunk at a party, described herself as having no morals and as being somehow hurtful to her family because she disclosed that she had been sexually abused by her brother.

Although the *Survey of Student Life* (Artz & Riecken, 1994) indicated that self-concept was not necessarily connected to participation in violence, the descriptions of self offered by the key informants left no doubt that their self-concept was tied to a sense of worthlessness.

This sense of worthlessness became even more clear when they talked about their bodies. In describing how they believed they should look, the key informants endorsed the standard for beauty identified and questioned by Wolf (1990) as a "mass disseminated physical ideal" which holds up the "gaunt youthful model" as the example of what all women must embody in order to have personal and social worth (pp. 11–12). Each girl saw herself through the eyes of those who might be looking at her and judged herself according to that mass disseminated ideal.

None of the key informants believed that she measured up. Instead, each believed that she was constantly in competition with other girls and, most of all, with the examples of ideal womanhood created by the entertainment and fashion industries. All the informants felt great pressure to be "thin and perfect."

The general acceptance that girls should be thin was indicated in the *Survey of Student Life* (Artz & Riecken, 1994) by the significant number of girls who reported stopping themselves from eating. Sally put it most clearly when she said that in her world, most boys and many girls believe that all young women should look like supermodel Cindy Crawford, "who is underweight, and has like a perfect body." Jenny, in describing her struggle with being bullied for being fat and her subsequent refusal to eat, made clear how difficult and painful nonconformity to socially sanctioned standards of female beauty can be. Marilee was so focused on competition from other females that she deliberately chose friends whom she considered not competitive, that is, not as attractive as herself.

All the key informants looked to males for acceptance and confirmation of their worth. For Jenny and Marilee, confirmation came from having a boyfriend. Jenny, in particular, placed a great deal of importance upon being sought after by boys, and was happy with herself only when receiving attention from males. Sally's confirmation of worth came from being accepted by male Skaters as more than a mere "poser." For Mary and Linda, confirmation was very much tied to acknowledgment from their fathers, something that they experienced only rarely. Molly's confirmation of worth came from being protected by her older brother — the same person who abused her.

Goals and aspirations

The desire for acceptance and acknowledgment from males is also revealed in the key informants' plans for the future. Their aspirations are very traditional: They want to get married and raise children, even though they have strong fears (even revulsion) with respect to pregnancy and childbirth. They have no career plans and no goals or plans for further education beyond finishing high school. They want to get jobs that are merely jobs — that is, a way of making money, seen as a means to achieve their central goal of marriage. Marilee and Jenny are so certain of marriage and children that they have made choices with these goals in mind, and thus, behave in very male-focused ways.

Growing up female

Overall, despite their desire and their efforts, positive acknowledgment from males is not a common experience for the key informants. Mostly, they see themselves as being discriminated against because of being female.

Sally spoke of being excluded from certain aspects of skateboarding and snowboarding because of being female. Jenny lamented being barred from boxing for the same reason. Mary talked about not being considered an able helper in her father's construction business, despite having demonstrated both skill and reliability, merely because she was female. She also talked of her extended workday serving her father and her brother and attending to all the domestic chores, including the care of the family's animals. Mary, Marilee, and Linda also described being emotionally and physically abused by their fathers. In general, in each of the key informants' households, the orientation is not one of equality and respect for women, but rather, the opposite.

Consistent with the significantly high levels of reported sexual abuse among violent girls generated by the *Survey of Student Life* (Artz & Riecken, 1994), all six key informants have received sexually abusive messages and sexually harassing or abusive treatment from males that "made them feel low." The degradation they experienced as part of being female was graphically illustrated by the examples they gave of sexual harassment at school (see Chapter Five, "Molly's Story"). Everyday life for them meant running a gauntlet of staring eyes, groping hands, and derogatory comments about their bodies. Although they despised such treatment, they saw it as an integral and inevitable part of being female. Similarly, they saw the males' behavior as so much a part of being male that they explained it (to themselves and to me) as being caused by hormones — physical urges beyond the control of the offensive boys.

As the key informants see it, there is nothing particularly positive about being female. A girl has to be vigilant about staying thin; she is restricted with regard to the kinds of activities she can undertake; she is less respected and less important than a boy. She is routinely subjected to sexual discrimination and harassment. If she attempts to take the initiative or experiment sexually, she is a "slut" and deserves a beating. If a woman has children, she faces a great deal of pain, and if her husband is present to see the "mess," she risks losing him because, through pregnancy and childbirth, her body becomes unattractive.

Role models

The notion that women achieve their greatest importance when they command attention from males was elaborated in the key informants' choice of role models. Sally, Marilee, Molly, Linda, and Jenny all named Madonna as their number one female idol. The reason they each gave was best expressed by Sally: "She can do anything she wants and not care what anybody thinks of her."

Yet, Madonna's power and freedom rest on her ability to capitalize on the sexual double standard. She derives her position primarily from displaying herself sexually, from "holding onto the sustained mass patriarchal gaze for as long as she can keep the public's attention" (hooks, 1994, p. 12). Far from being a symbol of female power and creativity, Madonna has played into exactly those images and values that serve to underline women's roles as sexual objects. She has become a major link in what hooks (1994) describes as "the marketing chain that exploits representations of sexuality and the body for profit, a chain which focuses on images that were once taboo," a chain aimed directly at those conventional consumers of pornography, men (pp. 14–15).

The role that Madonna offers to women is that of the classic whore. The joke is in her name, though I doubt that the girls who participated in this study understood this. They see her as powerful because she can get away with behavior that they can't. If they acted like her, someone — probably a group of girls — would beat them up. They see her as being able outdo all other women and attract the desiring gaze of millions of men, with no one to beat her at her game.

I feel my key informants missed the point here, because they failed to recognize Madonna's extreme dependence. They also missed the significance of her violent marriage to Sean Penn. Further, they missed the ignorance, and the danger and hate for females in Madonna's statement about male violence against women: "I think for the most part if women are in an abusive relationship and they know it and if they stay in it they must be digging it" (hooks, 1994, p. 17). Far from offering women freedom and power, Madonna offers them the most standard form of enslavement that exists for women.

Of the six key informants, only Mary did not completely accept all of the above. She believed that "sluts" deserved to be beaten; she accepted that males could and would treat females in demeaning ways. But she did not want to be like Madonna. She had given up on being thin and sexy and on attracting male attention through conforming to what, for her, were standards of beauty that were impossible to achieve. Instead, she concentrated on getting her father's attention through proving to him that she was as good as any male. She focused on correcting her father's behavior and making him over into the kind of man to whom she could relate. She saw nothing intrinsically useful or valuable in being female. She found value in emulating males, and described herself proudly as a tomboy. She did not understand that being one of the boys offers girls no autonomous value at all.

Oppressed group behavior and horizontal violence

In according women and girls so little intrinsic value, and particularly in selecting as targets for female-to-female violence girls whom they see as having lost all worth (because they appear to be sexually accessible), the key informants seem to be exhibiting what Roberts (1983; after Friere, 1971) calls "oppressed group behavior." Such behavior is premised upon an "attitude of adhesion to the oppressor" (Friere, 1971, p. 30), which demands that those who suffer at the hands of the dominant group turn upon members of their own kind whenever they behave in ways that are deemed unacceptable to the dominant group.

Because all standards and roles are prescribed by the dominant group, the subordinate group's greatest hope lies in achieving dominant-group standards and fully enacting the roles assigned to them. At the same time, another possibility is held out to the subordinate group: If their members could but emulate the dominant group well enough, they might be offered acceptance by it; perhaps even membership in it. (This is the approach Mary has taken.)

In the world in general, and in the life-worlds of the key informants in particular, males are the dominant, women the subordinate group. Further, as members of a subgroup of girls who come from homes where women are given even less value than usual, these six girls and others like them are yet more vulnerable to the internalization of oppressed group behavior. It is not surprising that they think of girls and women as they do. In accepting without question that girls and women must submit themselves to the needs and expectations of boys and men, the key informants make manifest the values that permeate their lives and engage in behavior that is characteristic of oppressed groups. Specifically, in the hope of gaining a measure of power, they engage in "horizontal violence" — that is, they beat each other up.

Roberts (1983) shows that such behavior does nothing more than support the status quo. Noting that leaders of powerless groups are generally controlling, coercive, and rigid, and that members of oppressed groups often spend most of their aggressive energy in hurting one another, Roberts (1983) suggests that such horizontal violence is a safe way to release tension: The threat posed by members of one's own group is never as great as that posed by the dominant group. When aggression is directed at members of the dominant group, little changes. Subordinate-group members can never fully assimilate, since they will always be members of the group to which they were, by definition, originally assigned.

Obviously, a girl or woman can never be a boy or a man, no matter how much she assumes the characteristics of males. In fact, too much emulation puts a girl or woman in danger of losing any kind of group membership and with it, any chance of belonging. Too much emulation leads to marginalization, the inability to belong either to one's group of origin (because one has assimilated so many characteristics of the dominant group) or to the dominant group (because of one's origins). Thus relegated to the fringes, a marginalized person has nowhere to go except to those who are similarly marginalized (Roberts, 1983). It is no accident that the six key informants are so well known to one another.

Friends and Friendship

The low value the six key informants placed upon women and girls also came through, in part, as they discussed their friends and their notions of friendship. Although all seemed to place importance upon friendship and all believed they should fight to defend their friends (another finding of the *Survey of Student Life* [Artz & Riecken, 1994]), their friendships with other girls were tenuous relationships that tended to shift over time. In some cases, these were alliances made on the basis of having a common female enemy rather than a genuine bond based on care and trust.

Each girl described a relationship with a "best friend" that involved ambivalence and conflict. Sally described her friendship with Adel, who betrayed her, as a close friendship, but one that involved loving to see each other get pushed around. Although Marilee considered that her friendship with Sarah required her to help Sarah beat up Sally, she also saw it as a relationship she didn't really want to bother with, one that she continued largely because Sarah was a good source of information about boys. In Mary's friendship with Cathy (the girl who beat up Molly), she saw herself as the one who prevented Cathy from descending further into violence, yet she herself was prepared to use violence against Cathy. Mary was also prepared to use violence against Tanya, her closest female friend. In Jenny's friendships, girls shifted from being enemies to friends and back again as they competed for male attention. This theme was mirrored in Marilee's friendships with girls.

During the time I spent meeting with Molly, Linda, and Mary as a group, I witnessed some of these shifts in allegiance. When Molly, despite swearing an oath of confidentiality to Linda and Mary, broke that oath and disclosed Linda's history of sexual abuse to others, she sacrificed Linda to her own immediate need for attention. Linda and Mary then banded together with Molly as their common enemy. Later, when Linda excluded Mary from a social outing, Mary became angry and was Linda's enemy for a time.

Mary was also "best friends" with Faye and Brent, yet cut her ties with both when they became friends with each other. While Mary was struggling with the changes in these dynamics, she phoned me several times to discuss her feelings of anger and loneliness. She wrestled with the question of whether she should beat up Faye, finally deciding against this, largely because I insisted that beating someone up was not a viable method for resolving a dispute. She, in turn, made it clear to me that refraining from violence, at least in this case, carried a high price for her: It meant that she would have to forego the cathartic experience of unleashing her anger against her friend and "letting her have what she deserved." Consistent with the notion that connections with boys are of greater value than connections with girls, Mary ultimately placed more importance on her friendship with Brent. Although she cut her ties with him as she did with Faye, it was the loss of her friendship with Brent that Mary mourned.

Sally's friendships with Beverley and Lorraine (the other two "beastie girls") were not as subject to the shifts in alliance that characterized most of the key informants' relationships. What struck me about this group of friends, however, was the underlying sense of isolation, especially from family, that brought these three together. In seeking one another out, and in seeking out groups like the Skates, the Rappers, and the Bloods, Sally and her friends seemed to be looking for somewhere to belong.

What the key informants sought from their affiliation with a group was attention and a sense that they had worth in other people's eyes, a feeling of safety, an identity, and a surrogate family. Further, they were willing to put themselves at considerable risk in order to achieve this.

Social Activities

The groups the key informants sought out engage in risky and potentially harmful behaviors. Drugs and alcohol are regularly misused, violence is a pastime as well as a means to an end, sex is largely akin to sexual abuse, and danger is glamorized.

The six key informants and their friends gather at corner stores, Seven-Eleven convenience markets, fast-food restaurants, shopping malls, and school yards. The main attraction of these public venues is other people and the possibility of excitement, any kind of excitement.

In imitating the Beastie Boys, Sally and her friends regularly take chances. They engage strangers on street corners in order to try to provoke some kind of action or reaction. Sally's romantic notions about gangs as safe havens and gang members as friendly people make her vulnerable to being drawn into activities that involve harm to herself and others. The same is true of Jenny, who referred to gangs with the same enthrallment that Sally did. Marilee is similarly attracted to people who participate in deviant and criminal activities, such as the "friend" who committed a drive-by shooting. These girls seemed to value the notoriety that they believed rubbed off on them as a consequence of knowing someone "really bad."

The *Survey of Student Life* (Artz & Riecken, 1994) indicated that violent school girls and boys considered parties of great importance, and parties were indeed very important to all the key informants. Mary's idea of a "really good time" was an all-night party at which 20 to 30 young people got together to drink and do drugs without interruption. At such parties (which happen almost every weekend at houses where the parents are away, or at the beach, or in some other place chosen for its remoteness from adults), "accidents" happen. People drink so much that they become violently ill, and in some cases, incur alcoholic poisoning. Sexual intercourse takes place in a way that leaves no participant free of the taint of having taken part, voluntarily or otherwise, in a degrading act. People drive cars while "under the influence," harming or killing themselves and others.

The adults involved in the key informants' lives have provided ample modeling of such behavior in that they themselves engage in just such activities. They sometimes provide not only the example but, as in Marilee's and Mary's cases, also the means, by purchasing alcohol for their children. Each of the girls had her first encounter with drunken behavior in her own family.

In all these social interactions one finds an ever-present undercurrent of violence. In fact, violence that seems poised to erupt at any moment is sometimes the focus of social engagement. Thus, fights don't only happen; they are arranged. Factions are formed, audiences gather, violence is orchestrated. As Mary pointed out, fighting is "entertainment sort of, a lot of people want to see somebody get their butt kicked in real life. It's kind of like TV."

Fighting between girls carries added entertainment value; it is, as Molly pointed out, not only physically, but also sexually exciting for the boys. According to Molly (and Mary, Linda, and Jenny, who concurred), boys like to watch girls fight because "it gets them pumped. It gets them excited, not in the physical, in the sexual." Thus — given the key informants' internalized attitudes of adhesion to the oppressor, their propensity for horizontal violence, and their need for attention from males — these girls fight to oblige their confreres.

The Rules of Violence

Besides its entertainment value, the key informants made it clear that for them, violence is not chiefly a matter of lashing out in the heat of the moment. Instead, it is a rule-bound and purposeful activity engaged in to redress the intolerable imbalances they perceive in their largely hierarchical social world. An imbalance usually arises when the rules, which form a kind of code of conduct, have been broken.

For example, when a grade eight girl "mouths off" a grade nine or ten girl, a lower-grade, lower-status girl has attempted to behave in a manner acceptable only for someone with higher status in a higher grade. That is, she is acting "cocky" when she should be subordinate, and thus, may rate a beating. Or, one girl may decide it is her right (usually because she is older or stronger or tougher or prettier or better established) to forbid others to wear certain kinds of clothing, yet another girl may wear those clothes anyway, either in defiance or out of sheer ignorance. In this case, the offending girl should "know better," and is now at risk for attack. Or, a girl has entered territory that is not her turf but is the turf of another girl (perhaps a "gang" girl); she looks the other over (or worse yet, looks at the girl's boyfriend) in a manner that is deemed provocative. Or, a girl has talked to other girls about her interest in a boy already designated as another's boyfriend; she may now be called a "slut" and may receive a beating from her peers.

Some rules, if broken, are sufficient in and of themselves to be construed as provocation to violence. Others need to be broken several times, or in combination, before they constitute cause for retribution. For example, mouthing off an older girl might not be enough cause for an immediate fight, but it will start the meter ticking in the countdown to provocation. Eyeing the wrong boy could start a fight (especially if the offender is dressed in a way that meets with the disapproval of the girl who has claimed the boy being eyed), but then again, it might merit only a strongly worded warning. Provocation, while definitely a rule-bound construct, is also governed to some degree by personal perception and mood (e.g., Mary gave Jenny a second chance, while Linda did not). However, talking about being interested in someone else's boyfriend is a clear violation of the code, an infraction almost certain to lead to the designation of "slut." This insult, in turn, rates highest on the list of possible provocations, and demands immediate redress.

If the rules are broken, girls will set upon each other, usually one-on-one, but often with help from a best friend, who is bound by further aspects of the code to lend such assistance. Others (sometimes as many as 300) will look on without attempting to stop the fight. Spectators too are bound by the code, which dictates their behavior be passive — to the point that few witnesses ever "snitch." The combatants will beat each other mercilessly until one, most often the one who has "brought the beating on herself" by breaking the code, is black and blue with bruises and bloody with cuts, usually to her face. The bruises are simply part of the action; the cuts are deliberate, put there by rings worn expressly as weapons. In the eyes of the assailants, no wrong has been done. Why not? Because (as all the girls I spoke with told me at one point or another) "I never hit anyone unless I have to," and "I only hit people who deserve it." For them, the beatings they dole out are punishment, and the punishment only fits the crime.

Shifting responsibility

This notion that hitting and beating one's chosen victim is the "right thing to do" bears further examination. At various times during our conversations, each of the six key informants told me she was against violence. All participated in the study because they saw themselves as contributors to violence prevention. But all of them also felt completely justified in beating those girls whom they had beaten. Further, in every case, the perpetrator found ways to shift the responsibility for the beating onto the person whom she was beating. None of the key informants found her way to feeling empathy for her victim. As each girl saw it, she was meting out just punishment, "doing the right thing."

In shifting the moral and causal responsibility for their violent action from themselves to their victims, the key informants appeared to recreate their parents' ways of making sense of their own punitive and violent behavior. When lashing out against, berating, and physically beating their daughters, these parents regularly blamed the girls for creating the feelings and behaviors that the parents exhibited. Using the premise "look what you made me do" as justification, the parents (and the key informants themselves) locate the source of their own violence in those whom they attack, and thereby excuse themselves from responsibility for their actions.

In constructing others as deserving of punishment, the key informants always believe that their own actions are both just and inevitable (i.e., determined by their victims). True to symbolic interactionist notions that people "act towards each other and toward things in terms of the meanings that these … have for them, and these perspectives are the basis for their reality" (Prus, 1994, p. 19), the key informants beat their victims because of the meanings they impute to their victims' behaviors.

This way of making sense of aggressive and violent behavior is reminiscent of Katz's (1988) analysis of the dynamics between interrogator and interrogee in a war zone. Interrogators routinely escalate the amount of physical assault and torture that they visit upon interrogees in the name of "having to" keep up the pressure in order to achieve their goal of procuring the required information. Beginning with the premise that the captured interrogee is undoubtedly somehow connected to the enemy, the interrogator moves forward on what Katz calls the "paths of determinism," which demand that he fulfill his obligation to extract the necessary intelligence. Citing the "Americal Rule" (sic) employed by the U.S. military in Vietnam as an example ("If he wasn't a Vietcong then, he sure as hell is one now"), Katz (1988, p. 6) notes:

> At the start, interrogators were often unsure of the political sympathies of the interrogee, but in the end it did not matter. Either the interrogee was a Vietcong sympathizer or, if not, the eminently dispassionate reasoning went, he was likely to turn hostile after being slapped unjustly. In either case, it was reasonable after a while to consider his failure to cooperate as being motivated by malevolence. At that point, the interrogee's hostility is blocking the progress of the interrogation and thus is provocative: the *interrogee* is giving the *interrogator* a hard time!

Marilee, in making sense of her involvement in beating Sally, used just such a rationale. Citing the determinants that Sally had (a) expressed an interest in Sarah's boyfriend, (b) apparently called

Sarah a "slut" behind her back, and (c) in the course of attempting to resist being beaten, broken one of Marilee's nails and bled onto Sarah's sweater, Marilee construed Sally's behavior as the cause of what followed.

Indeed, each of the key informants, in describing her involvement in physical violence against others, expunged herself of responsibility in the name of being forced to respond as she had because of her victim's behavior. This construction of the victim as the original assailant clearly recalls the reasoning used by the informants' parents when attacking them.

Noticeably absent in this way of viewing victims is the "different voice" — the voice of a morality of care and response to others — described by Gilligan (1983) in her work on the moral development of women and girls. Gilligan and her colleagues (Gilligan, Ward, & Taylor, 1988; Gilligan, Lyons, & Hanmer, 1990; Brown & Gilligan, 1992) have conducted research with students at the Emma Willard School, an independent high school for girls in Boston, from 1981 to 1984, and the Laurel School, an independent coeducational high school in Cleveland, from 1985 to 1989. They have consistently found that adolescent girls are strongly motivated by relational concerns and by a desire to help others — even, on occasion, at the expense of self. Although Gilligan and her colleagues have never made the claim that all girls approach life in this way, they have stated that girls, more than boys, demonstrate the inclination to avoid conflict and understand moral problems in the light of a commitment to the preservation of relationships. They found little evidence of victim blaming and the displacing of moral responsibility from assailant to victim in the way that Katz (1988) and the key informants describe it.

Victim blaming as a phenomenon was not, however, identified by Katz (1988); it was previously recorded and explored by psychologists focusing on moral development. Arbuthnot (1992) points out that nearly all the studies examining moral reasoning of delinquents (male and female) that he reviewed give examples of shifting moral and causal responsibility from assailant to victim in just the manner displayed by the key informants in this study. Basing his analysis on Kohlberg (1969, 1984), Arbuthnot suggests that such moral reasoning is limited and indicative of Stage 1 and Stage 2 (of a possible six stages) of Kohlberg's Stages of Sociomoral Reasoning. These stages are described by Kohlberg as "preconventional" (Colby & Kohlberg, 1987,

p. 18) and circumscribed by a social perspective that is both self-centered and self-serving.

In Kohlberg's terms, in Stage 1 of moral development, an individual exhibits a "heteronomous morality [one that is subject to external controls] which equates right behavior with concrete rules backed by power and punishment" (Arbuthnot, 1992, p. 286). In Stage 2, an individual takes an individualistic utilitarian approach, in which "right behavior is that which serves one's own interests," and one is "aware of others' needs in an elementary fashion, but not of others' rights" (Arbuthnot, 1992, p. 286). Thus, fairness is "strict, rigid, [and] concrete," and "reciprocal agreements are pragmatic" (Arbuthnot, 1992, p. 286).

According to Kohlberg and Colby (1987), one can expect to find a clear relationship between age and stage of moral judgment. For example, one typically finds Stage 1 and Stage 2 moral reasoning at or around age 10. At age 13 to 14, there is usually evidence of a move from Stage 2 to Stage 3, with a concomitant perspectival shift to a "conventional" level of moral reasoning. This implies that the individual is now able to see beyond his or her own immediate needs or desires to the good of the group and, later, the good of society (Colby & Kohlberg, 1987, p. 18). In Stage 3, an individual exhibits the need to be a good person, the desire to care for others, and a belief in the Golden Rule. If such reasoning is not found by the age of 13 or 14, the individual is said to exhibit a developmental delay (Arbuthnot, 1992; Colby & Kohlberg, 1987).

In light of the above, the question then arises: Are we to take the key informants' behavior as the outcome of a symbolic interaction in which they have pursued the "good" by constructing as necessary, though undesirable, the use of violence against someone who has violated or threatened group norms? Or, are we are to take their behavior as the outcome of delayed moral development? The answer to this question is beyond the scope of this study; it is posed as groundwork for further research.

Porter (1991) provides some direction for such an undertaking. She suggests that, by construing moral decisions as the outcomes of underlying developmentally driven cognitive structures, systems such as Kohlberg's fail to take into account both the agency of persons as self-interpreting beings and the personal context of moral dilemmas. It is Porter's contention that if one is to understand moral judgment, one must first of all understand the interpretative, contextual basis of that judgment. To that end, one must engage the interpretative self of those involved and work from there. If one were to engage another person's interpretative self with the notion in mind that this individual suffers from a developmental delay and must therefore be stimulated to mature along appropriate lines, one may foreclose the kind of dialogue that can promote understanding — and with it, change.

Further Dimensions of Violence

Along with the shifting of moral and causal responsibility for their violent actions from themselves to their victims, the key informants share one other similarity with the interrogators described by Katz (1988): They are drawn further into violence by the sensual dimensions of participating in violent behavior.

As Katz (1988) describes it, assailants appear to experience first of all an imperative to attack their victims based on construing the victim as the cause of the aggressor's displeasure. This engenders a heightened sense of excitement and passion, along with a seductive compulsion to engage in violence until that passion is spent. According to Katz, the emotions that seem to be most potent in fueling the assailant's moral righteousness are frustration, humiliation, shame, hurt, and anger, all of which call forth a need to redress a perceived imbalance of power (Katz, 1988, pp. 4–11).

In justifying their involvement in violence, the key informants singled out these same emotions. For them, humiliation especially — that is, being seen to be put down, threatened, or otherwise undercut, either through word or deed — called forth their anger and their need to retaliate. Thus engaged, the assailant's emotions and sensations serve to heighten the conviction that the assailant must act.

In describing what it felt like to engage in violence, the key informants talked about excitement, adrenaline rushes, and the feeling of "getting pumped." They described the anger and rage they felt towards their victims, and the sense of well-being and power they experienced when they had beaten someone up. They mentioned the importance of discharging their anger against the victim who had, after all, caused that anger in the first place.

The emotional quality of their violent interactions can be further understood through attending to the key informants' language.

Describing one's victims as "sluts," "total bitches," "cocky little bitches," "assholes," or "jerks" suggests a unilateral construction of one's opponents as detestable and worthy only of contempt. As I have said elsewhere (Artz, 1994), the words we use are the windows to the worlds in which we live. That is, the words that we choose in order to describe our experience reveal how we have interpreted that experience. This is not a new notion, but one that has been considered and explored by others.[1]

If we listen to the language of the key informants, we can hear echoes of life worlds that are harsh and mean and crude. As Marilee said, "the world is a piece of shit"; or, as Linda and Mary believe, it is a place where one is forlorn and lonely, "outcasted"; and where, as Jenny says, "you've gotta watch your back." This is a graphic indictment of a life-world in which violence and abuse are part of the fabric of everyday life.

Violence in Schools

Schools are sites for everyday violence. Much of the violence in which the key informants were involved took place in school corridors, school yards, on the way to and from school, in front of the corner stores, and in the shopping malls closest to the schools. While schools and school districts don't cause violence, they do provide the ground for the social networks that support it: They draw together all the young people of a certain age in a given area and demand that they operate within a certain set of rules, in a certain building, under the guidance and supervision of a relatively small number of adults.

With few exceptions, most people between the ages of five and 18 go to school. In the province of British Columbia, where this study was undertaken, one cannot legally leave school before the age of 15, and school boards are obliged to provide all students within their jurisdiction with educational programming until they attain that age.

The key informants most often met their victims, and were themselves selected by others as targets, while they were at school. Yet, students alone are not responsible for all school conflict. Educators, administrators, and support staff each make their own contributions to the overall climate, which is on occasion hostile. It may further be argued that structural aspects of the education system, such as graduated grades and the investment of authority and power in educators and administrators (i.e., the older and stronger) over students (i.e., the younger and weaker), become — along with examples set by rigid and controlling parents — models for the rule-bound and hierarchical system the students themselves set up in order to control one another. Within the forced confinement of a school building, human dramas are enacted that necessarily involve rubbing up against other people in ways that are not always optimal or pleasant. Invariably, conflict arises; and when it does, violence is sometimes the result.

In the *Survey of Student Life* (Artz & Riecken, 1994), 28.2% of students (males and females) reported that they agreed with the statement, "If I don't like my teacher, it's okay to act up in school." High-deviant girls, and girls who identified themselves as having beaten up another kid at least once in the past year, reported subscribing to this notion with an agreement rate of 41.9%, while girls who were not in the high-deviant/violent group reported an agreement rate of 11.9%.

The key informants in this study believed that actions from school personnel or other students demanded aggressive and violent reactions whenever they (a) showed the key informants a lack of respect, (b) subjected them to a loss of status or power, or (c) perpetrated an injustice against them. Whether these reactions were directed against their teachers and school administrators or against fellow students is immaterial. For the key informants, violence is not necessarily desirable, but it is necessary. When they resort to it, it is because they perceive that they must.

In the last chapter of this book, I offer some suggestions on how schools may help to change this perception.

NOTES

1. For example, the philosopher Wilhelm von Humboldt (1767–1835) wrote that, because of the mutual dependency of thought and word, language is not so much a means of representing the truth that has already been ascertained, as it is a means of discovering the truth not previously known (cited in Edwards, 1967, p. 74).

CHAPTER TEN

WHAT IS TO BE DONE?

> What would the ideal program for girls include? There are no easy answers to this particularly since the literature evaluating programs is quite lean, and especially so in regard to programs for girls. Further, a fair number of components of model programs rely on family-strengthening strategies; these need to be reviewed with care, given the gendered nature of family life and girls' special problems within families. (Chesney-Lind & Shelden, 1992, p. 198)

> Readers may be disappointed if they expect to learn of many innovative, effective programs. Many evaluations of particular approaches do not deal with gender issues and frequently the evaluated programs do not even serve girls. (Chesney-Lind & Shelden, 1992, p. 183)

WHAT THE KEY INFORMANTS WANT

Like the participants in the *Survey of Student Life* (Artz & Riecken, 1994), the key informants of this study place a high value on being respected and liked, and on belonging. They want their parents and their teachers to listen to them and to treat them as if they have value and importance. They want their friends to do the same, and they want their peers — that is, those with whom they interact at school and in their social milieu — to give them what they believe is their due. This means that younger students should defer to older students, and no one should behave as Jenny does, that is, be "mouthy and cocky and try to act like King Shit," especially if she is "merely" a grade eight student in the presence of grade tens. For the key informants, hierarchies make sense, and given their internalized oppression, this comes as no surprise.

Being heard and being acknowledged seem to take precedence over just about everything else. Over and over, the key informants emphasized the importance of being heard and of receiving respect and attention. Positive attention is best, but negative attention is better than no attention at all.

Status, too, is important. It can be achieved through acquiring a "tough rep" as surely as it can through more conventional means, such as good grades and participation on school teams. Notoriety has its attractions; at least it ensures being known.

Being feared, or knowing people who are feared, also has its uses to the key informants. It offers a sense of security, however false. As Sally said after her beating: "I have like tons of friends in gangs and I'm not even scared."

When I asked how girls should be dealt with vis-à-vis their participation in violence, Mary (acting as a spokesperson for violent girls during a two-day community think tank on youth violence) said:

> Girls who get into trouble probably have some sort of self-confidence problems, and they need to figure out who they are, like by going to counseling. And, like, I think they should get community work, not just community hours. They should do something which is working within the community, doing something constructive instead of just sweeping grounds or whatever, something they can learn from instead of the punishment-type thing, something they might want to carry on after it's all done... .
>
> And their parents need counseling, their fathers need help, they're like the main source of the problem, and their mothers need something like a "Speak Out" group, a group where you get together with a bunch of people and learn to tell your feelings and thoughts and things instead of just being in a corner and being quiet. The mothers need to learn to be their own person and not be ordered around by their husband or being pushed around by their husband. If they're not being pushed around then they can get out of the situations they're in ... .
>
> And the victims need help, they need to get their self-conscious built, or their self-esteem built, because most people don't try to steal other people's boyfriends and go around calling people sluts and whatnot. There's gotta be something wrong there. Seems to me that those people are doing things the wrong way, trying to get on top in a negative way, and then they get pounded on. When you're a teenager you're in kind of a conflict position where you have to keep your own position and not let people put you down.

On the subject of violence prevention and intervention, Mary offered several suggestions:

1. With regard to the large number of students who choose to be spectators when there is a fight:

> Watching fights is just a normal occurrence. I mean if there's a fight happening, then everyone goes, "Oh, oh, I wanna see it." It's sort of like an entertainment-type thing 'cause they're bored 'cause there's nothing else to do, and it's not like it's an everyday occurrence. So there's some people where they're just like going, "I wanna be there," kind of thing. I remember last year they tried to suspend people who were viewing fights, and there ended up being so many people around the fights that they couldn't suspend everybody so — I think if

they sorta prepared people or like suggest and say, "Look, it's not right," and teach it in schools or family life skills, or life skills in grade eight, or something in grade nine or ten — You could get a teacher, you could stop it... .

2. With regard to suspensions:

... If you suspend someone, they should give them an in-school suspension and get them to work like with the victims, not just their victims, but other victims, so they can see how victims are feeling, and how the victims' families are feeling. In-schools [suspensions] work better than regular suspensions, I mean I was suspended for being mouthy with my teacher and I went to the beach every day. Got a nice suntan for a week ... .

3. With regard to treatment of victims:

... [Usually] the victim doesn't wanna go back to school. But I think if they got her together [with the girl who beat her up] the day it happened or the day after or whatever, when she's feeling better and she wants to come, if there's an environment where she knows she's safe, then she can come to school and talk it out with the other girl, and she can say her thoughts and feelings and how she's been hurt, not only physically, but other ways ... and the other girl [the one who beat her up] can say her thoughts and feelings and how she's been hurt ... .

4. With regard to the use of counselors:

The counselors' area is kind of a safe place, and it's used, but not with people like — With friends and stuff, you can talk it out, but with people who aren't really your friends, and you just don't like 'em, and say someone wants to beat them up, they're not gonna talk it out, they're gonna go ahead and do it and then talk about it after, 'cause there's no real connection that can get them in there, unless the person that's gonna get beat up comes in and says, "Look, this person, I've heard threats that she was gonna beat me up" — they often know it's gonna happen to them — so you can get them down and ask them why ... . But you gotta watch it, 'cause when you're angry, you don't wanna work it out ... . But I think there needs to be a lot of talking done, people need to talk to each other.

To summarize: Mary says that for her, violence among adolescent females needs to be understood as a problem that has its beginnings in families where parents need help along with their children, where fathers are violent and "push around" mothers who "need to learn to be their own persons," and girls lack self-confidence and "don't know who they are." According to Mary, adolescent female violence also needs to be understood as a problem that involves both perpetrators and victims — victims who have the same kinds of problems with self-confidence that perpetrators have; victims and perpetrators who need to be able to talk to one another in a climate of safety, begin to understand one another's feelings and thoughts, and thereby begin to develop the empathy and connectedness that make the resolution of problems possible.

For Mary, connectedness seems to play a key role, because from her perspective, girls are more willing to talk with those whom they can consider "friends and stuff" — that is, with those whom they know and hold in some regard. But anger management is also key here, because when anger sets in, it overrules the girls' willingness to talk, even with friends. Therefore, something is needed that helps girls deal with anger, so that talking and listening can take place.

As well, Mary believes that teachers and counselors have a major role to play in the prevention of violence. Mary suggests that teachers and counselors, and the skills they teach and the rules they make with regard to what is right and wrong, will have some impact on students' behavior.

Mary's comments ring a hopeful note. If troubled and particularly violent girls nevertheless still have faith in teachers and counselors, this suggests that teachers and counselors who are trained in violence prevention could be instrumental in reducing violence among adolescent girls.

In part, this faith in the power of teachers and counselors may have something to do with the hierarchical universe in which Mary and the other key informants live. Since they believe that being older equates with having more power and a concomitantly greater share of respect, they may be willing to give certain adults, especially those who don't abuse their power, the authority to stop fights and to create rules for what is right and what is wrong.

For Mary and for the other key informants, those counselors who have listened and paid attention to the feelings and thoughts of their clients have been role models for constructive problem solving. It is to these people that Mary and the other girls have turned in seeking alternatives for violence.

It was my experience that being listened to and being treated with respect (i.e., being treated as if what one has to say is important) meant so much that none of the key informants engaged in violence while she was involved in this research project. Instead of resorting to violence, they called me or their counselor to discuss alternatives. Even when the alternatives did not appear to be as satisfying as "belting" someone, to my knowledge, the girls refrained from resorting to violence because they knew that their counselors and I did not hold with it as a way of settling conflict. On reflection, I find this to be significant, because it suggests that there may be a great deal of value in the relationships that the counselors and I built with the six key informants with a view to preventing their further engagement in violence.

Emerging Patterns

In contemplating all that I have heard and seen in the course of this study, what stands out for me are the apparently clear patterns in the key informants' lives that have prepared them for involvement in violence:

- All come from families with many generations of experience with violence, alcohol misuse, and a generalized dysfunction that has left them with a less than helpful way of constructing self and world.

- All have internalized notions of being female that assign low general worth to women, hold that women achieve their greatest importance when they command the attention of males, and support the entrenchment of the sexual double standard. They have learned to accept the objectification of women and support the monitoring of women's sexuality; thus, they monitor one another's sexual activities closely, and judge any girl or woman harshly if she shows signs of engaging in "unsanctioned" sex (i.e., sex that is not legitimated through a long-term relationship; also flirting, or other kinds of sexually based interaction, especially with males who are already spoken for).

- In their immediate families, and in their social circle, the key informants have been exposed to no forms of conflict resolution other than those that settle disputes through threat, intimidation, and violence. They have internalized a way of perceiving those who displease them that shifts moral and causal responsibility for their own displeasure onto those with whom they are displeased, and thus makes lashing out and punitive action justifiable.

- As well, as is always the case with oppressed groups, the key informants have accepted their own and others' subordination to hierarchies built upon power and domination to such a degree that they become extremely incensed with those of their own kind whom they consider below them on the ladder, who dare to buck the system. They do, of course, buck the system themselves, especially with adult authority figures, but only when in their eyes, these people displease or otherwise stymie them, thus provoking retaliation.

- Finally, given their extensive personal experiences with emotional, physical, and sexual abuse, they are quick to anger, and quick to assume that others "have it in for them." Yet, they are also strangely blind to risk and danger, probably because the terrain is so familiar. The known seldom appears dangerous.

When the key informants engage in violence — which they do most often with girls just like themselves — they enact all that they have come to take as given and exhibit a classic form of oppressed group behavior (as discussed in Chapter Nine). At some level, some of the girls (e.g., Mary and, to a lesser extent, Jenny) realize they are doing this, but changing is difficult. It means giving up the only form of status and power that they understand.

WHERE TO GO FROM HERE?

Violence prevention and gender issues
Programs that focus on the treatment of delinquency, like most theories of delinquency, rarely deal with gender issues (Chesney-Lind & Shelden, 1992; Gordon, 1988). Most programs that serve females derive from programs originally designed for males.

Programs specifically concerned with violence prevention are typically gender neutral. That is, they operate on the assumption that "one size fits all" and that no special consideration need be given to male–female differences when examining participation in and diversion from violence.

Gender neutrality, or gender blindness, also prevails in school-based violence prevention. An inventory of some 50 violence prevention programs (including school-based programs) offered in the community in which this study was done showed that only seven (five adult-focused, and two child- and youth-focused programs) concerned themselves with violence against females (Orom, 1995). Only one of the seven offered any additional programming specifically designed for violent females.

In Canada, as elsewhere, school systems attempt to address the issue of youth violence through both policy and curriculum initiatives. Often, the first line of defense against violence is the development of strict discipline policies, codes of student conduct, and structured consequences for offenders, including temporary suspension and even expulsion. For the most part, violence prevention curricula have as their goal the development of a variety of pro-social attitudes, skills, and knowledge intended to help students resolve conflict in peaceful and non-violent ways. Rarely do such programs address gender differences in youth involvement in violence.

As Ted Riecken and I surmised elsewhere (Artz & Riecken, 1994), this gender blindness can perhaps be explained by the fact that the forerunners of such curricula are to be found in the character-education movements first seen in the United States early in the 20th century, and later in the moral-education and values-education movements of the 1970s in Canada and the United States (Leming, 1993). Such programs typically do not concern themselves with gender. In a review of the literature on character education, Leming observes that to date, there is little empirical evidence to indicate that such programs, whether policy or curricular, are effective in changing student behavior. Leming (1993) notes:

> With the caveat that the present research base is small, disparate, and inconsistent, we can offer the following observations:
> • Didactic methods alone — codes, pledges, teacher exhortation and the like — are unlikely to have any significant or lasting effect on character.
> • The development of students' capacity to reason about questions of moral conduct does not result in a related change in conduct. Apparently, one cannot reason one's way to virtuous conduct.
> • Character educators should not expect character formation to be easy. Schools that expect easily achieved and dramatic effects will be disappointed. (p. 69)

Lockwood (1993) offers a further critique of such programs and also questions the assumption that changes in behavior will arise from systematic teaching of values and morals alone. Leming's (1993) and Lockwood's (1993) observations are troubling, particularly in light of two recent studies that suggest antiviolence curricula have the opposite effect from what was expected.

In a study done by the Department of Evaluation of the Saginaw Michigan Public School Board (1991), a district-wide school safety project was evaluated in its third year of operation. Objectives for the project were: (a) the employment and training of home-school liaison officers, (b) establishment of an advisory council, (c) development and implementation of school-based initiatives, and (d) reductions in violence and vandalism. It was found that by the third year of the program, reports of criminal or delinquent acts had *increased* by 47%.

A similar study (Madak & Bravi, 1992) conducted in Canada examined the effects of the Second Step Curriculum, a popular antiviolence program developed in Seattle, Washington, and used extensively in schools in Western Canada. Madak and Bravi (1992) found that the total number of behavioral incidents *increased* during the second year of the project.

The two studies raise questions about the efficacy of such programs when they appear to be associated with an increase in the very behaviors they are designed to reduce. Madak and Bravi (1992) hypothesize that the increase in behavioral incidents noted in their study may be the result of teachers being "hyper-vigilant" in reporting such behavior as a result of being exposed to the program. It is difficult to assess the validity of this hypothesis, although it should be noted that a similar explanation (i.e., hypersensitivity) is sometimes offered for the large statistical increase in reported youth crime (Frank, 1994).

Evidence from research studies that call into question the effectiveness of such character development and violence prevention programs indicates that one of the reasons such programs fail is their inability to recognize the complexity of the issue of violence among young people. Leming (1993) writes that "character develops within a social web or environment. The nature of that environment, the messages it sends to individuals, and the behaviors it encourages and discourages are important factors to consider in character education" (p. 69). Lockwood (1993) comments that "at minimum, some mix of psychological, situational, and sociological variables are involved in determining behavior" (p. 73). Gender and its effects upon persons and groups must be included for consideration in this mix of variables.

Complex roots of female violence

Clearly, the problem of youth violence, both male and female, is bigger than the school systems which, up to now, have been the main agencies responsible for trying to address and modify the behavior of young people. Youth violence is a complex social issue that is borne of multiple origins.

Data from this study point directly to family dysfunction, abuse, and neglect as part of the grounding that prepares school girls for participation in violence. I have found what many others[1] before me have found, in setting themselves the goal of understanding the lives of violent children.

Although the participants in the *Survey of Student Life* (Artz & Riecken, 1994) were mostly white, and the six key informants of this study were all white and comparatively more affluent and privileged than the participants in Campbell's (1984, 1991) studies, Chesney-Lind and Koroki's (1985) study, and Chesney-Lind and Shelden's (1992) overview of girls' delinquency and juvenile justice, the lived experiences of my key informants are similar to those of the participants in the other studies.

The families of the six key informants are characterized by the same kinds of problems with alcohol misuse, marital discord, and family violence encountered by the participants in the above-mentioned studies. Despite their mothers' claims of family unity as evidenced by enduring marriages and professions of "closeness" to other family members, the key informants' experiences with family are largely negative. The social bond that is premised upon attachment, seen by Hirschi (1969) to contribute to the containment of delinquency (see Chapter One), is not operative here. Instead, the key informants report experiencing a kind of enmeshment with family members that violates their personal boundaries and leaves them in a state of emotional abandonment.

The key informants' families are battlegrounds organized along traditional lines. Men rule over women, who are charged with the care and control of the children. On the surface, these families, while they are not "ideal patriarchal" families because the fathers are blue-collar workers and the mothers also work, are nonetheless similar (by virtue of their traditional organization) to those described by Hagan (1987) as the kinds of families that generally have lower rates of female delinquency. That is not the case here, however.

Although males are dominant and the women take care of the children, these families are producing girls who are violent. In these families, dominance is synonymous with petty tyranny and the negation of women. The gender divisions that are modeled and reinforced serve to produce internalized oppression and appear to contribute to the horizontal violence exhibited by the key informants. Further, these families also model a way of interpreting others' behavior that supports the shifting of moral and causal responsibility for one's actions onto those same others.

In suggesting that the internalization of victim blaming is central to the final step towards violence, I join Katz (1988) in pointing out that sociological and psychological factors alone are insufficient for an understanding of why some people engage in violence. If we are to work effectively, both at understanding how violence happens and at creating interventions that serve to prevent violence and its rationalization, I believe we must take into account how people make sense of their violent behavior beyond the psychosocial factors that give context to their experience.

After all, not all people who have been abused become abusers (Gelles & Straus, 1988). Thus, more must be at work than past experience alone. So far, an understanding is missing from the literature of how girls make sense of and rationalize their behavior. Such an analysis would move beyond the confines of moral-developmental and character education. I believe that there is much to be learned from exploring this area further.

In concluding that sexual abuse and sexual harassment play an important role with regard to the key informants' low sense of self-worth and negative views of other girls and women, I have raised issues previously suggested by Chesney-Lind and Koroki (1985) and Chesney-Lind and Shelden (1992). I take this line of inquiry one step further by suggesting that the key informants, and others like them, may extend their negative view of females by making moral judgments about their predominantly female victims. That is, they have drawn the conclusion that girls and women deserve to be beaten for certain behaviors (those judged as unacceptable according to a rigid reading of the sexual double standard), and thus exhibit horizontal violence and other oppressed group behaviors. Here, too, is an area for future inquiry into female violence, particularly in the light of attempts to understand it as the dark side of feminism (Adler, 1975; McGovern, 1995).

In my view, the judgments of women exhibited by the key informants do not arise because these girls are becoming more emancipated. Rather, this arises because within their life-worlds, they still apply narrow notions of male-focused behavior as the standard for what is right and good for women. If I am correct, this insight may be significant for preventing the perpetuation of violence across generations, especially female-to-female violence: Any such interventions must emphasize the valuing of women not in male terms, but as individuals who have worth in and of themselves as women.

Violence prevention in schools

Gelles and Straus (1988), in their exhaustive study on the causes and consequences of abuse in the American family, suggest that "sexual inequality is a prime cause of family violence" and that "eliminating sexism can prevent violence in the home" (p. 203). Evidence provided by the key informants of this study suggests that sexual inequality also has a major role to play in the violence participated in by adolescent school girls outside their homes. By extension, eliminating sexism may contribute substantially to preventing violence among these girls. Violence prevention programming aimed at adolescent school girls should focus on violence against women and should not assume that it is only males who act violently towards females.

The participants in this study (and others) have spoken eloquently about their experiences with abuse and their resulting anger and emotional pain. This suggests that any violence prevention programming we envision — including programs aimed at adolescent school girls — should include an abuse-survivor recovery component that addresses the female experience in positive and strength-giving ways.

Finally, in view of the loneliness and abandonment described by the key informants, and which has been linked by other researchers to deviance, delinquency, and violence (Hirschi, 1969; Jensen & Eve, 1976; Cernkovich & Giordano, 1987), we must find the means to help young women participate in our social institutions in ways that are important and relevant to them. That is, we must enable them to experience respect, affirmation, and connectedness. If we do not, they will pay every price asked of them in order to matter to someone, regardless of how destructive the relationship. And we, as a society, will pay the cost of their demise.

Keeping Violent Girls in Mind

Chesney-Lind and Shelden (1992) suggest that if we are to serve delinquent girls with regard to programming, we must always keep in mind their special needs vis-à-vis their experiences with sexual objectification and brutalization. I believe this applies to violence prevention programming in schools, as well. In all that we do, we must count gender in.

Evidence from several U.S. studies indicates that intervention in early childhood has a significant impact in reducing antisocial and criminal behavior later in life (Hechinger, 1994). Often, such programs involve both parents and children, and offer parents the chance to develop constructive, non-violent child-rearing skills. The goal of such programs is the development of healthy and stable parent–child relationships that lay the foundations for children's future interactions with peers and society. Given the findings of the present study, effective parent education for preventing violence must also include education and training in gender equity.

Some programs in violence prevention include not only parents, but other community members as well. MacDougall (1993) writes:

> A growing number of successful violence prevention/safe school initiatives throughout Canada share a common feature. They are products of partnerships. Pooling experience, skills, talent, and expertise better utilizes resources. Marrying previously fragmented groups towards a goal of reducing violence increases benefits to children, youth and families. Partnerships include educators, parents, students, police, government officials, artists, social service and mental health workers and others.

In Canada, an example of such partnerships is to be found in a program created by the Wellington Board of Education in Guelph, Ontario. In 1990, in response to growing community concerns about youth violence, the Wellington Board brought together representatives from education, police, social services, the Crown Attorney's Office, and parents. The mandate of this group is to develop and maintain cooperative strategies to reduce youth violence.

The Family Violence Prevention Project of the Community Child Abuse Council of Hamilton-Wentworth in Ontario is a similar collaborative effort. This project involves over 25 organizations and agencies representing school boards, social service agencies, health care providers, and government (MacDougall, 1993).

Given the small number of evaluations that have targeted violence intervention projects, more research is clearly needed. It appears, though, that the most successful programs are more broadly based in approach and, through collaboration, take into account contextual, environmental, familial, social, and gendered dimensions of violence — and do so at an early age.

Crime statistics in North America indicate that violence among young people, and especially young women, is on the rise. School systems have also noted this increase. Thus, it cannot be disputed that violence intervention and prevention are currently among our most pressing issues. Further, it makes sense, given the critical role that schools play in the socialization of young people, that schools should be the sites to begin the campaign against violence.

Teachers recognize the importance of sexism in school violence. In a survey on violence in schools (Macolmson, 1994), about one half of the teachers who participated said they believe that sexism plays a role in instigating violence at school. If school-based violence prevention programs are to be successful, they must move beyond merely transmitting violence-related curricula to students and must be grounded in the following principles:

- Early intervention. Waiting until young people reach adolescence before providing intervention compounds the problem.

- Involvement of students, parents, and community agency personnel with educators in the development of program initiatives and curricula that are meaningful to those for whom they are intended.

- Collaboration among students, parents, community-based agencies, and other community members in the implementation of co-developed programs and curricula.

- Continuous monitoring and evaluation of the implementation process in order to verify that programs are, in fact, achieving their purpose.

- A focus on gender and inequity. Questions of gender can no longer be ignored or subsumed into more general questions. Violence, sex, and gender must be studied, understood, and dealt with together.

All the current work of the Youth Violence Project focuses on gender. Thus far, it is clear that the gender differences identified in the self-report data of Phase I (described in Chapter Two) persist. In a related study (Artz & Blais, 1995), a number of resources designed to educate teens about sexual harassment and date rape were explored (see Appendix II). These resources provide useful information about male-to-female violence and make important points about gender equity, but do not address female-to-female violence.

Programs and materials that seek to prevent male violence against females are of paramount importance, especially because the majority of females will almost certainly encounter such violence at some point in their lives (Statistics Canada, 1993). It must now be recognized that most female-to-female violence is also a form of sexual harassment, given that it is so often perpetrated as a means of keeping female sexuality under control. It must therefore be included in any kind of programming that seeks to deal with sexual harassment.

The two kinds of violence against women, male-to-female and female-to-female, have their origins in the same belief systems. These hold that females are inferior to males and are, in the last analysis, sexual objects. Such beliefs are still deeply rooted in many aspects of our culture, and are especially visible and audible in media aimed at young people. The images of girls and women that predominate on television, in the movies and particularly in rock music and the videos that promote it, are overwhelmingly sexist and misogynist. Violence prevention programming must take into account the systemic ways in which girls and women are sexually misused and exploited, and must help both females and males find constructive ways to understand and relate to females.

Given the dominance of the male-focused perspective of females, it is no surprise that most girls grow up seeing themselves through the eyes of males. In families that devalue women, it takes little for girls to progress from a negative vision of women to overt violence against them. A thorough understanding of gender is thus central to any understanding of female violence, and integral to all violence prevention programming in the future.

Notes

1. See Flowers, 1990, for an overview.

References

Adler, F. (1975). *Sisters in crime*. New York: McGraw-Hill.

Ageton, S. (1983). The dynamics of female delinquency, 1976–1980. *Criminology, 21*, 555–584.

Anderson, D. (1991). *The unfinished revolution: The status of women in twelve countries*. Toronto: Doubleday.

Aoki, T. (1987). *Toward understanding curriculum orientations*. Unpublished manuscript.

Arbuthnot, J. (1992). Sociomoral reasoning in behavior-disordered adolescents. In J. McCord & R. Tremblay (Eds.), *Preventing antisocial behavior*. New York: The Guilford Press.

Artz, S. (1994). *Feeling as away of knowing: A practical guide to working with emotional experience*. Toronto: Trifolium Books.

Artz, S., & Blais, M. (1995). *An evaluation of an awareness and violence prevention project directed at sexual harassment, abuse and date rape among teens*. Unpublished report to sponsor, Victoria, BC: British Columbia Ministry of Education, Gender Equity Branch.

Artz, S., & Riecken, T. (1994). The survey of student life. In *A study of violence among adolescent female students in a suburban school district*. Unpublished report, British Columbia Ministry of Education, Education Research Unit.

Ashbury, H. (1928). *The gangs of New York*. New York: Alfred Knopf.

Attacks on trendy teenagers not just kid's stuff. (1993, March 21). *Victoria Times Colonist*.

Atwater, E. (1992). *Adolescence*. Englewood Cliffs, NJ: Prentice Hall.

Auty, S., Dempsey, M., Duggan, S., Lowery, G., West, G., & Wiseman, D. (1993). A dialogue on the nature and extent of the problem. In G. West (Ed.), Violence in the schools, schooling in violence. *Orbit, 24* (1), 1–5.

Ayto, J. (1990). *Bloomsbury dictionary of word origins*. London, UK: Bloomsbury Publishing.

Balkan, S., & Berger, R. (1979). The changing nature of female delinquency. In C. Knopp (Ed.), *Becoming female: Perspectives on development*. New York: Plenum.

Beaten at playground, boy, 11, wins at chess. (1993, April 13). *Victoria Times Colonist*.

Becker, H. (1963). *Outsiders: Studies in sociology and deviance*. New York: Macmillan.

Belenky, M., Clinchy, B., Goldberger, N., & Tarule, J. (1986). *Womens' ways of knowing: The development of self, voice and mind.* New York: Basic Books.

Berger, R. (1989). Female delinquency in the emancipation era: A review of the literature. *Sex Roles, 21* (5/6), 375–399.

Bibby, R., & Posterski, D. (1992). *Teen trends.* Toronto: Stoddart.

Binder, A., Geis, G., & Bruce, D. (1988). *Juvenile delinquency: Historical, cultural, legal perspectives.* New York: Macmillan.

Blumer, H. (1969). *Symbolic interactionism: Perspective and method.* Englewood Cliffs, NJ: Prentice Hall.

Boothe, J., Bradley, L., Flick, M., Keough, K., & Kirk, S. (1993, February). The violence at your door. *The Executive Educator,* 16–21.

Brenauer, J., & Rasmussen, D. (Eds.). (1984). *The final Foucault.* Cambridge: MIT Press.

Brenner, M., Brown. J., & Canter, D. (Eds.). (1985). *The research interview: Uses and approaches.* Orlando, FL: Academic Press.

Brown, L., & Gilligan, C. (1992). *Meeting at the crossroads.* New York: Ballantine Books.

Brown, W.K. (1977). Black female gangs in Philadelphia. *International Journal of Offender Therapy and Comparative Criminology, 21* (3), 221–228.

Burbank, V.K. (1987). Female aggression in cross-cultural perspective. *Behavior Science Research, 21* (1–4), 70–100.

Burgess, E.W. (1928). The growth of the city. In R.E. Park, E. Burgess, & R.D. McKenzie (Eds.), *The city.* Chicago: University of Chicago Press.

Cameron, E., deBruijne, L., Kennedy, K., & Morin, J. (1994). *British Columbia Teachers' Federation task force on violence in schools: Final report.* Vancouver, BC: BCTF.

Campbell, A. (1984, 1991). *The girls in the gang.* (2nd ed.) New York: Basil Blackwell.

Campbell, A. (1986). Self-report by fighting females. *British Journal of Criminology, 26,* 28–46.

Campbell, A. (1987). *Self-definition by rejection: The case of gang girls.*

Canadian Crime Statistics (1995). Catalogue #85-205. Ottawa, ON: Statistics Canada.

Canadian Review of Sociology and Anthropology, 27, 137–156.

Cernkovich, S., & Giordano, P. (1979). A comparative analysis of male and female delinquency. *Sociological Quarterly, 20,* 131–145.

Cernkovich, S., & Giordano, P. (1987). Family relationships and delinquency. *Criminology*, *25*, 295–321.

Charon, J. (1979). *Symbolic interactionism: An introduction, an integration.* Englewood Cliffs, NJ: Prentice Hall.

Chesney-Lind, M., & Koroki, J. (1985). *Everything just going down the drain: Interviews with female delinquents in Hawaii.* Hawaii: University of Hawaii Youth Development & Research Center report.

Chesney-Lind, M., & Shelden, R. (1992). *Girls' delinquency and juvenile justice.* Pacific Grove, CA: Brooks/Cole.

Chilton, R., & Datesman, S. (1987). *Gender, race and crime: An analysis of urban arrest trends, 1960–1980.* Paper presented at the annual meeting of the American Sociological Association.

Cloward, R., & Ohlin, L. (1960). *Delinquency and opportunity.* New York: Free Press.

Cohen, A. (1955). *Delinquent boys: The culture of the gang.* New York: Free Press.

Colby, A., & Kohlberg, L. (1987). *The measurement of moral development: Theoretical foundations and research validation.* (vol. 1). Cambridge: Cambridge University Press.

Cole, M., John-Steiner, V., Scribner, S., & Souberman, E. (1978). *L.S. Vygotsky — Mind in society: The development of higher psychological processes.* Cambridge: Harvard University Press.

Cormier, L., & Hackney, H. (1993). *The professional counselor: A process guide to helping.* Boston: Allyn & Bacon.

Cowie, J., Cowie, V., & Slater, E. (1968). *Delinquency in girls.* London, UK: Heinemann.

Deegan, M. (1987). Symbolic interactionism and the study of women: An introduction. In M. Deegan & M. Hill (Eds.), *Women and symbolic interactionism.* Boston: Allyn & Unwin.

Denboer, R. (1994). *CRD demographic atlas.* (1994). Victoria, BC: Capital Regional District.

Dietz, M., Pruz, R., & Shaffir, W. (1994). *Doing everyday life: Ethnography as human lived experience.* Toronto: Copp Clark Longman.

Durkheim, E. (1933). *The division of labor in society.* (G. Simpson, trans.) New York: Free Press.

Edwards (Ed.). (1967). Von Humboldt. *The encyclopedia of philosophy.* New York: Collier MacMillan.

Evans, E.D., & Warren-Sohlenberg, L. (1988). Patterns of analysis of adolescent behavior towards parents. *Journal of Adolescent Research, 3* (2), 201–206.

Faludi, S. (1991). *Backlash: The undeclared war against American women.* New York: Anchor/Doubleday.

Federal Bureau of Investigation. (1988, July). *Crime in the United States, 1987.* Washington, DC: U.S. Government Printing Office.

Figueria-McDonough, J., Barton, W., & Sarri, R. (1981). Normal deviance: Gender similarities in adolescent subcultures. In M. Warren (Ed.), *Comparing male and female offenders.* Newbury Park, CA: Sage.

Flowers, R. (1990). *The adolescent criminal: An examination of today's juvenile offender.* Jefferson, NC: McFarland & Company.

Fowler, H. (1965). *A dictionary of modern English usage.* New York: Oxford University Press.

Fox Keller, E. (1990). Gender and science. In J. McCarl Nielsen (Ed.), *Feminist research methods: Exemplary readings in the social sciences.* San Francisco: Westview Press.

Frank, F. (1994). Violent youth crime. In *Canadian social trends: A Canadian studies reader.* (vol. 2). Toronto: Thompson Educational Publishing.

Friere, P. (1971, 1984). *Pedagogy of the oppressed.* New York: Continuum.

Geertz, C. (1973). *The interpretation of cultures.* New York: Basic Books.

Geertz, C. (1988). *Works and lives: The anthropologist as author.* Stanford: Stanford University Press.

Gelles, R., & Straus, M. (1988). *Intimate violence: The definitive study of the causes and consequences of abuse in the American family.* New York: Simon & Schuster.

Giallombardo, R. (1980). Female delinquency. In D. Shichor & D. Kelly. (Eds.), *Critical issues in juvenile delinquency.* Lexington, MA: Lexington Books.

Gilligan, C. (1982). *In a different voice: Psychological theory and women's development.* Cambridge: Harvard University Press.

Gilligan, C., Lyons, N., & Hanmer, T. (Eds.). (1990). *Making connections: The relational world of adolescent girls at Emma Willard School.* Cambridge: Harvard University Press.

Gilligan, C., Ward, J., & Taylor, J., with Bardige, B. (1988). *Mapping the moral domain.* Cambridge: Harvard University Press.

Giordano, P., & Cernkovich, S. (1979). On complicating the relationship between liberation and delinquency. *Social Problems, 26,* 467–481.

Giordano, P., Cernkovich, S., & Pugh, M. (1986). Friendships and delinquency. *American Journal of Sociology, 91,* 1170–1202.

Goetz, J.P., & LeCompte, M.D., (1984). *Ethnography and qualitative design in educational research.* Montreal: Academic Press.

Gordon, L. (1988). *Heroes in their own lives.* New York: Viking.

Grosser, G. (1951). *Juvenile delinquency and contemporary American sex roles.* Unpublished doctoral dissertation, Harvard University.

Habermas, J. (1971). *Theory and practice.* Boston: Beacon Press.

Hagan, J. (1988). *Structural criminology.* New Brunswick: Polity Press.

Hagan, J. (1990). The structure of gender and deviance: A power-control theory of vulnerability to crime and the search for deviant role exits. *Canadian Review of Sociology and Anthropology, 27* (2), 137–156.

Hagan, J., Gillis, A., & Simpson, J (1985). The class structure of delin-quency: Toward a power-control theory of common delinquent behav-ior. *American Journal of Sociology, 90,* 1151–1178.

Hagan, J., Simpson, J., & Gillis, A. (1987). Class in the household: A power-control theory of gender and delinquency. *American Journal of Sociology, 92,* 788–816.

Hamilton, J. (1993). *It's a jungle out there. In Leading the way to violence free schools.* Conference handbook, British Columbia School Trustees Association/British Columbia Teachers' Federation Conference. Vancouver, BC: BCSTA.

Hancock, E. (1989). *The girl within.* New York: Fawcett Columbine.

Hechinger, F. (1994) Saving youth from violence. *Carnegie Quarterly, 33* (1), 1–15.

Hindelang, J., Hirschi, T., & Weis, J. (1981). *Measuring delinquency.* Newbury Park, CA: Sage.

Hirschi, T. (1969). *Causes of delinquency.* Berkeley: University of California Press.

Hoffman-Bustamente, D. (1973). The nature of female criminality. *Issues in Criminality, 8* (Fall), 117–136.

hooks, b. (1994). *Outlaw culture: Resisting representations.* New York: Routledge.

Hopper, C.B., & Moore, J., (1990). Women in outlaw motorcycle gangs. *Journal of Contemporary Ethnography, 18* (4), 363–387.

Horowitz, R. (1983). *Honor and the American dream.* New Brunswick, NJ: Rutgers University Press.

Horowitz, R. (1986). Remaining an outsider: Membership as a threat to research rapport. *Urban Life, 14,* 238–251.

Horowitz, R. (1987). Community tolerance of gang violence. *Social Problems, 34*, 437–450.

Jagger, A., & Bordo, S. (1990). *Gender/body/knowledge: Feminist reconstructions of being and knowing.* New Brunswick, NJ: Rutgers University Press.

James, J., & Thornton, W. (1980). Women's liberation and the female delinquent. *Journal of Research in Crime and Delinquency, 17*, 230–244.

Jenkins, J. (1994). *Resolve I: Resolving violence through education, an anti-violence curriculum for senior secondary students.* Campbelltown, NSW: University of Western Sydney, Macarthur.

Jensen, G., & Eve, R. (1976). Sex differences in delinquency. *Criminology, 13*, 427–448.

Juvenile weapons arrests double. (1995, November 13). *The Globe & Mail.*

Katz, J. (1988) *Seductions of crime: Moral and sensual attractions of doing evil.* New York: Basic Books.

Kelly, D. (1993) *Deviant behavior: A text-reader in the sociology of deviance.* New York: St. Martin's Press.

Klicpera C., & Klicpera B. (1996). Die situation von "Tatern" und "Opfern," agresiver handlung in der schule. *Praxis der Kinderpsychologie und Kinderpsychiatre, 45*, 2–9.

Kirby, S., & McKenna, K. (1989). *Experience, research, social change: Methods from the margins.* Toronto: Garamond Press.

Klein, M. (1971). *Street gangs and street workers.* Englewood Cliffs, NJ: Prentice Hall.

Kohlberg, L. (1969). Stage and sequence: The cognitive developmental approach to socialization. In D. Goslin (Ed.), *Handbook of socialization theory and research.* Chicago: Rand McNally.

Kohlberg, L. (1984). *Essays on moral development: The psychology of moral development.* (vol. 2). San Francisco: Harper & Row.

Konopka, G. (1966). *The adolescent girl in conflict.* Englewood Cliffs, NJ: Prentice Hall.

Konopka, G. (1983). *Young girls: A portrait of adolescence.* New York: Hayworth Press.

Kostash, M. (1987). *No kidding: Inside the world of teenage girls.* Toronto: McClelland & Stewart.

Larson, Goltz, & Hobart (1994). *Families in Canada: Social context, continuities and changes.* Toronto: Prentice Hall Canada.

Lather, P. (1991). *Getting smart: Feminist research and pedagogy within the postmodern*. New York: Routledge.

Leading the way to violence free schools. Conference handbook, British Columbia School Trustees Association/British Columbia Teachers' Federation Conference. Vancouver, BC: BCSTA.

Leming, J. (1993). Synthesis of research: In search of effective character education. *Educational Leadership, 51* (3), 63–71.

Leontyev, A. (1981). *Problems of the development of mind*. Moscow: Progress Publishers.

Lockwood, A. (1993). A letter to character educators. *Educational Leadership, 51* (3), 72–75.

Lombroso, C., & Ferrero, W. (1895). *The female offender*. New York: Philosophical Library.

MacDougall, J. (1993). *Violence in the schools: Programs and policies for prevention. A report from the Canadian Education Association*. Toronto: CEA.

McGovern, C. (1995). You've come a long way, baby. *Alberta Report, 1* (33), 24–27.

Mack, B. (1994). Mission impossible. *Grand Royale* magazine, a division of Grand Royale Entertainment, available on the Internet through the Beastie Boys home page: http://www.nando.net.music/gm/BeastieBoys/../BeastieBoys/press

Madak, P., & Bravi, G. (1992). *Second step: A violence prevention curriculum in a western Canadian elementary school. An evaluation*. ERIC Document No. ED 350 542.

Mahoney, M. (1991). *Human change processes: The scientific foundations of psychotherapy*. New York: Basic Books.

Malcolmson, J. (1994). *Violence in schools: An overview of findings from the "Teaching in the 90's Survey."* Vancouver, BC: British Columbia Teachers' Federation.

Mathews, F. (1994). *Youth gangs on youth gangs*. Ottawa: Solicitor General Canada.

Mawby, R. (1980). Sex crimes: Results of a self-report study. *British Journal of Sociology, 31*, 526–543.

Mead, M. (1934). *Kinship in the Admiralty Islands*. New York: American Museum of Natural History.

Merton, R. (1938). Social structure and anomie. *American Sociological Review, 3*, 672–682.

Miller, E. (1986). *Street women: The illegal work of underclass women.* Philadelphia: Temple University Press.

Miller, W. (1958). Lower class culture as a generating milieu of gang delinquency. *Journal of Social Issues, 14,* 5–19.

Mishler, E. (1986). *Research interviewing.* Cambridge: Harvard University Press.

Morash, M. (1986). An explanation of juvenile delinquency: The integration of moral reasoning theory and sociological knowledge. In W.S. Laufer & J.M. Day (Eds.), *Personality theory, moral development, and criminal behavior.* Lexington, MA: Lexington Books.

Morris, A. (1987). *Women, crime and criminal justice.* New York: Basil Blackwell.

Morris, R. (1965). Attitudes towards delinquency by delinquents, nondelinquents and their friends. *British Journal of Criminology, 5,* 249–265.

Mundy, C. (1994). Where the wild things are. *Rolling Stone,* Issue 688, pp. 45–53 and 73–74.

Novak, M. (1978). *Ascent of the mountain, flight of the dove: An invitation to religious studies.* New York: Harper & Row.

Nye, F. (1958) *Family relationships and delinquent behavior.* New York: Wiley.

Olweus, D., Block, J., & Radke-Yarro, M. (1986). *Development of antisocial and prosocial behavior: Research, theories, and issues.* Orlando, FL: Academic Press.

Orom, C. (1995). *Violence prevention in the community: A report and inventory of prevention initiatives in the community of Victoria.* Victoria, BC: Community Social Planning Council.

Osborne, J. (1994). Some similarities and differences among phenomenological and other methods of psychological qualitative research. *Canadian Psychology, 35* (2), 167–189.

Pecukonis, E.V. (1990). A cognitive/affective empathy training program as a function of ego development in aggressive adolescent females. *Adolescence, 25* (97), 59–76.

Police Management Information System Summary Statistics, 1977–1991. Victoria, BC: Queen's Printer.

Pollack, O. (1950). *The criminality of women.* New York: Barnes.

Porter, E.J. (1991). *Women and moral identity.* North Sidney, Australia: Allen & Unwin.

Prus, R. (1994). Approaching the study of human group: Symbolic interaction and ethnographic inquiry. In M. Dietz, R. Pruz, & W. Shaffir

(Eds.), *Doing everyday life: Ethnography as human lived experience*. Toronto: Copp Clark Longman.

Rabinow, P. (Ed.). (1984). *The Foucault reader*. New York: Pantheon.

Reckless, W. (1961). *The crime problem* (3rd ed.). New York: Appleton-Century-Crofts.

Reiss, A. (1951). Delinquency as the failure of personal social controls. *American Sociological Review, 16*, 196–207.

Richards, P., & Tittle, C. (1981). Gender and perceived chance of arrest. *Social Forces, 59*, 1182–1199.

Rigby, K. (1996). *Bullying in schools and what to do about it*. Melbourne: The Australian Council for Educational Research.

Roberts, S. (1983, July). Oppressed group behavior: Implications for nursing. *Advances in Nursing Science*, 22–30.

Rogers, C. (1957). The necessary and sufficient conditions for therapeutic personality change. *Journal of Consulting Psychology, 21*, 95–103.

Ryan, C., Mathews, F., & Banner, J. (1993). *Student perceptions of violence*. Toronto: Central Toronto Youth Services.

Saginaw Public Schools. (1991). *School safety project: Product evaluation, 1990–1991*. Saginaw Public Schools, Department of Evaluation Services. ERIC Document Number, ED 343 267.

Schur, E. (1972). *Labeling deviant behavior*. New York: Harper & Row.

Schur, E. (1984). *Labeling women deviant*. New York: Random House.

Shaw, C. (1930). *The jack roller*. Chicago: University of Chicago Press.

Shaw, C., & McKay, H. (1931). *Social factors in juvenile delinquency*. Chicago: University of Chicago Press.

Shaw, C., & McKay, H. (1942). *Juvenile delinquency in urban areas*. Chicago: University of Chicago Press.

Short, J. (1968). *Gang delinquency and delinquent subcultures*. Chicago: University of Chicago Press.

Simon, R. (1975). *Women and crime*. Lexington, MA: Lexington Books.

Singer, S., & Levine, M. (1933). Power-control theory, gender and delinquency: A partial with additional evidence on the effects of peers. *Criminology 26*, 627–647.

Slade, P. (1984). Premenstrual emotional changes in normal women: Fact or fiction? *Journal of Psychosomatic Research, 28*, 1–7.

Spradley, J. (1979). *The ethnographic interview*. New York: Holt, Reinhardt & Winston.

Statistics Canada (1993). *Violence against women survey: Survey highlights*. Ottawa: Author.

Steffensmeir, D. (1978). Crime and the contemporary American woman: An analysis of changing levels of female property crime, 1960–1975. *Social Forces, 57*, 566–584.

Steffensmeir, D., & Cobb, M. (1981). Sex difference in urban patterns, 1934–1979. *Social Problems, 29*, 37–50.

Steffensmeir, D.J., Steffensmeir, R.H., & Rosenthal, A.S. (1979). Trends in female violence. *Sociological Focus, 12* (3), 217–227.

Summary Statistics: Police Crime, 1985–1994 (1995). Vancouver, BC: Police Services Division, Ministry of the Attorney General.

Sutherland, E. (1939). *Principles of criminology*. Philadelphia: Lippincott.

Sutherland, E., & Cressey, D. (1978). *Criminology* (10th ed.). Philadelphia: Lippincott.

Teen beating suspects remanded. (1993, April 13). *Victoria Times Colonist*.

Thrasher, F. (1927). *The gang: A study of 1,313 gangs in Chicago*. Chicago: University of Chicago Press.

Toby, J. (1957). Social disorganization and stake in conformity: Complementary factors in predatory behavior in hoodlums. *Journal of Criminal Law, Criminology and Police Service, 48*, 12–17.

"Tremendous" increase in violence among girls. (1993, October 15). *Victoria Times Colonist*.

Tutt, N. (1991). The future of the juvenile justice system. In Jungen-Tas, Boendermaker, & van der Laan (Eds.), *The future of the juvenile justice system* (pp. 107–129). Acco Leuven: Netherlands.

Tutt, N. (1988). Report to the European Council of Ministers, Council of Europe of the Expert Committee on Juvenile Crime. Council of Europe, the Hague, Netherlands.

Van Maanen, J. (1988). *Tales from the field*. Chicago: University of Chicago Press.

van Manen, M. (1977). Linking ways of knowing with ways of being practical. *Curriculum Inquiry, 6* (3), 205–228.

Warren, M. (Ed.). (1981). *Comparing female and male offenders*. Beverly Hills: Sage.

Wilson, J., & Herrnstein, R. (1985). *Crime and human nature*. New York: Simon & Schuster.

Wilson, S. (1977). The use of ethnographic techniques in educational research. *Review of Educational Research, 47* (1), 245–265.

Wolcott, H. (1975). Criteria for an ethnographic approach in research in schools. *Human Organization, 34* (2), 111–127.

Wolf, N. (1991). *The beauty myth.* Toronto: Vintage Books.

Appendix I
Tables of Survey Results

Table A-1
PARENTAL OCCUPATION by PERCENTAGE REPORTED

Parent	Profes- sional	Manag- erial	Clerical	Service	Manual	Military	Self- Employed
Mother (n=833)	21.1%	5.5%	31.6%	30.0%	7.6%	1.2%	3%
Father (n=1,084)	12.7%	8.7%	3.5%	25.6%	32.0%	12.5%	5%

Table A-2
PARENTAL EDUCATION by PERCENTAGE REPORTED[†]

Parent	Less Than High School	High School	Trade or Busi- ness School	University Degree	Graduate Degree
Mother (n=1,086)	13.1%	44.6%	13.0%	20.3%	9.1%
Father (n=1,002)	16.9%	37.0%	17.2%	17.3%	11.7%

[†] In interpreting these data, it is important to keep in mind that these percentages are based on students' knowledge of their parents' occupation and education. This knowledge may be less than completely accurate, since over 30% of students indicated that they did not know the level of their parents' education. However, these figures do correspond to those provided in local census data.

Table A-3a
Familial differences for males and females

Family Dynamics	Nonhitting Females (n=556)	Hitting Females (n=147)	Nonhitting Males (n=367)	Hitting Males (n=396)
Family life is "very important"	46.4%	35.4%* less when compared with nonhitting females and nonhitting males	42.5%	33.8%
Enjoyment from mother not applicable	1.3%	9.5%* more nonapplicable when compared with all other groups	2.5%	3.5%
Afraid of being physically abused at home	6.5% Yes	18.4%* Yes more often when compared with all other groups	4.8% Yes	3.3% Yes
Have been physically abused at home	6.3% Yes	19.7%* Yes more often when compared with all other groups	3.0% Yes	9.6% Yes

*Significant at $p < .0001$, chi-square

Table A-3b
Familial differences for males and females

Family Dynamics	Nonhitting Females (n=556)	Hitting Females (n=147)	Nonhitting Males (n=367)	Hitting Males (n=396)
Smoked without parents' permission	46.4% Never	**29.3%*** Never less often when compared with all other groups	66.2% Never	**41.4%*** Never less often when compared with nonhitting male
Lied about where they had been or whom they were with	29.7% Never (in the past year)	**11.6%*** Never (in the past year) less often when compared with nonhitting females and nonhitting males	43.1% Never (in the past year)	**18.2%*** Never (in the past year) less often when compared with nonhitting female and nonhitting males
Stayed out all night without parents' permission	68.7% Never (in the past year)	**36.1%*** Never (in the past year) less often when compared with nonhitting females and nonhitting males	69.8% Never (in the past year)	**35.9%*** Never (in the past year) less often when compared with nonhitting female and nonhitting males
Deliberately ruined something their parents valued after an argument	89.4% Never (in the past year)	**70.1%*** Never (in the past year) less often when compared with nonhitting females and nonhitting males	91.0% Never (in the past year)	**72.2%*** Never (in the past year) less often when compared with nonhitting female and nonhitting males

*Significant at $p < .0001$, chi-square

Table A-4
Group membership of survey participants, percentage indicating affiliation

Relationships and Group Membership	Nonhitting Females (n=556)	Hitting Females (n=147)	Nonhitting Males (n=367)	Hitting Males (n=396)
Rappers	13.5%	**31.3%*** when compared with nonhitting females and non-hitting males	10.9%	**24.2%*** when compared with nonhitting females and non-hitting males
Bangers	11.5%	**29.3%*** when compared with nonhitting females and non-hitting males	9.5%	**24.2%*** when compared with nonhitting females and non-hitting males
Skates	5.2%	8.2%	4.6%	5.1%
Total % claiming group member-ship in Rappers, Bangers, and Skates	30.2%	**68.8*** when compared with nonhitting females and non-hitting males	25.0%	**53.5%*** when compared with nonhitting females and non-hitting males

*Significant at $p < .0001$, chi-square

Table A-5
SElf-reported importance of belonging to a group or gang and having the right clothes (percentage reporting "very important")

Important Peer Group Dimension	Nonhitting Females (n=556)	Hitting Females (n=147)	Nonhitting Males (n=367)	Hitting Males (n=396)
Belonging to a group or gang	20.4%	38.5%* when compared with nonhitting females and non-hitting males	18.3%	37.0%* when compared with nonhitting females and non hitting males
Having the right clothes to fit your group or gang	26.2%	41.8%* when compared with nonhitting females and non-hitting males	24.0%	30.1%* when compared with nonhitting females and non-hitting males

* Significant at $p < .0001$, chi-square

Table A-6
SElf-reported levels of damaging school property and endorsing acting-out against teachers

Behavior and Attitude	Nonhitting Females (n=556)	Hitting Females (n=147)	Nonhitting Males (n=367)	Hitting Males (n=396)
Damaged school property at least once or twice in the past year	12.4%	32.0%* when compared with nonhitting females and non-hitting males	18.7%	42.6%* when compared with nonhitting females and non-hitting males
Endorsed "If I don't like my teacher, it's OK to act up in school"	13.1%	27.2%* when compared with nonhitting females and non-hitting males	15.1%	33.3%* when compared with nonhitting females and non-hitting males

* Significant at $p < .0001$, chi-square

TAblE A-7
SElf-REpoRTEd iNTERpERSONAL VALUES COMPARISON FOR NONHITTINQ FEMALES ANd MALES

Interpersonal Values (rated as "very important")	Nonhitting Females (n=556)	Nonhitting Males (n=367)
Friendship	91.9%	76.6%*
Being loved	77.3%	53.1%*
Concern for others	69.4%	40.6%*
Respect for others	66.9%	49.6%*
Forgiveness	66.2%	40.9%*
Honesty	64.2%	46.3%*
Politeness	42.1%	33.5%*
Generosity	41.2%	28.3%*
Being respected	71.0%	55.3%*

* Significant at $p < .0001$, chi-square

TAblE A-8
SElf-REpoRTEd iNTERpERSONAL VALUES COMPARISON FOR FEMALES

Interpersonal Values (rated as "very important")	Nonhitting Females (n=556)	Hitting Females (n=147)
Friendship	91.9%	91.2%
Being loved	77.3%	74.1%
Concern for others	69.4%	68.0%
Respect for others	66.9%	61.2%
Forgiveness	66.2%	55.8%
Honesty	64.2%	49.7%*
Politeness	42.1%	34.0%
Generosity	41.2%	30.6%
Being respected	71.0%	66.7%

* Significant at $p < .001$, chi-square, but *not* at $p < .0001$

TAble A-9
Self-reported interpersonal values comparison for males

Interpersonal Values (rated as "very important")	Nonhitting Males (n=367)	Hitting Males (n=396)
Friendship	76.6%	69.9%
Being loved	53.1%	46.7%
Concern for others	40.6%	35.1%
Respect for others	49.6%	36.9%*
Forgiveness	40.9%	33.6%*
Honesty	46.3%	31.1%*
Politeness	33.5%	21.0%*
Generosity	28.3%	21.2%*
Being respected	55.3%	50.0%

*Significant at p <.0001, chi-square

TAble A-10
Self-reported moral judgment comparison for nonhitting females and males (percentage indicating agreement)

Moral Judgment	Nonhitting Females (n=556)	Nonhitting Males (n=367)
If someone has something you really want, it's OK to make them give it to you	4.1%	12.8%*
It's OK to punch or hit someone when you're having an argument	8.3%	20.7%*
Fighting is a good way to defend your friends	14.0%	31.4%*
It's OK to use threats to get what you want	6.1%	10.7%*
If I don't like my teacher, it's OK to act up in school	13.1%	15.1%*
It's OK to damage buildings and property as a way of getting even	3.4%	7.9%*
Right or wrong is a matter of personal opinion	83.7%	80.7%
The use of marijuana should be legalized	51.5%	43.5%

*Significant at p <.0001, chi-square

Table A-11
Self-reported moral judgment comparison for females (percentage indicating "agree" and "strongly agree")

Moral Judgment	Nonhitting Females (n=556)	Hitting Females (n=147)
If someone has something you really want, it's OK to make them give it to you	4.1%	16.3%*
It's OK to punch or hit someone when you're having an argument	8.3%	36.0%*
Fighting is a good way to defend your friends	14.0%	42.2%*
It's OK to use threats to get what you want	6.1%	22.5%*
If I don't like my teacher, it's OK to act up in school	13.1%	27.2%*
It's OK to damage buildings and property as a way of getting even	3.4%	11.6%*
Right or wrong is a matter of personal opinion	83.7%	92.3%*
The use of marijuana should be legalized	51.5%	66.0%*

*Significant at $p < .0001$, chi-square

Table A-12
Self-reported moral judgment comparison for males (percentage indicating "agree" and "strongly agree")

Moral Judgment	Nonhitting Males (n=367)	Hitting Males (n=396)
If someone has something you really want, it's OK to make them give it to you	12.8%	26.8%*
It's OK to punch or hit someone when you're having an argument	20.7%	50.1%*
Fighting is a good way to defend your friends	31.4%	63.4%*
It's OK to use threats to get what you want	10.7%	31.0%*
If I don't like my teacher, it's OK to act up in school	15.1%	33.3%*
It's OK to damage buildings and property as a way of getting even	7.9%	24.0%*
Right or wrong is a matter of personal opinion	80.7%	86.1%
The use of marijuana should be legalized	43.5%	66.5%*

*Significant at p <.0001, chi-square

Table A-13

Self-reported moral judgment comparison for hitting females and nonhitting males (percentage indicating "agree" and "strongly agree")

Moral Judgment	Hitting Females (n=147)	Nonhitting Males (n=367)
If someone has something you really want, it's OK to make them give it to you	16.3%	12.8%
It's OK to punch or hit someone when you're having an argument	36.0%*	20.7%
Fighting is a good way to defend your friends	42.2%	31.4%
It's OK to use threats to get what you want	22.5%*	10.7%
If I don't like my teacher, it's OK to act up in school	27.2%*	15.1%
It's OK to damage buildings and property as a way of getting even	11.6%	7.9%
Right or wrong is a matter of personal opinion	92.3%*	80.7%
The use of marijuana should be legalized	66.0%*	43.5%*

*Significant at p <.0001, chi-square

Table A-14
Self-reported moral judgment comparison for hitting females and males (percentage indicating "agree" and "strongly agree")

Moral Judgment	Hitting Females (n=147)	Hitting Males (n=396)
If someone has something you really want, it's OK to make them give it to you	16.3%	26.8%
It's OK to punch or hit someone when you're having an argument	36.0%	50.1%
Fighting is a good way to defend your friends	42.2%	63.4%*
It's OK to use threats to get what you want	22.5%	31.0%
If I don't like my teacher, it's OK to act up in school	27.2%	33.3%
It's OK to damage buildings and property as a way of getting even	11.6%	24.0%
Right or wrong is a matter of personal opinion	92.3%	86.1%
The use of marijuana should be legalized	66.0%	66.5%

*Significant at $p < .0001$, chi-square

Table A-15
PARTICIPANTS' SELF-ASSESSMENT ON QUESTIONS OF SELF-CONCEPT (PERCENTAGE ANSWERING THAT THIS STATEMENT DESCRIBED THEM "FAIRLY WELL" OR BETTER)

Self-Concept Questions	Nonhitting Females (n=556)	Hitting Females (n=147)	Nonhitting Males (n=367)	Hitting Males (n=396)
I am well liked	94.6%	97.3%	91.0%	90.9%
I am good-looking	67.3%	72.1%	76.3%	78.3%
I can do most things well	80.0%	73.5%	**91.5%*** when compared with all females	**89.3%*** when compared with all females
I have lots of confidence	69.5%	66.0%	**81.7%*** when compared with all females	**82.6%*** when compared with all females

*Significant at $p < .0001$, chi-square

Table A-16
RATINGS OF SELF-CONCEPT, MEAN SCORE COMPARISONS FOR MALES AND FEMALES

Self-Concept Questions	Females (n=703)	Males (n=763)
I am well liked	3.20	3.14
I am good-looking	2.79	**2.90***
I can do most things well	2.97	**3.19***
I have lots of confidence	2.79	**3.12***

*Significant at $p < .0001$, chi-square

Table A-17

GENDER COMPARISONS OF PERSONAL AND SOCIAL CONCERNS (PERCENTAGE REPORTING "VERY SERIOUS" OR "VERY IMPORTANT")

Social and Personal Concerns	Nonhitting Females (n=556)	Hitting Females (n=147)	Nonhitting Males (n=367)	Hitting Males (n=396)
AIDS	87.6%*	85.2%*	72.9%	75.9%
Child abuse	80.7%*	84.5%*	57.5%	60.9%
Racial discrimination	71.0%*	71.7%*	54.9%	50.1%
Teenage suicide	70.8%*	70.5%*	48.7%	47.1%
Violence against women	67.7%*	67.1%*	46.1%	46.4%
The environment	67.1%*	67.6%*	58.0%	56.2%
The unequal treatment of women	55.6%*	67.8%**	31.4%	35.8%
Violence in schools	52.8%*	37.1%†	46.0%††	37.8%
Drug abuse	64.1%††	52.1%††	59.2%††	48.2%
Alcohol abuse	59.8%*	48.6%	53.5%††	42.9%
Youth gangs	50.3%*	47.8%*	41.9%††	37.1%
Native–white relations	34.9%*	38.2%*	24.6%	26.5%
The economy	38.5%	32.5%	43.4%	38.1%
Global awareness	33.0%*	16.0%†	22.0%	17.7%
Spirituality	29.0%*	23.5%	19.3%	18.9%
Cultural group or heritage	15.5%	13.5%	12.8%	12.2%

* Significant at $p < .0001$, chi-square. All significant differences apply to an overall comparison with males

** This significant difference applies to a comparison with nonhitting females and all males

† This significant difference applies to a comparison with nonhitting females

†† This significant difference applies to a comparison with hitting males

Table A-18
Participants' responses to questions relating to ambition (percentage reporting "a great deal" or "very important")

Ambition Questions	Nonhitting Females (n=556)	Hitting Females (n=147)	Nonhitting Males (n=367)	Hitting Males (n=396)
How much enjoyment do you receive from your job?	(n/a=54.0%) 18.8%	(n/a=58.5%) 14.8%	(n/a=55.3%) 18.3%	(n/a=43.2%) **26.7%*** significant difference when compared with hitting females
How important is working hard?	43.5%	35.9%	44.38%	34.85%
How important is success in what you do?	64.3%	59.2%	68.6%	61.4%
How much does pressure to do well in school bother you?	22.9%	31.5%	25.1%	31.5%
How much does never having enough time bother you?	35.0%	36.3%	29.5%	40.3%
How much does the question of what you are going to do when you finish school bother you?	21.3%	23.1%	20.1%	33.1%
Do you agree or disagree that anyone who works hard will rise to the top?	84.6% Agree	72.2% Agree	85.2% Agree	78.7% Agree

* Significant at $p < .0001$, chi-square

TablE A-19
Participants' responses to questions relating to money

Monetary Questions	Nonhitting Females (n=556)	Hitting Females (n=147)	Nonhitting Males (n=367)	Hitting Males (n=396)
Do you have a job during the school year?	38.4% Yes	42.0% Yes	35.6% Yes	47.23% Yes
How many hours per week do you work?	20.03% 10 hrs. or more	29.6% 10 hrs. or more	23.5% 10 hrs. or more	33.5% 10 hrs. or more
What is your hourly wage? (% reporting $7/hour or more)	12.68%	**26.7%*** significant when compared with hitting females	41.22%	**50.0%*** significant when compared with all females and non-hitting males
Do you receive a weekly allowance?	55.3% Yes	66.2% Yes	58.0% Yes	60.9% Yes
What is your weekly allowance? (% reporting over $25)	5.6%	**17.7%*** significant when compared with nonhitting females and non-hitting males	6.22%	**13.2%*** significant when compared with nonhitting females and nonhitting males
How much does the lack of money bother you? (% reporting "a great deal")	29.5%	33.8%	31.2%	**45.7%*** significant when compared with nonhitting males and females and hitting females

* Significant at $p <.0001$, chi-square

Table A-20
Participants' responses to four quality-of-life questions (percentage reporting "very important")

Quality-of-Life Questions	Nonhitting Females (n=556)	Hitting Females (n=147)	Nonhitting Males (n=367)	Hitting Males (n=396)
How important is a comfortable life to you?	62.0%	54.9%	69.2%	55.7%
How important is intelligence to you?	40.7%	42.4%	50.6%	41.4%
How important is humor to you?	64.5%	61.9%	64.5%	60.9%
How important are your looks to you?	28.8%	33.3%	35.7%	45.9%

Table A-21
Participants' responses to social support network questions

To Whom Will You Turn Re: Money?	Nonhitting Females (n=556)	Hitting Females (n=147)	Nonhitting Males (n=367)	Hitting Males (n=396)
Parents	52.2%	40.0%	50.4%	44.2%
Friends	25.9%	35.7%	22.6%	25.6%
School counselor	0.0%	0.0%	0.3%	0.3%
Minister or priest	0.0%	0.0%	0.3%	0.3%
Adult friend	0.4%	2.1%	0.8%	1.4%
No one	18.3%	20.2%	25.1%	27.5%
Other	2.3%	1.4%	0.6%	0.8%

TAble A-22
PARTiciPANTS' RESPONSES TO SociAL SUPPORT NETWORk qUESTioNS (CONT'd)

To Whom Will You Turn Re: Relationships?	Nonhitting Females (n=556)	Hitting Females (n=147)	Nonhitting Males (n=367)	Hitting Males (n=396)
Parents	7.7%	10.6%	11.3%	7.9%
Friends	80.6%	77.3%	59.6%	67.3%
School counselor	0.9%	0.0%	0.9%	0.5%
Minister or priest	0.2%	0.0%	0.3%	0.8%
Adult friend	1.1%	1.4%	1.7%	2.1%
No one	7.9%	9.2%	25.4%	19.5%
Other	1.5%	1.4%	0.8%	1.9%

TAble A-23
PARTiciPANTS' RESPONSES TO SociAL SUPPORT NETWORk qUESTioNS (CONT'd)

To Whom Will You Turn Re: Sex?	Nonhitting Females (n=556)	Hitting Females (n=147)	Nonhitting Males (n=367)	Hitting Males (n=396)
Parents	14.7%	11.2%	12.3%	11.4%
Friends	49.3%	59.4%	34.2%	46.2%
School counselor	1.9%	0.7%	0.9%	1.3%
Minister or priest	0.6%	0.0%	1.2%	1.1%
Adult friend	1.6%	2.8%	1.5%	2.1%
No one	28.6%	25.2%	47.4%	35.1%
Other	3.3%	0.7%	2.6%	2.9%

Table A-24
PARTICIPANTS' RESPONSES TO SOCIAL SUPPORT NETWORK QUESTIONS (CONT'd)

To Whom Will You Turn Re: Fun?	Nonhitting Females (n=556)	Hitting Females (n=147)	Nonhitting Males (n=367)	Hitting Males (n=396)
Parents	4.1%	0.7%	5.4%	4.3%
Friends	88.0%	90.7%	78.1%	78.1%
School counselor	0.0%	0.7%	0.0%	0.3%
Minister or priest	0.0%	0.0%	0.6%	0.8%
Adult friend	0.0%	0.0%	0.3%	1.6%
No one	7.1%	7.1%	14.2%	14.4%
Other	0.7%	0.7%	0.8%	0.5%

Table A-25
PARTICIPANTS' RESPONSES TO SOCIAL SUPPORT NETWORK QUESTIONS (CONT'd)

To Whom Will You Turn Re: Right and Wrong?	Nonhitting Females (n=556)	Hitting Females (n=147)	Nonhitting Males (n=367)	Hitting Males (n=396)
Parents	48.6%	32.6%	49.7%	36.0%
Friends	30.6%	38.0%	18.2%	25.8%
School counselor	1.4%	2.9%	1.1%	2.3%
Minister or priest	0.2%	0.7%	0.9%	0.8%
Adult friend	2.5%	3.7%	1.7%	2.3%
No one	14.0%	19.7%	27.3%	29.6%
Other	2.7%	2.2%	1.1%	1.9%

Table A-26
Participants' responses to social support network questions (cont'd)

To Whom Will You Turn Re: School?	Nonhitting Females (n=556)	Hitting Females (n=147)	Nonhitting Males (n=367)	Hitting Males (n=396)
Parents	51.6%	37.5%	53.5%	39.1%
Friends	27.7%	36.0%	18.8%	24.7%
School counselor	7.6%	13.2%	8.4%	10.4%
Minister or priest	0.0%	0.0%	0.6%	1.1%
Adult friend	1.9%	2.2%	0.3%	2.9%
No one	8.7%	10.3%	16.8%	20.7%
Other	2.1%	0.7%	1.7%	1.1%

Table A-27
Participants' responses to social support network questions (cont'd)

To Whom Will You Turn Re: Careers?	Nonhitting Females (n=556)	Hitting Females (n=147)	Nonhitting Males (n=367)	Hitting Males (n=396)
Parents	60.0%	44.9%	65.7%	52.0%
Friends	13.2%	21.0%	10.6%	12.6%
School counselor	5.3%	10.9%	2.1%	4.8%
Minister or priest	0.0%	0.7%	0.9%	1.1%
Adult friend	1.2%	1.5%	2.4%	4.0%
No one	17.3%	19.6%	16.4%	24.4%
Other	2.2%	1.5%	1.8%	1.1%

Table A-28
Participants' responses to social support network questions (cont'd)

To Whom Will You Turn Re: A Major Problem?	Nonhitting Females (n=556)	Hitting Females (n=147)	Nonhitting Males (n=367)	Hitting Males (n=396)
Parents	32.1%	27.2%	52.9%	37.9%
Friends	48.0%	51.2%	26.4%	34.6%
School counselor	5.7%	5.6%	2.4%	4.5%
Minister or priest	0.2%	6.4%	1.2%	1.1%
Adult friend	3.7%	4.8%	1.2%	5.1%
No one	5.3%	4.8%	13.2%	14.3%
Other	5.1%	4.8%	2.7%	2.5%

Table A-29
Level of being bothered by fear of attack

How often does the fear of being attacked or beaten up bother you?	Nonhitting Females (n=556)	Hitting Females (n=147)	Nonhitting Males (n=367)	Hitting Males (n=396)
A great deal or quite a bit	25.8%	20.6%	18.4%	20.4%
Little or none	74.2%	79.4%	81.6%	79.6%

Table A-30
Percentage of participants fearing attack at school

Are you afraid of being physically attacked at school?	Nonhitting Females (n=556)	Hitting Females (n=147)	Nonhitting Males (n=367)	Hitting Males (n=396)
Yes	17.6%	17.4%	19.8%	20.6%
No	82.4%	82.6%	80.2%	79.4%

Table A-31
PERCENTAGE of participants fearing being beaten by a gang of kids

Are you afraid you might be beaten up by a gang of kids?	Nonhitting Females (n=556)	Hitting Females (n=147)	Nonhitting Males (n=367)	Hitting Males (n=396)
Yes	21.2%	16.6%	25.1%	21.5%
No	78.8%	83.4%	74.9%	78.5%

Table A-32
PERCENTAGE of participants staying away from school because of fear

Have you ever stayed away from school because you were afraid?	Nonhitting Females (n=556)	Hitting Females (n=147)	Nonhitting Males (n=367)	Hitting Males (n=396)
Yes	12.5%	12.9%	5.8%	9.2%
No	87.5%	87.1%	94.2%	90.8%

Table A-33
PERCENTAGE of participants fearing physical abuse at home

Are you afraid you might be physically abused at home?	Nonhitting Females (n=556)	Hitting Females (n=147)	Nonhitting Males (n=367)	Hitting Males (n=396)
Yes	6.6%	18.5%*	3.3%	4.9%
No	93.4%	81.5%	96.7%	95.1%

* Significant at $p < .0001$, chi-square

Table A-34
PERCENTAGE of participants fearing sexual assault

Are you afraid you might be sexually assaulted?	Nonhitting Females (n=556)	Hitting Females (n=147)	Nonhitting Males (n=367)	Hitting Males (n=396)
Yes	28.0% when compared with all males	37.2%* when compared with all males and nonhitting females	4.1%	7.7%
No	72.0% when compared with all males	62.8%* when compared with all males and nonhitting females	95.9%	92.3%

* Significant at $p < .0001$, chi-square

Table A-35
PERCENTAGE of participants fearing sex against their will

Are you afraid you might be talked into having sex with your boy/girl-friend against your will?	Nonhitting Females (n=556)	Hitting Females (n=147)	Nonhitting Males (n=367)	Hitting Males (n=396)
Yes	14.3% when compared with all males	22.4% when compared with all males and nonhitting females	2.8%	8.2%
No	85.7% when compared with all males	67.6% when compared with all males and nonhitting females	97.2%	91.8%

* Significant at $p < .0001$, chi-square

Table A-36
PERCENTAGE of PARTICIPANTS who hAVE bEEN victimizEd by A gANg of kids

Have you ever been a victim of a gang of kids?	Nonhitting Females (n=556)	Hitting Females (n=147)	Nonhitting Males (n=367)	Hitting Males (n=396)
Yes	4.1%	10.2%	6.0%	14.9%* when compared with nonhitting males and female
No	95.9%	89.8%	94.0%	85.1%* when compared with nonhitting males and female

* Significant at p <.0001, chi-square

Table A-37
PERCENTAGE of PARTICIPANTS who hAVE bEEN ATTACkEd whilE goiNg TO OR FROM school

Have you ever been attacked on your way to or from school?	Nonhitting Females (n=556)	Hitting Females (n=147)	Nonhitting Males (n=367)	Hitting Males (n=396)
Yes	3.6%*	5.4%*	10.2%	18.9%*
No	95.9%*	89.8%*	94.0%	85.1%*

* Significant at p <.0001, chi-square

Table A-38
PERCENTAGE of PARTICIPANTS who hAVE bEEN physicAlly AbusEd AT hOME

Have you ever been physically abused at home?	Nonhitting Females (n=556)	Hitting Females (n=147)	Nonhitting Males (n=367)	Hitting Males (n=396)
Yes	6.3%	19.9%*	3.0%	9.6%
No	93.7%	80.1%*	97.0%	90.4%

* Significant at p <.0001, chi-square

Table A-39
Percentage of participants who have been sexually abused

Have you ever been sexually abused?	Nonhitting Females (n=556)	Hitting Females (n=147)	Nonhitting Males (n=367)	Hitting Males (n=396)
Yes	11.2%*	23.5%*	0.8%*	4.5%*
No	88.8%*	76.5%*	99.2%*	95.5%*

* Significant at $p < .0001$, chi-square

Table A-40
Percentage of participants who have been talked into sex against their will

Have you ever been talked into having sex with your boy/girlfriend against your will?	Nonhitting Females (n=556)	Hitting Females (n=147)	Nonhitting Males (n=367)	Hitting Males (n=396)
Yes	7.3%	13.7%*	2.8%	7.1%
No	92.7%	86.3%*	97.2%	92.9%

* Significant at $p < .0001$, chi-square

Table A-41a
Participants involved in rule-breaking, deviant, and delinquent behaviors (percentage reporting "very often") (all differences significant at $p < .0001$, chi-square)

Behavior	Nonhitting Females (n=556)	Hitting Females (n=147)	Nonhitting Males (n=367)	Hitting Males (n=396)
Smoke without parents' permission	20.4% significantly higher than nonhitting males	38.4% significantly higher than nonhitting males and females	6.8% significantly lower than all other groups	27.6% significantly higher than nonhitting males
Lie to parents	12.6% significantly higher than nonhitting males	31.5% significantly higher than nonhitting males and females	4.7% significantly lower than all other groups	23.5% significantly higher than nonhitting males and females
Stay out all night without parents' permission	1.6%	8.9% significantly higher than nonhitting males and females	2.5%	15.2% significantly higher than nonhitting males and females
Skip classes	4.9%	17.7% significantly higher than nonhitting males and females	3.8%	16.4% significantly higher than nonhitting males and females
Skip school	4.0%	17.7% significantly higher than nonhitting males and females	3.6%	15.8% significantly higher than nonhitting males and females
Steal little things that don't belong to you	2.7%	12.9% significantly higher than nonhitting males and females	2.7%	14.9% significantly higher than nonhitting males and females

Table A-41b
Participants involved in rule-breaking, deviant, and delinquent behaviors (percentage reporting "very often") (all differences significant at $p < .0001$, chi-square)

Behavior	Nonhitting Females (n=556)	Hitting Females (n=147)	Nonhitting Males (n=367)	Hitting Males (n=396)
Deliberately ruin parents' property after an argument (1–2x/year or more)	10.6%	**29.9%** significantly higher than nonhitting males and females	9.0%	**28.8%** significantly higher than nonhitting males and females
Damage others' property for fun	0.5%	**3.4%** significantly higher than nonhitting males and females	1.6%	**10.4%** significantly higher than nonhitting males and females and hitting females
Take something from a store without paying	1.6%	**8.9%** significantly higher than nonhitting males and females	2.2%	**13.9%** significantly higher than nonhitting males and females
Break into a place to look around	0.2%	**4.8%** significantly higher than nonhitting males and females	0.0%	**9.6%** significantly higher than nonhitting males and females and hitting females
Purposefully damage school property	0.5%	**2.1%** significantly higher than nonhitting males and females	0.8%	**5.8%** significantly higher than nonhitting males and females
Carry a weapon	0.9%	**6.2%** significantly higher than nonhitting males and females	2.2%	**16.9%** significantly higher than nonhitting males and females and hitting females

Table A-41c
Participants involved in rule-breaking, deviant, and delinquent behaviors (percentage reporting "very often") (all differences significant at $p < .0001$, chi-square)

Behavior	Nonhitting Females (n=556)	Hitting Females (n=147)	Nonhitting Males (n=367)	Hitting Males (n=396)
Smoke weekly or more	29.1% significant when compared with nonhitting males	56.5% significant when compared with nonhitting males and females and hitting males	9.9% significantly lower than all other groups	32.2% significant when compared with nonhitting males
Drink alcohol weekly or more	11.3%	26.9% significantly higher than nonhitting males and females	8.5%	27.0% significantly higher than nonhitting males and females
Smoke marijuana weekly or more	10.5%	26.5% significantly higher than nonhitting males and females	8.8%	27.2% significantly higher than nonhitting males and females
Use other illegal drugs weekly or more	3.5%	17.9% significantly higher than nonhitting males and females	3.3%	15.8% significantly higher than nonhitting males and females
Use over-the-counter drugs weekly or more	10.6%	15.0%	6.3% significantly lower than all other groups	10.7%
Stop oneself from eating in order to lose weight weekly or more	10.9% significantly higher than nonhitting and hitting males	13.8% significantly higher than nonhitting and hitting males	1.7%	3.3%

Appendix II
Resource List*

Pamphlets
Dating Violence Prevention (March 1993)
Child Abuse Prevention Program for Adolescents
The Canadian Red Cross Society, B.C./Yukon Division

Working Together to Understand and Stop Sexual Harassment (1992)
Stop Sexual Harassment
King County Sexual Assault Resource Center
P.O. Box 300
Renton, WA 98057

Surviving Sexual Assault: Stress and Relaxation (1991)
King County Sexual Assault Resource Center
P.O. Box 300
Renton, WA 98057

The Abuse Began Just After We Started Going Out:
  What Young Women Should Know About Abuse by their Boyfriends
Battered Women's Support Services
P.O. Box 1098, Postal Station A
United Way Affiliated Agency
Vancouver, B.C. V6C 2T1

Booklets
Just A Kiss: A Photo Novella About Dating Violence (1993)
Battered Women's Support Services
P.O. Box 1098, Postal Station A
Vancouver, B.C. V6C 2T1

Today's Talk About Sexual Abuse: A Booklet for Teens
Project 1993–94 (© 1994)
Victoria Women's Sexual Assault Centre

* This resource list was developed by Monica Blais, MA.

Manuals

*Healthy Attitudes, Healthy Relationships: Men Working to
  End Men's Violence Against Women*
by Kathleen Folliot, Kimberley Morrison, and Michael Kaufmann
Prepared by White Ribbon Campaign
Activities for Classrooms and Schools
CAW/TCA Canada
The White Ribbon Campaign
220 Yonge Street, Suite 104
Toronto, ON M5E 2H1

*Flirting or Hurting: A Teacher's Guide on Student-to-Student
  Sexual Harassment in Schools (Gr. 6–12)* (1994)
by Nan Stein and Lisa Sjostrom
NEA Professional Library Publication
National Education Association
Washington, DC

Dating Violence Prevention: Overview and Response, Part III (1993)
by Judi Fairholm, RN, BScN
The Canadian Red Cross, B.C./Yukon Division

So What's It To Me: Activity Guide Sexual Assault Information for Guys
by Gayle M. Stringer and Deanne Rants-Rodriguez (1987)
King County Rape Relief
1025 S. Third
Renton, WA 98055

Accompanying Booklet — *So What's It To Me: Activity Guide Sexual Assault
Information for Guys* (1989)

Top Secret: A Discussion Guide
by Billy Jo Flerchinger and Jennifer J. Fay (1985)
Network Publications
Santa Cruz King County Rape Relief

Accompanying Booklet — *Top Secret: A Discussion Guide* (1982)
King County Sexual Assault Resource Center
P.O. Box 300
Renton, WA 98057

Sexual Harassment and Teens: A Program for Positive Change
by Susan Strauss and Pamela Espeland (1992)
Free Spirit Publishing
Minneapolis, MN

Dating Violence: A Discussion Guide on Violence in Young People's Relationships
by Debra J. Lewis (1994)
Battered Women's Support Services
P.O. Box 1098, Postal Station A
Vancouver, B.C. V6C 2T1

Books
No Is Not Enough: Helping Teenagers Avoid Sexual Assault
by C. Adams, Jennifer Fay, and Jan Loreen (1990)
Martin Import Publishers
San Luis Obispo, CA

Videos
When Dating Turns Dangerous
Sunburst Communications (1995)
Pleasantville, NY

Other Resources
Viraj — Programme de prévention de la violence dans les relations amoureuses des jeunes
(1) Animation classe
(2) Session de perfectionnement
(3) Guide de participation à la session de perfectionnement
Gouvernement du Québec
Ministère de l'Éducation
Québec, 1993

Responding to Sexual Assault in Schools — Towards Zero Tolerance:
   A Discussion Paper
by Catherine Stewart (1992)
Catherine Stewart & Associates

Index